CW00337269

80p

THE CHAMPIONS OF FORMULA 1

THE CHAMPIONS OF
FORMULA 1

From Fangio to Piquet

KEITH BOTSFORD

Stanley Paul

London   Melbourne   Auckland   Johannesburg

Stanley Paul and Co. Ltd

An imprint of Century Hutchinson Ltd

Brookmount House, 62–65 Chandos Place
Covent Garden, London WC2N 4NW

Century Hutchinson Australia (Pty) Ltd
PO Box 496, 16–22 Church Street, Hawthorn, Melbourne, Victoria 3122

Century Hutchinson New Zealand Ltd
191 Archers Road, PO Box 40-086, Glenfield, Auckland 10

Century Hutchinson South Africa (Pty) Ltd
PO Box 337, Bergvlei 2012, South Africa

First published 1988

Set in Linotron Sabon by
Rowland Phototypesetting Ltd
Bury St Edmunds, Suffolk
Printed and bound in Great Britain by
Mackays of Chatham Ltd, Chatham, Kent

British Library Cataloguing in Publication Data

Botsford, Keith
    The champions of formula 1.
    1. Racing cars. Racing, to 1987
    I. Title
    796.7'2'0904

ISBN 0-09-173694-3

Contents

Introduction

This book is a series of portraits of world champion (and other) drivers I have known. It does not pretend to be a comprehensive history of the sport, but it does have one singularity, in that it begins with Jackie Stewart and not with Giuseppe Farina, who won the first title in the so-called 'modern' period of F1 racing which began in 1950. That is because Farina, Fangio, Ascari, Hawthorn, the two Hills, Brabham, Clark, Surtees, Hulme and Rindt belong in my mind to another world. If Enzo Ferrari could write of Farina as being capable of 'committing the most astonishing follies' and if Farina continued racing for a great number of years, that is but one of a hundred signs saying that was another epoch in the sport. He is also supposed to have had a 'difficult and disagreeable' temperament: to which one can only comment that so do many modern drivers, only they cannot afford to show it in the ways Farina did. Mowing down ten spectators in Argentina is but another way of saying the same thing: that in those days, they did things differently. Mind you, I have seen Argentines stray onto the track even in my day, but the cops thought they were terrorists and hauled them away. Today's sport is more sanitary.

When you read about Juan Manuel Fangio – I have met the man a few times, infinitely taciturn, even slower of speech than Carlos Alberto Reutemann – and you hear how Juan Perón (he of Evita fame), a dictator among many with a passion for motor cars and panoply, sponsored a whole school of Argentine drivers and built the Autodromo in Beunos Aires for them, you know that you're in another world. Imagine! Back then they thought drivers were what counted! Fangio's record, of course, is quite fantastic: five world championships, four of them in a row between 1954 and 1957. Alfa Romeo, then not the pale simulacrum of recent years, Mercedes, Lancia/Ferrari, Maserati. Great stuff, but how can one possibly compare his achievement with that of a Stewart, a Lauda or a Prost? In his first championship, only five constructors took part: Alfa, Ferrari, Maserati, Talbot and Gordini. There were only eight races. The season began in late May on the Swiss Bremgarten circuit, a park with handsome trees, and finished in Barcelona in October. Would it happen today that after a handsome pile-up in Monaco, Fangio 'saw the yellow danger flag being waved by a marshal . . . and immediately braked hard. As he reached the melee, a marshal directed him round the wrong side of the tangled cars so that his Alfa was blocked in. With his powerful, beefy arms Fangio heaved on the back wheels of his Alfa, slowly reversing the car and then accelerating round the stationary cars and on with the race'?

No, it would not. That belongs to an era of unsentimental and unprofessional privateering. As did the man. His only link with modern racing seems to have been his profound lack of affection for Ferrari. Certainly what happened at Monza in 1956, when Fangio had to retire and thus allow Stirling Moss to win the championship, could not happen today. His team-mate, Peter Collins, lying second, came in for a routine tyre check and, seeing Fangio's plight, simply handed his car over to him, saying, 'I've got plenty of opportunity in the future.' Fangio took the championship with those shared points and Collins's action bespeaks something slightly better than gentle-manliness. Presumably the two men liked each other and even gave a thought to each other. I do not see this happening among the Mansells and Piquets, but then, so we're always told, back then men raced for themselves.

Fangio's great qualities – and one must remember, in considering his record, that he drove almost exclusively in winning cars – seem to have been strength, endurance and tenacity. The rest of the equipment of a grand prix driver was taken for granted: he was quick and he was precise. He was also in some ways a precursor of more modern drivers: intensely professional, utterly absorbed in the sport, he had very little else going on 'on the side' – unlike some of his contemporaries. He was neither personally rich nor highly educated (to be a racing driver today is to exclude the latter) and consequently racing was, quite literally, his life.

Alberto Ascari, the son of the great pre-war driver Antonio, was of a type equally rare today: placid, gentle, plump, genial, full of restraints and self-discipline; his ego seems not to have bothered him at all. Not unlike Stewart, he fancied driving from the front rather than, like Lauda in our own day, harrying from behind, and, as one biographer puts it, he 'knew so precisely his own and his car's limitations the number of accidents in which he was involved were very few. It was rare indeed for him to finish other than completely relaxed and without signs of fatigue.' Which sounds slightly like an obit for a period. That is, Ascari could, and chose to, drive within his limits; he was not out to prove anything because he took his talent for granted; the bonanzas of a championship meant relatively little to him. By all reports, he was also imperturbable: when in 1955 at Monaco his Lancia's brakes locked up and he bounced off the bales of hay and the bollards by the harbour, his car plunged into the water; within a few seconds his helmet bobbed up to the surface and then Ascari himself was hauled up onto a boat with little more than a broken nose.

That hay gives it all away, plus the open cockpit, the driver position, the rowboat that picked him up (today you can't get into Monaco harbour with anything less than an ocean-going liner), the casualness of the whole event. Its only link with modern racing is that then, as now, Monaco remains a hazardous race which ought to be abandoned, jettisoned, done away with, eliminated.

The first Brit on the roster of champions was Mike Hawthorn, a graduate of Kingston Technical College and then a student at the College of Aeronautical Engineering in Chelsea, London: in short, a mechanical type who appeared at races in white overalls and a bow tie. Hawthorn's first car, the Cooper-Bristol, was also a precursor of sorts: simple, economical, relatively unsophisticated, it was short on power but also far less over-engineered than its Italian rivals. So was the man. When God called him to Maranello, Hawthorn hardly leaped at the chance: he wasn't sure he wanted to be a full-time racing driver and he was even less sure that he wanted to drive for a foreigner. And part of the reason for that had to be that to work at Ferrari was to be slightly more 'professional' than to drive for oneself. In fact, Hawthorn took some time to adapt: he liked a joke, he grinned a lot and a good part of the Scuderia thought the young man wasn't taking his racing quite seriously enough.

It makes pleasant and anachronistic reading to hear that Hawthorn and Fangio, heading the field at Reims, were locked in combat and that 'when Fangio moved over to crowd Hawthorn out, Mike, grinning broadly, held his ground and wagged his finger warningly'. The best we get today is a furiously clenched fist. And who today would care that Hawthorn, excused for medical reasons (kidney trouble), failed to do his National Service? So far as I know, both France and Italy have compulsory military service to this day, but I have noticed no drivers of repute driving on brief furloughs and donning their uniforms after a race. After the great Le Mans disaster in which Hawthorn was peripherally involved but Pierre Levegh and eighty-four spectators were killed, Hawthorn 'appeared utterly broken, he blamed himself completely for the accident and vowed that he would never race again'. The only modern thing about that is that Mike was coaxed back into a car. But he had the same reaction again when Peter Collins went off at the Pflanzgarten at the Nürburgring in West Germany: again he wanted to quit.

But two incidents make the differences between then and now even clearer. Towards the end of Hawthorn's championship year, his Ferrari spun off the track in Oporto, Portugal; getting out of his car, he managed to push-start it again and take a vital second place, only to be disqualified at the finish for pushing his car against the direction of the race. So Stirling Moss intervened to insist that Hawthorn had been pushing his car on a footpath and not on the circuit and should therefore keep his points. Then in the final race, at Casablanca, in Morocco, when Hawthorn *had* to finish second to become champion, Graham Hill eased off to hand Hawthorn his own second place and the title. It is nice to remember that sportsmanship was then fashionable.

The Brabhams, Hills, Clarks and the rest of the world champions up to Jackie Stewart were all infected by the same spirit, yet as the years went by the beginnings of the modern spirit were being felt. In Graham Hill's dourness on the track and Jim Clark's technical perfection there are outlined characteristics of the modern driver. Hill was personally an extrovert; I have seen him being charming and I have seen him being far from charming, a failing that often accompanies an excess of drink. Graham was clearly one of the first to cultivate an 'image' for himself: in advertising terms, had advertising been of any real importance at the time, he was good news: tall, handsome, toothy, bristly-moustached, every inch the hero. On the circuit, he had much bravado, a lot of wildness and a constant tendency to try too hard, so much so that at one early race he was black-flagged for 'repeated revolutions', i.e. uncontrolled spins.

Taking his career as a whole, however, Graham has to be called a naturally dogged and often unlucky driver. He stayed loyal to BRM for six long years, winning just one championship with them in 1962 and another with Lotus in 1968, a title that almost certainly would not have been his but for the death of Jim Clark. Out of 176 races, Graham culled only fourteen victories: not because he lacked the talents, but because by the Sixties, victories were getting much harder to come by and the sport was growing ever more competitive. Then, too, as the sport developed, more and more young drivers (Graham didn't start racing until the relatively late age of twenty-five and was still racing in 1975 when he was pushing fifty) pushed their elders and betters harder and harder, which tended to work on Graham's nerves. Where in his earlier days he raced with able but less competitive drivers like Richie Ginther, by 1965 he had Jackie Stewart by his side; then, when he moved to Lotus, he had Jim Clark first and then Jochen Rindt, neither of them the sort of men who thought seniority in racing counted for much.

His last years were relatively unhappy. Lotus was not then, any more than it was to be later, a happy team: there was rivalry within, Chapman was dictatorial, he had off-track preoccupations. Two years' racing for his friend Bernard Ecclestone's Brabham did little to advance Graham's reputation: as others waxed, he waned. In nature, he was a transitional figure between the old world and the new. One of the first to admit publicly that he enjoyed racing for money, he was also inclined to self-denigration and occasional melancholy. On the other hand, in his up periods, he was much more like today's drivers than the earlier Hill, who said it was no coincidence that he chose a job he could do sitting down (he was also an accomplished rower). He recognized the competitive drive that kept him going for so many years: through driving, he said, he learned to master cars and master himself, and cars expressed his character and his mood. He thought of himself as an optimist, but in the few conversations we had – I met him only in the year he died in a plane crash – I was compelled to view him as something of a melancholic. The two are not incompatible. They were just different parts of the same character. The man who wanted to be a musician or a comedian, and who forced himself to learn from failure, was also a man of great tenacity, concentration and ambition. Nothing could put him down, not even the most appalling accidents, and, as he said, he wanted to win every race he entered. That's already a modern statement.

Greatly different from Hill and much closer to the modern age was Jochen Rindt, once quoted as saying, 'No one knows how long you have to live. So it is everyone's duty to put into his life all he can.' Jochen was a rich boy to start with: his parents, however, were both killed in an air raid when Jochen was a year old, so he grew up with his grandparents in Graz, Austria; grew up to be pretty wild, too. He was also impudent, mischievous, imprudent and completely self-confident. Also a driver on the ragged edge of danger, also a car breaker, also a hero. In short, one of the wild and woolly ones.

It did not last for ever. By 1966, Jochen had matured; his ego had calmed down, his style had improved. But the progress of his career – apart from stunning successes in F2 – had not kept pace with his own growing mastery. He had indifferent years in indifferent cars and he was in danger of fading into some obscurity in the face of new rivals such as Jacky Ickx and Stewart. The solution was Colin Chapman and Lotus, who needed a replacement for Clark and for Clark's first replacement, Jackie Oliver. Rindt insisted on being joint Number One with Graham Hill. That was to sour 1969, as Hill did not intend to yield, either on the track or within the team. In Barcelona, both Hill and Rindt suffered serious crashes when their aerofoils failed. It was the end of a period of unbridled and uncontrolled experiment in the sport, the last gasp of an old technology that was about to be replaced by stringent rules and an ever-increasing concern with driver safety.

By the end of that year, as one writer puts it, 'Jochen was in a difficult no-man's land between notoriety and fame'. He had won his first championship race at the end of his fifth full season of racing; what he hadn't shown was that he was championship material, that he knew when *not* to win, when to place and how to conserve his car. With Graham Hill's disastrous accident at Watkins Glen putting him out of contention, Jochen became the undisputed Number One at Lotus and he and Chapman began to enjoy a far better understanding. But when the new Lotus 72 was inaugurated at Jarama, it still needed a great deal of development work. Rindt didn't drive that shark-headed, ultra-light car again until Zandvoort. Where at Monaco, in the old car, he had driven one of his finest and most combative races to beat out the ageing Jack Brabham, in Holland Jochen led from lap three right to the end.

But that was also the race at which Jochen took his decision to retire at the end of the season: his great friend Piers Courage had died in appalling circumstances on the track and Rindt's wife, the lovely Nina, was insistent. Jochen agreed, but said he could not just retire in midseason: not and maintain his self-respect. So he soldiered on, winning the next three races, at Clermont-Ferrand, Brands Hatch and Hockenheim, in a row. In Austria he was beaten by Ickx and the Ferraris were mounting a challenge to his championship lead. To be champion, he needed to win at Monza.

I have heard many reports of that final Saturday practice when Jochen's car first weaved slightly and then went into a crash barrier, its nose going under the rail and striking a supporting post. Jochen's injuries were terrible and he died almost immediately. The car was impounded, investigations made and there are plenty who will still tell you that Chapman's design was at fault, and that once again he had sacrificed a driver on the altar of speed. The image that remains in my head from the stories I've heard is that of a sudden silence falling all over Monza, a long wait, and then the bad news. And in fact, I have relived that moment a number of times: to the point where a sudden silence during a race or practice has become an almost certain harbinger of disaster. If all the drivers stop, it means that one of their number has suffered disaster. Nowadays, only the flutter-flutter-flutter of the rescue helicopter is an equally bad omen.

Rindt's death marks the close of an era as Jackie Stewart's career marks the beginnings of a new one. Rindt was the last of the hugely flamboyant figures whose pictures stare at one from picture books, Stewart the first of a new breed which turned motor racing into a profession rather than an occasional occupation, a way of life or a way of tempting death.

The first thing to note about the new period is its concentration on money and the intrusion of politics. The former is largely the work of Jackie Stewart, whose assiduous pursuit of sponsorship in the sport and whose financial demands were far greater than those of any preceding driver. Jackie set the standards by which others were judged and once money, big money, entered the sport, it was inevitable that drivers would be competing as much for money as for love of the game. The politics of the sport had little to do with Jackie—though he was from his earliest days a strong proponent of greater track safety – but rather more to do with the creation of racing teams that were as professional as the drivers. Once those banded together, as constructors, and began to exert an influence on the sport's ruling body in Paris, the FIA (International Automobile Federation), it followed as night follows day that the sport could no longer be left in the hands of amateurs: amateurs were fine but they should not drive, should not race, should not promote circuits or control regulations. That was the business of the pros.

None of these developments were really foreseeable when Stewart began racing; by the time he retired, they were firmly in place. The reasons were very simple. Firstly, big money, big sponsors, demanded something in return for their money: exposure. That meant the televising of racing. It meant the tarting-up of circuits. It meant creating more equal conditions for racing and thus imposing regulations which made the cars more equally competitive. It also meant doing something about safety: death on the track may bring the average fan to a circuit; on the box at home it is decidedly bad for business.

The reason safety became important was equally simple. Technology had made such strides, cars had grown so much faster and, in seeking to limit their weight, so much frailer, that something had to be done. Many circuits, it was well known, were no longer adapted to the new speeds. Monaco was one of them, but Monaco had a bankroll and prestige to keep it on the calendar. But many other circuits simply disappeared or were asked to make major modifications while other new ones were created to take their place. In France, Reims, Rouen and Clermont-Ferrand went; the old circuit in Mexico was abandoned; Watkins Glen was dropped, so were Mosport and Mont Tremblant in Canada; Montjuich first and then Jarama went in Spain and Interlagos in Brazil; Spa in Belgium was dropped for thirteen years while it was re-designed: the famous Nürburgring suffered the same fate. A driver of the early Sixties, resurfacing in the Eighties, might be forgiven for finding his world a totally altered place.

All these changes enforced new alliances and new power groups. As drivers grasped at economic power, sponsors became ever more vital to the sport: Marlboro and its colleagues in the tobacco industry, for instance, became almost totally dominant: a survey I did showed that almost 70 per cent of a $1.5 billion business was controlled by tobacco interests. Because big sponsors came in, the cars became correspondingly more expensive: one did not fix up wrecked cars, one brought on a new one; one did not work in a garage but in an ultra-modern plant with the latest available technology. Where in Jackie Stewart's day a F1 car might have been developed and built for under $100,000, by the mid-Eighties, the sum required ran into the millions.

Where major financial influences are present, politics will rear its head. Thus the once simple matter of establishing rules, a calendar, eligibility and such became matters of grave contention: as many races were being won (particularly by Ferrari) around the boardroom table or in private meetings in the best restaurants as were won on the track. It became a matter of pride to steal a march on the competition: by political if not by racing means.

Television vastly increased the world's familiarity with the sport. That meant that it had to be dressed up and sold to the public. In the process, a lot of the old racing values went by the board and racing, like many another sport, found itself becoming a source of power, a way for a man to climb up in the world. Where one rises, another must fall, and the lingering wars of the Seventies scarred many. Racing fell into three camps: the constructors, principally English, gathered under the banner of FOCA (the Formula One Constructors' Association) led by Bernard Ecclestone; the sporting authorities under the FIA led by the choleric Jean-Marie Balestre; and a third force vaguely representing a Latin coalition, led by the Machiavellian Enzo Ferrari, which sought to gain advantage by the quarrels between the other two groups.

The issue was clearly power, the question of who controlled motor racing. And I find to hand, in an old *Sunday Times* piece, a succinct view of what each of the parties thought of the other. First, Balestre speaking about the constructors: 'Let me tell you something, those people don't know what they're in for, they don't understand power, they're just little men playing with toys, making cars in garages: who do they think they are? They don't own motor sport.'

And second, Bernard Ecclestone on Balestre and his cronies at the FIA: 'Who the hell is FISA? They are a bunch of nobodies, they appointed themselves and they think they own racing, when all they really have is a bunch of clubs around the world and self-important people living off the back of the sport.'

The sulphurous quality of the exchange is fully representative of the spirit of modern racing; inevitably, such attitudes filtered down to drivers and you will find some of their quarrels detailed in the pages that follow.

What has changed most in the years I have been observing the sport is style, the style of the people involved. I have watched drivers, constructors, sponsors, officials, PR men, advertisers, groupies and almost everyone grow rich; I have watched their progressive aliena-tion from both their roots and the sport. I have watched their lives grow more sumptuous and their souls more stressful. On the first day I went to a racing weekend I lunched in downtown Barcelona with James Hunt; today we would never have so much leisure. I don't think the people themselves have changed: just their perception of life has drifted further away from my own. By their natures they now have to garrison their privacy with the toys of affluence; travel has abolished their sense of place, their hotels are international look-alikes and time is something they don't have. Where they once competed on tiny tracks for the sheer hell of it, they now compete to see who owns the bigger jet, the faster boat, the most cars, go-karts and houses. Where they once had a loyal mechanic or two helped out by a devoted wife, they now live among accountants, lawyers and managers. For a band-aid and a brave face, substitute the private jet-set doctor who works only for you. For loyalty, substitute greed.

I don't think it's ultimately their fault. The times are to blame and the overall commercialization of sport worldwide. I am not one who thinks commercialization is necessarily an evil; certainly drivers are entitled to be paid handsomely for risking their lives. But commerce need not enter the bloodstream; it should not block the kind of human relations which these drivers of an earlier day enjoyed. It has. And, as the sport is capable of killing, so money has killed off its joy.

But then people are intrinsically interesting and drivers, as a race, are complex and disturbed personalities, far richer than one might expect. I hope this book offers some small insight into their enclosed and secretive society.

Jackie Stewart

Jackie had finished racing by the time I got involved in the sport, but it is utterly fitting that this collection of drivers' portraits should begin with Jackie: not only because he was a great champion, not just because he changed the course of the sport, but because he's really never been away. His influence on F1 racing, both while he was in it and after he retired, probably remains greater than that of any other single driver. He is also, by a long shot, one of its most interesting and articulate characters.

I remember particularly well a long discussion we had on a bright sunny day in Austria in 1983, on the subject of the relative importance of car and driver. We had two statements before us: Teddy Mayer's of McLaren, who had asserted that drivers were 'just interchangeable light bulbs: you plug them in and they do the job' and Bernard Ecclestone's classic, 'no driver is worth more than $25,000'. A good beginning for Stewart, who thought both statements rubbish.

'The talent required to drive a machine to the ultimate of its ability is the same as always. Very little has changed. The same inherent chemical element is present today as when the sport began. Machines exist to be interpreted and understood.' He went on to call the relationship between man and machine a marriage. 'In all my years of motor racing, I can only think of a couple of times when I mastered the machine as at the Nürburgring in 1968. It was foggy, rainy and aquaplany: that day, the machine was my passenger. Otherwise, I was always doing my best to reconcile a difficult marriage.'

I then quoted to him a remarkable analysis of how drivers must use their minds. Didier Pironi, who was one of the brightest ones, had said, 'Driving is more a state of mind than the use of intelligence. The driver's problems are psychological rather than intellectual. But that said, and God's gift and the will to succeed apart, all has to be harnessed to the mind. Making a machine work may be mostly "feel", but that "feel" has to be translated through the mind and conveyed to the machine.'

Jackie agreed, so I asked him why constructors like Mayer and Ecclestone so looked down on drivers. 'Perhaps they may think the sport is in a period of relative driving mediocrity,' answered Jackie. 'The constructors and team-managers have enjoyed for some years now such unrealistic power and influence, have commanded so much attention, they have begun to think of themselves and their cars as the stars. Were a great talent to appear, all that sort of talk would be hushed. No team-owner had the guts to belittle a Clark or a Fangio.'

Or, Jackie might have added, a Stewart. Ferrari had the temerity to do so with Lauda, another remarkable talent, and Niki didn't put up with it. And to my recollection, no one for whom Prost has ever driven has had a bad word to say about him, save at the very end of Prost's career with Renault, when other factors that had nothing to do with driving intruded. In the modern era, those three must be bracketed together: they, with Piquet – who, despite his achievements, is rarely mentioned in the same company – have totally dominated the sport for the last twenty years.

The first time I ever spent any time with Jackie was also my baptism into driving around a circuit *fast*. Elf had arranged that Jackie take me around Monaco and the experience – of living through what a grand prix driver lives through every time he races – remains engraved on my mind. There are two parts to the experience. One is myself, white-knuckled and terrified, as Jackie heads past the Casino towards the open sea at something like 150 m.p.h. Ahead is a concrete wall, beyond it the water, fifty metres down; somewhere, I think I know, there is a sharp right-hand turn. There is no notable deceleration, but I don't know that my mind was recording anything but fear, nor is there any particular screech or roll, but suddenly we're around the corner and accelerating down towards the tunnel and Jackie's saying, 'You can relax now, Keith.' The other part is Jackie, to whom going round that tight course as fast as Elf's insurance would allow him to is a mere nothing.

I learned from that outing that there is in top-level racing, as well as intelligence, a physical dimension which is vastly important. There are, of course, a few physically awkward, gawky, uncoordinated drivers. To watch Reutemann on a tennis court, for instance, was painful; even Hunt, a splendid athlete, really lacked that sort of fluency which expresses real 'style'; Jody Scheckter, doing almost anything, was incredibly clumsy. But most of the real champions have a physical quality in common: there is no doubt that they *see* better than most of us. I believe firmly that John McEnroe is not lying when he says he sees the small print on a tennis ball, and Jackie himself has often referred to his vision as a paramount essential in driving. Certainly depth-perception and rapid reflexes in adjusting what is *seen* standing still to oneself moving at great speed, is essential: that corner in Monaco must have appeared to Jackie exactly as it was: such-and-such a distance away, to be approached at such-and-such an angle, such-and-such a speed and so on. The other essential attribute is obviously that of being able to link what one perceives through the brain to what one is doing with one's body.

Well, Jackie was a shooting champion before he was ever a driving champion and, listening to him recently at Gleneagles, when he was taking my neophyte self through the task of shooting at moving targets, I was conscious of how simply Jackie takes these complicated relations between brain and body. The very words he uses, to 'sight', to 'follow', to 'go through', to 'relax', are all part of a physical vocabulary. They are things we tell our eyes or our muscles and limbs to do: much practised, they probably come more readily, but the body needs constant reminding. In a way, mentally, there is no such thing as a 'natural' driver. But there are those for whom the task is easier than it is for most. They are especially gifted and I can hardly think of a sport in which the eye is not the essential informer of the mind.

But there is, of course, a lot more to Jackie than an eye. There is an extraordinary record in racing at all levels, but especially in F1. Jackie's grandfather was a gamekeeper, his father owned a garage, his brother Jimmy raced before him – until a bad accident at Le Mans in 1954 – and Jackie himself started at twenty-one, in 1960. His early career was with Ecurie Ecosse and largely in endurance racing: until the moment when, in 1964, his path crossed that of Ken Tyrrell. Ken has often told me the story of how Jackie came to drive single-seaters: how he had lost a driver in F3 (Teddy Mayer's brother Timmy) and how John Cooper had reported to him (belatedly, Ken says, because he'd already spotted Jackie) that there was some tiny Scot going around whom he absolutely must sign. Ken did and Jackie promptly produced results: on his first day's testing he was as quick as Bruce McLaren; in his first race he won and scored eleven victories in thirteen starts.

The next year, 1965, he had his choice of three F1 teams competing for his services and chose BRM: as he has said, he wanted to be in a team 'where they wouldn't rush me, a team where I wouldn't be battling for my place every time I took the grid, a team where I could learn from a man like Graham Hill'. The result of that first year? His first victory (at Monza) ahead of Graham Hill, Dan Gurney, Luigi Bandini and Bruce McLaren and a third place in the championship behind his fellow Scot Jim Clark and his mentor Graham Hill.

The next two years were not at all successful, and there were reasons for that which Jackie himself will admit. First, that he was pushing himself too far too fast, that his appetite was outstripping his ability and his knowledge of the sport. And that was, at least in part, a consequence of another attribute that is highly marked in the man. Put at its baldest, Jackie was a young man on the make. Not so much for fame, but for money. No sooner was he in the sport than he was already scheming to make his first million; he has never stopped scheming since, to make many more than the first. It is simply an appetite, like any other, and Jackie can be at his funniest when he is mocking this propensity in himself: the endless appearances, the systematic use of his celebrity, the unlimited sponsorships, the directorships, the new business ventures, the life that is taken up, 100 per cent, in 'making it' and, having made it, in making some more. Jackie's greed is no more, really, than an inversion of the competitive spirit he showed in shooting, racing and everything else he did.

Then, too, Jackie made a misjudgement in 1966 and 1967: he stayed in BRM when that team was already on the slippery slope towards oblivion. In terms of engineering, the BRMs were behind their time; the cars gave endless trouble; Jackie's dissatisfactions grew; accidents intervened, especially at a rain-soaked Spa where Jackie went off the track at high speed and lay trapped in his car, his shoulder broken, his ribs cracked and petrol from his ruptured tanks soaking through his overalls, burning his skin.

One bit of good news in 1966, however, was when Ken Tyrrell brought a new Matra to England for Jackie to test. Though he found the new car handled very well, it didn't immediately have the success it might have had in F2, partly because Jackie missed a number of races after his Spa accident; it improved the following year with a Cosworth engine, but by then he was already thinking of what his next move in F1 would be. There was a (typically) abortive contact with Ferrari, but meanwhile Ken Tyrrell had persuaded Matra to upgrade their F2 car to F1 specifications. It was a race to get the car ready in time. In South Africa, Jackie was already on the front row of the grid but the engine gave up on him. Then in practice for the next race, at Jarama in Spain, he suffered another accident, severely damaging his wrist. He had to scratch at Monaco and did not return until Spa, nearly a month later: there, despite a wrist-brace and a lot of pain, Jackie led the whole race until he ran out of fuel, finishing fourth after a pit-stop. At Zandvoort, on another rainy day, Jackie lapped the whole field except Jean-Pierre Beltoise, to win his second grand prix.

At Rouen, he finished third, a lap down, and at Brands Hatch, crucified by the pain in his wrist and driving mostly one-handed, the best he could do was sixth place. Then, in the race Jackie refers to above, the only time the car was his passenger, at the Nürburgring, again in pouring rain, Jackie scored one of the most remarkable victories ever notched up, winning by something over four minutes from Graham Hill. The conditions were appalling and Jackie's mastery absolute. I may not have seen the race, but I've had enough people describe both the race and Jackie's driving to know what a result it was. By Monza, Jackie was still well down on his former team-mate Graham Hill, now driving in a Lotus, and Jackie retired with engine problems while Hill had a wheel fall off. Canada was next, at the old Mont Tremblant circuit, and Hill's fourth place was worth two more points than Stewart's sixth. Jackie and Hill then did a one-two at the Glen, leaving the championship to be decided in Mexico. Jackie had a nasty puncture in practice on the 150-m.p.h. straight and though he was not injured, his Matra was only just repaired in time for the race. A sick engine cost Jackie the championship.

It was all different in 1969. The MS-80 was a winning car and Jackie pulverized the opposition. Though the old car was used in South Africa, Jackie promptly started the new season with a convincing win, repeating the feat in Spain, at Montjuich in Barcelona. At Monaco, his drive-shaft failed and all he had to show for the race was his twenty-two laps in the lead. At Zandvoort, Clermont-Ferrand and Silverstone, he won handily and though he had only third and fifth gears, Jackie virtually clinched the championship with his second place at the Nürburgring. At Monza, he beat Jochen Rindt by a few feet and the championship was his, even though he did not win another race that season.

The 1970 season produced the only posthumous champion in the history of F1, Jochen Rindt, who was killed in practice at Monza. By that year, Ken Tyrrell had some sponsorship money from Ford and abandoned the Matra in favour of a Robin Herd–designed March. The car had the usual teething problems and was not the equal of either the Lotus or the Ferrari, and Jackie's only victory of the year was at Barcelona. But the last three races of the season were in the new Tyrrell. Designed by Derek Gardner, it was a world-beater; by the time it was fully developed during the 1971 season, Jackie was again able to run away with the championship, scoring nearly twice as many points as his nearest rival, Ronnie Peterson. Even his new team-mate, the much-lamented François Cevert, won at the Glen in that car.

Not only was it a superior car, but quite clearly the engines which Ford furnished for Jackie and the Tyrrell team were quite exceptional. Jackie retired only once that year because of his engine and won six races, just as he had in his previous championship in 1969. Was there any reason to doubt that 1972 would be just as successful? If there were, they were not immediately apparent, because in Argentina, Jackie led from start to finish. But in South Africa, after having been in the lead for forty-three laps, he had to retire with a seized gear-box. By Spain, Jackie was beginning to feel the first twinges of the ulcer which was to hamper him for some time and keep him out of racing properly – and out of Belgium altogether – until July.

The ulcer was no real surprise. Jackie lived at a high pitch, he was making hay while the sun shone, he was spreading himself thin with a young family and as many interests as he could cram into the year; for someone always highly strung, always working at a high pitch of nervousness, an ulcer was the logical consequence. At Clermont-Ferrand, however, he came back and brought the famous 003 to its final win. The 005 followed the troubled 004. It should have started at Brands Hatch, but Jackie crashed it and had to race again in the 003. Emerson Fittipaldi was having a triumphant year at Lotus, he led the championship and wasn't about to yield it up: the best Jackie could do was a second. Then at the Nürburgring, the 003 ran its last race, with Regazzoni pushing him off. The 005 came into its own in North America at the end of the season, but by then Fittipaldi had the championship wrapped up.

Jackie's third and final championship, 1973, was another story, with the season starting in ascending order: a third place in Argentina was followed by a second in Brazil and a victory in South Africa. A retirement in Spain was followed by another win in Belgium and triumph in Monaco. The midseason was disappointing, but by the end of July, in Holland and a fortnight later in Germany, Jackie had notched up his fourth and fifth victories of the season and a second place in Austria put him well in the lead. Monza was to be decisive for his championship, and Ken Tyrrell has written that it was Jackie's finest race, not least because he knew he led the championship and because, having already decided to retire, he needed to do no more than the minimum, particularly since he was starting only from sixth place on the grid. During Sunday morning warm-up, Jackie's engine – his and the team's favourite – went off and had to be replaced. As if that were an omen, the race itself went just as badly and after nine laps Jackie had to come in to change a deflating tyre. With a minute wasted, Jackie rejoined the race in nineteenth place. In no time at all, he was faster than he had been in practice, something I have never seen since in a race by a leading driver. Nine laps later, he was thirteenth; at the halfway mark, eighth; seventh came when Niki Lauda went off spectacularly; sixth when he overtook a faltering Mike Hailwood; fifth when on lap fifty-five he overtook Reutemann after many laps of cat and mouse with the Argentine, never an easy man to get by; fourth, his finishing position, when his team-mate François Cevert gallantly waved him by.

As that was a race in which Lotus, knowing that Fittipaldi was planning to leave, had given no team orders to Ronnie Peterson to be obliging to Fittipaldi, Ronnie won – as he could have done several times previously – and with Ronnie's win, Fittipaldi was eliminated from the title race. That was Jackie's third championship in the bag and there was to be only one more race for him, his ninety-ninth, in Canada, where he finished fifth. The Glen would have been his hundredth race, but Cevert was tragically killed in practice and Ken withdrew his Tyrrells. It was an unhappy end to a great career, but Jackie's decision to retire had been taken long before: in April.

The decision was as rational a move as every other move in Jackie's career. Though we have several times discussed the subject of retirement, in connection with other drivers, on his own withdrawal from the sport I would rather let Jackie have the word. Jackie wrote in 1974, explaining his reasons, that 'when the racing bug bites, it is often impossible to shake it off... It can be the world's most exhilarating sport, but it can also be the most cruel.' Like many another driver, Jackie had clearly contemplated the risks he was taking; he had had several severe accidents, so he knew what was involved; he knew the odds. But when his friend and fellow Scot Jim Clark died in 1958, Jackie – like so many others – simply rationalized and sublimated that fact: 'Somehow his death had become impossible to accept. It had been a freak accident. It didn't seem to apply to me.'

But friends continued to die: Jo Schlesser at Rouen a few months later. 'I suppose that I was still naive and intoxicated by the candyfloss world that racing can seem to be.' What one can read between the lines was that Jackie wasn't yet a champion, that he knew he was good enough to be one and that the pressures and opportunities to make money were too good to be passed up. In 1969, he won his first championship. Retire? 'It never even entered my mind.' *Ipse dixit.* After all, success brings its own rewards: and demands. The rewards are goodies; the demands keep a driver too occupied to think too much.

The 1970 season brought a less efficient car – a good moment for a driver to pack it in. For Jackie, it also brought a number of painful reminders that in those days, perhaps only a trifle more than now, driver mortality was a fact of life. First was the death of Bruce McLaren during testing. Then came the horrifying death of Piers Courage at Zandvoort, when despite many a brave effort, Courage died in his flaming car. 'I saw Piers's helmet lying on the track, so I knew whose car it was . . . That was the first time I was to see pain and suffering at close quarters.' What was worst for Jackie, in a way, was the follow-up: the melancholy task faced by his wife Helen as she and Courage's wife Sally had to pack up Piers's things back at the Bouwes Palace. Gathering up the relicts is a hard business at the best of times, and Jackie had to know how the task, carried through with Helen's usual bravery, would have affected her.

Then Jochen Rindt was killed at Monza in practice:

I was to see the effect, in my own home, on my own children, that such tragedy could bring. Both Piers and Jochen were close friends of our children, as well as of ours. It is a strange thing continuing to do something by choice which has taken the lives of your close friends . . . It is difficult to explain to those you love why you want to go on doing the same thing . . . the easy thing is to avoid looking at reality, to run away from it. And the easiest way to escape is just to slip back into the cockpit of a racing car. Once in there and on the track, all the awkward questions are forgotten. You are anaesthetized: no more pain, no more conscience, no more guilt.

Let it be said here that Jackie is not one of the wild ones; he was never, like a Villeneuve or a Depailler, a death-seeker; his thrills did not come from risk, from playing Russian roulette with life, and unlike them, he had everything to live for. I interpose that merely to point up that when Jackie talks of 'guilt' and 'conscience' and 'pain', these were perfectly real things to him. He was *consciously* continuing to race.

Then in 1972, Jo Bonnier was killed at Le Mans. That put a direct pressure on Jackie's family. As he puts it:

Helen had been hurt by Jochen [Rindt's] death but somehow, perhaps because it was near the end of the racing year, we both seemed to mend before the next season got underway. I do remember that that was the first time I wondered if I could bring myself to retire . . . Perhaps I needed more courage to retire than to carry on. But with Bonnier's death, it was different. Especially with Helen. 'I could now see the strain was beginning to tell.' Then came the day when his own two sons came home and asked their mother 'when *their* Daddy was going to be killed, because *all* racing-driver daddies got killed'.

Even by April 1973, when the final decision had been taken, it still weighed heavily on Jackie: so much so that he finally sought advice from an Anglican priest and prayed God to give him enlightenment. With that, 'something came out of me . . . it was like having an unbearably heavy weight cut loose.' Mediaeval theologians would have called it an incubus: racing was Jackie's devil, his familiar, and it had to be cut out, exorcized.

The record was anyway there: three world championships, twenty-seven grand prix wins – a record that remained untouched for fourteen years until Alain Prost finally beat it – and a meteoric career.

Since I didn't know Jackie in his racing years, I can only speak of his character as I've known it since 1975, a period by which he had already become obsessed with driver safety and a real force in improving conditions for drivers. It is an observable fact that the greatest drivers I have known have all been highly safety conscious: a sign that their minds ruled their instincts. But driver safety was far from being Jackie's only hobby horse and the first thing I noticed about Jackie – and I don't think he'll hold it against me to say so – was his incredible garrulity. There wasn't any subject on which Jackie would not discourse: at length. In another, this might be offensive. But in fact, Jackie had by then given so much thought to the sport, to its rules, its techniques, its politics, its characters, that he was unendingly fascinating. The only thing that could get one down – as it eventually did his American television followers – was his high-pitched, breathless, Scots delivery. It was only a decade later that Jackie began to learn how to listen to others. Otherwise, it was always what Jackie said that counted.

But I have an explanation for that. The fact is that Jackie is so fully occupied, every minute of the day, every day of the year, that he is under a sort of compulsion to do everything, including talk, faster than anyone else. He exists in a series of time-capsules, deeply aware of personal responsibilities, of demands made on his time, of kindnesses he wishes to offer, but nonetheless often unable to escape from the maelstrom he has created around himself. Some of that has to be insecurity and often I have thought that what makes Jackie run is the fear that if he stops running the world will all fall apart about him.

Then, too, there are overriding ambitions in Jackie. There is the ambition, desperately normal in the self-made man, to be recognized, to leave a mark on the world. To those bred in greater ease, I suppose this is one of his less attractive sides. You can't exactly call it social climbing, because Jackie is, financially and in terms of celebrity, already at the top. Still, a suspicion lingers that the gamekeeper's grandson would like to be the laird, and I think it scandalous that Jackie's rewards from a nation whose standard-bearer he has so long been, should be a mere OBE. But it is well known that there is a prejudice against awarding the bigger gongs to those who have fled England: especially for Switzerland. Still, it is something unrequited in Jackie and it curiously twists his character, making him sometimes use people on his upward path.

Another ambition has been financial reward, and it is a lucky man who escapes a conversation with Jackie without being reminded of his various positions, his bankers, his lawyers, his accountants and his courtiers. That, too, is explicable, and though Jackie himself puts it down, with much humour, to being a Scot, it is more likely the product of a powerful drive to succeed left over from his motor-racing days. Just as I am sure twenty-seven victories seemed utterly insufficient to Jackie – and had he not retired, he was certainly fit enough and a good enough driver, given the right cars, to which he would have had total access, to notch up another fifteen or twenty – I am sure that his first million seemed a trifle.

Jackie is, I suspect, a far more complex personality than most people give him credit for. He has a passion for information and a like passion for exactness in whatever he does. Absolutely punctilious, he is prone to mood swings which only the exhilaration of activity can overcome. I have known others like Jackie, not in motor sport but in other areas. I have seen the growth of obsession, the inability to leave well enough alone, to relax, to play enough, to be oneself at all times. Once I talked with a doctor about one such personality, asking if in his opinion X did not need psychiatric help, just so he could let go a little. My friend answered that he wouldn't for the life of him ever tinker with such a volcano: 'If I did,' he said, 'the whole man might fall apart.'

I think that is true of Jackie. You take the whole man as he is, foibles and all. Take out a single cog and the gears might grind to a halt.

Emerson Fittipaldi

When I first knew Emerson, the days of his glory were in the past. He was still driving for the McLaren team, this time with the amiable German Jochen Mass, but the team had fallen on relatively lean times, and Emerson, a man short on patience and long on a sense of his own worth – and with two championships to his name – was a sometimes angry and often frustrated man.

Emerson had begun his career with Lotus in 1970, scoring his first grand prix victory at Watkins Glen in 1971. He had steadily improved his performance in the shadow of Jochen Rindt and, with Rindt's death at Monza in 1970, he had inherited the mantle of Number One driver and, by 1972, had won his first championship at Lotus.

A short but commanding figure with bristling sideboards, an underslung slouch and a heavily ridged face, Emerson is not the sort of Brazilian most people expect to meet. Though he was fully capable of relaxation, what marked him most was a restless irritability. That is because Emerson wasn't truly a Brazilian, but a Paulista. The Paulistas are to Brazil what the Milanese are to Italy: they are the businessmen, the ones with the energy and the drive and, as a consequence, they are disliked by the rest of the Brazilians. São Paulo is a place of immigrants and, as is obvious by his name, Emerson's paternal heritage is Italian; his mother is Russo-Polish. In many ways, therefore, Emerson is a cross-breed. There is a part of him which always loved the soft life of the Brazilian beaches, the sun, the sea, the sport, the girls; and there is another part of him that is quite ruthless, highly organized, very self-promoting and ambitious.

In many ways, the dichotomy derives from his own family. As Emerson's father, Wilson Sr, is a journalist, I got to know him quite well in my early years in the sport. Wilson is a typical F1 fanatic, an enthusiast who is excited, vicariously, by the sport and can see no wrong in any aspect of it. Both the Fittipaldi brothers, Wilson Jr, known as Wilsinho, and Emerson, three years his junior, were strongly pushed towards motor racing by their father's enthusiasm. In a nation which is as sports-crazy as Brazil, and which has produced a number of greatly distinguished drivers, of which Emerson was the first world champion, the interest is hardly surprising. If you had the money and the leisure in Brazil, and Emerson's family gave him both – though not so lavishly as, say, Piquet's family – motor racing was something perfectly natural. Brazil is a huge country and the car – and hence competitive cars – is very much part of national life.

Brazil is also a country of frontiersmen, pioneers – *bandeirantes*, they are called – and it would be an understatement to say that ethics and morals play a relatively small part in the art of being Brazilian. It is a place of wide expanses, immense opportunity, widespread corruption, constant violence, sexual laissez-faire and general fantasy, appalling gulfs between rich and poor, between survivors and the condemned. All these factors have some role in Emerson's make-up, but it is that old Paulista go-ahead mentality that made him one of the most disciplined, most consistent and, in his prime, ablest of drivers. It was the same mentality that led him into the *folie de grandeur* of thinking that, having been a champion driver, he was also fitted to run a motor-racing team – indeed, to think that he was better fitted to do so than those for whom he had worked and driven.

Thus Emerson's career breaks into three parts: his years as a champion and at the top of the F1 drivers' hit parade, his years as an unhappy and frustrated team-manager and his last years as an itinerant driver in search of a lost career.

Everyone who raced against him in his good years says roughly the same thing: as a driver, Emerson was enormously consistent, not especially aggressive, very thoughtful and possessed of an excellent racing technique, the source of which was undoubtedly a long apprenticeship spent in motor-cycle racing, karting, Formula Vee, in Renault Gordinis, sports-car racing and so on. On his arrival in England in 1969, he signed on at the Jim Russell school and raced in Formula Ford, passing from there to F3, winning the championship, and moving on in 1970 to F2 for Lotus.

Even in those early days, accounts of Emerson's races all speak of his smoothness, his restraint, his carefulness. It was also sometimes said that he was 'mediocre' and 'uninspired'. The truth is – and it is an old truth in F1 racing – that a driver is often only as good as his car. In a poor car, it takes a driver of great aggressivity and unbounded self-confidence to make such a car even moderately competitive. Keke Rosberg and Alan Jones, among others, were always in the thick of things even when they were driving what each of them calls a 'shit-box'. Emerson, on the other hand, required a good machine, solid backing, a lot of mental caressing, to perform at his best. When confident, few drivers were in his ultimate class, technically; when unconfident, he could be quite ordinary.

For Emerson 1972 was a fine year: with a full season in F1 behind him and with a winning car, he drove with assurance, confidence and verve, though still finicky if conditions were not favourable to him, as at Monaco in the rain. It is detracting nothing from his ability as a driver to say that his first championship, in 1972, he owed to a markedly superior car. The fact is that he had much to do with the development of that car, that he worked hard, drove cleanly and finished steadily: those are the marks of a real champion rather than a flash in the pan. He carried into 1972 the kind of driving which had made his reputation in 1971, and if you study the fact-sheets for that year – the inaugural race at Paul Ricard in France is a good example – you will see Emerson well back on the grid and yet prevailing in the end to finish well enough.

So it was that in 1972 the knowledge that consistency paid off, that concentration was necessary, that racing went to the prudent as well as to the bold began to pay off for Emerson. In Argentina, he was betrayed by his car, but after a bad fright in practice at Kyalami when a wheel came off, he came in second behind Denny Hulme after race-leader Jackie Stewart lost all the oil in his gear-box. By then, and with a couple of non-championship wins under his belt, Emerson and the whole Lotus team knew they were onto a winner in 1972. Not all the Lotus problems had been solved – the car was still very light at the front and had trouble coming out of the corners – but it was certainly thoroughly competitive and Fittipaldi's confidence was high: especially when he won going away at Jarama in Spain, with only Ickx's Ferrari providing any real opposition.

Monaco, however, was to be a set-back. It was a track which Emerson had never favoured, it rained and the best Emerson could do, after a couple of sorties, was third behind Beltoise and Ickx. The next race was at Nivelles in Belgium and Emerson took both pole and the race, leading for seventy-seven of the eighty-five laps. That brought him to Clermont-Ferrand for the French Grand Prix firmly in the lead of the championship but with a bad bout of flu. Despite not knowing the circuit and rain during practice, he scored another second place behind Stewart, who had recovered from an ulcer. Emerson and Jackie swopped positions at Brands Hatch, with both of them missing gears at critical points and having to drive some time in oil thrown up by Ickx's Ferrari.

Fittipaldi's victory made the championship score 43 points to the pretender and 27 to the reigning champion. If Jackie were to close the gap, it would have to be at the Nürburgring. There, Emerson made a superb start but got caught in traffic at the first left-hander. Ickx was leading, Peterson (in a March) behind him and Regazzoni was as usual making life difficult for those behind him. Stewart lay behind. Eventually Emerson got past Regazzoni and then Peterson, whose car was more like a wrestling opponent than a smooth machine. But just as Fittipaldi was beginning to think he might be able to make up Ickx's fifteen-second lead, his gearbox went off and caught fire and Emerson made a hasty emergency exit. Another victory in the incandescent heat of Austria, where Stewart had led for twenty-three laps, brought Emerson to Monza with the title within his grasp: he needed just three points to clinch the championship.

The race weekend, however, was one in which, Emerson had said, 'everything went wrong'. First, the transporter bringing his race car crashed on the autostrada and two of his mechanics were injured. It looked like the run of Lotus troubles at Monza – Clark's run-in with von Trips, Rindt's death – was continuing to dog the team. A spare car was in Chamonix and Emerson was the one who went to fetch it, so that he was exhausted by the time free practice began on Thursday afternoon. Then the newly installed chicane turned out to be a terrifying obstacle, though Emerson still preferred it to the old flat-out curve. A series of mechanical difficulties in setting up the car caused further problems and on Friday he had constant braking problems; an experiment on Saturday did little to change matters for the better – Emerson finished practice in sixth place. Finally, on Sunday morning Emerson woke up to find it raining – and Monza is not the track for rain, nor is rain a help to someone on the third row of the grid.

Meanwhile, Chapman had flown in from his palatial home on Ibiza and was in his usual itchy, touchy, irritable pre-race state. Relaxation was impossible to him: not just because he was a superb 'detail' man, looking into absolutely everything that could affect the outcome of a race, but because he was by nature a thoroughly driven and often neurotic man. I often suspected a touch of sheer paranoia in Colin on race weekends: as though he felt that the gods out there were all conspiring to deprive him of his advancement and rights. It would blow away with victory, it would calm itself off circuit, but at the track – always impeccably attired, natty, cleaned and scrubbed – he fairly sizzled.

That day, the rain mercifully stopped, but Emerson was close to being late, as he often was. He jumped into the car for warm-up and the brakes were as bad as ever. The front discs were changed and that was all that could be done. But Colin remained, in Emerson's own account, very twitchy: winning meant a great deal to him, he was the arch-competitor and in a way he also wanted to take revenge on a track which had both hurt and humiliated him.

Not long before the race started, a fuel leak developed in the cockpit. Shut up in the motor-home with Colin while the mechanics desperately mopped up the mess and changed the fuel bag, Emerson was reasonably sure he wouldn't be able to race. Hindsight says that if the Lotus mechanics hadn't worked so hard and so efficiently and if Emerson hadn't been able to race, Jackie Stewart's two victories in the last grands prix of the season would have given him the championship. That was how close it was, and as Emerson once said to me, he learned that weekend, sweating out the last half-hour before the start, that when you're running for the championship, you simply can't give anything away: give Stewart an inch and he would have taken a yard.

Even when the change had been made, in the nick of time, the questions remained in Emerson's mind: would the engine work? Would the fuel go through satisfactorily? Would the cockpit be full of fumes?

In the event, and despite a last-minute change to the rear roll bar, as Eddie Dennis has said, Emerson's calm won out. Where 'you see little bits of nervousness showing on other drivers, moving their hands, fiddling with the mirrors, feeling their switches, he just sits there . . .' Dennis said. And I can testify to that. Like his compatriot Nelson Piquet, Emerson in the cockpit is a somnolent cat.

The race, and the championship, were won at Monza, but not without difficulty due to Emerson's fear of running out of fuel, which he conserved with characteristic prudence.

The year 1973 came close to repeating the triumphs of 1972 but, as usual in F1, other cars were catching up with the Lotus, though not in qualifying, for 1973 was the year in which Ronnie Peterson notched an astonishing nine pole positions and a place on the front row in twelve of the season's fifteen races, as against one and five for Emerson, Peterson finishing a mere three points behind Fittipaldi. That year also saw Jackie Stewart end his racing career with his third championship, with Emerson as his runner-up.

In 1974, Emerson decided to move from Lotus to McLaren, a move dictated by the kind of restlessness and self-interest which characterize most racing drivers and, more than possibly, by the fact that 1974 was the year in which the multi-million-dollar multinational, Philip Morris, took over the sponsorship of the McLaren team. It is safe to say that Emerson made a leap in earnings by joining McLaren. A former world champion who had narrowly missed a second championship, he had a position of huge popularity in an important market for Marlboro (Brazil), exactly the kinds of characteristics needed to develop a new car, and fitted in temperamentally very well with the racing 'philosophy' of the McLaren boss Edward Everett Mayer – known on the circuit as 'the Wiener' due to his squeaky voice, short stature and constant presence.

In many ways, McLaren was an early, if not the first, prototype of the modern racing team, and it did indeed seem as though Emerson fitted in very well. In the first place, its very structure, financially and administratively, was 'corporate' in nature. Mayer is a Yale-trained lawyer, his background is equally in racing and business, he knows the value of money and how to extract it from sponsors and also was among the first to appreciate, in the changing nature of the sport, that the big bucks and the big battalions give any team a better chance of achieving championship results. Smart-liveried, amply motor-homed, luxurious to a degree, fully equipped with the best that money could buy in research and development, McLaren made a thoroughly businesslike and professional attack on the championships.

It was to be a championship forged from hard-earned placings against a very closely balanced opposition. Peterson, who stayed behind with Lotus, began the season with a pole position in Argentina but failed to finish; Emerson won one of his three races at home in Brazil; but it was already plain that the main opposition was going to come from Regazzoni and Lauda and the Ferraris, who were on one of their ascendant curves, Lauda in fact winning his first grand prix in Spain in April. Ronnie won at Monaco, outlasting both Rega and Niki, and from there to the very end of the season, Fittipaldi had to fight hard to keep his place among the front runners. In July, after Jody Scheckter carried off the race at Brands Hatch, the point situation was: Lauda 38, Fittipaldi 37, Regazzoni and Scheckter 35. At the Nürburgring, Emerson failed and fell seven points behind Lauda and four behind Jody. In Austria, Clay was the only leader to score any points, and in Italy, while Ronnie won his third race, Fittipaldi scored an important second place to keep his chances alive. His narrow victory at Mosport over Regazzoni put the two men equal on points with one race to go at Watkins Glen, with Scheckter still in with an outside chance, and when Rega retired, Emerson settled in behind Reutemann, Pace and Hunt for the fourth place which was to give him the championship.

As runner-up to Niki Lauda in the 1975 championship, a year of Ferrari triumph, Emerson further consolidated his reputation. In Jochen Mass, the amiable, brave, sometimes outrageous German driver, Emerson had the perfect foil for his own hard-headed attitude towards 'building' championships, and his character – at the time I met him – was, I think, best described by Jackie Stewart, who noticed that Emerson was amiable, easy-going, fun-loving, relaxed and serious about his job, but 'you don't drive a racing car because you are all nice. When you are driving a racing car and you are taking it up to the limit, you *can* be nice, you can be charming, but somewhere there are undercurrents going for you that make you a pretty aggressive individual.'

The truth was that for four years Fittipaldi had come close to dominating motor racing in the way Jackie had before him: after two indifferent early years learning his trade, he had been champion twice (in 1972 and 1974) and come second in 1973 and 1975. It was only natural, part of his family ethos and his own psychological make-up, that he would seek new fields to conquer. Remembering my conversations with him at the end of 1975 and the beginning of 1976, it was clear that he wanted fresh fields to conquer, that he thought he had more than proved himself as a racing driver and that he thought he could, with no great difficulty, follow a Bruce McLaren, for instance, and make his own way in cars of his own.

The manner of his handling his departure from McLaren was, however, characteristically inept. For a long time, Emerson simply failed to sign the contracts which would have kept him in front-rank racing. Neither McLaren nor their sponsor, Marlboro, could figure out what was going through Emerson's mind. There were rumours of all sorts and I recall Teddy Mayer speculating on the subject at the time. He felt that Emerson was going through a hard time in his own life, that he was confused, that he was having marital problems, that Brazil and his family were getting him down: in other words, that Emerson was under a lot of pressure.

Whatever the reasons, the result was a disaster for him personally. He managed three points in 1976 driving his own Copersucar Ford, 11 in 1977, 17 in 1978, 1 in 1979, 3 in 1980 and absolutely nothing in 1981, the year when he finally stopped racing his own cars and quit F1.

The whole enterprise was ill-founded from the start. As his team's sole driver, Emerson suffered the usual fate of one-car teams: development was hampered, accidents or breakdowns prevented the team from making its mark and the management and financing of the team distracted Emmo from the task at hand, which was to win races. In theory, Emerson's brother Wilson Jr, or Wilsinho, was to look after the team's administration and sponsorship. This was a task for which Wilson Jr, who had been at best an indifferent driver himself, was palpably unfitted. Much more choleric than his brother – who was never in those years very far from outright rudeness – Wilson offended people, and important people, right and left. He had stubbornness and tenacity, but no real knowledge of the development or maintenance of cars; Emerson, who did, was constantly frustrated and increasingly disaffected. His mood turned, and though he could, off the track, retain much of his charm, on the track or at race meetings, very little of this was evident.

The team was underfinanced from the start and indeed, some of the finance Emerson did get – like some of the companions and hangers-on he began to attract in those years – was distinctly off-colour. Copersucar, the Brazilian sugar giant and Emerson's chief sponsor, found itself in serious political trouble when it turned out that it was indirectly financing the vigilante groups who kept São Paulo in a state of severe political repression during those years. The revelation of these connections clearly did not help Emerson greatly in the ever more sophisticated world of F1 and the truth of the connection, plus Emerson's failure to succeed with a Brazilian team, affected his popularity back home to a substantial extent. Inside F1, it was known that Emerson could have gone on driving for a major team and many thought it a pity that he had not stuck to doing what he knew best. Likewise, in that same world, where financial probity may not be widespread in general but is strictly enforced within the sport, Copersucar's interminable financial difficulties, its frequently delayed payments, its general insecurity and inability to meet its commitments, took their toll of most people's tolerance.

It was widely thought, for instance, that too much of the team's money was going to the Fittipaldi family and too little into the preparation of the car. Emerson was offended by these suggestions and reacted with characteristic vehemence. My own view is that he did not understand, nor admit to himself, the extent of his own error in starting off on his own without experienced and able people around him. That is, he thought he was still the amiable, easy-going champion he had been, when in reality he was a harried man who was beginning to learn about defeat and humiliation.

It is also true that when a decline sets in in F1, it is very difficult to retain one's status. Those of us who remember the horrid cruelties applied to Frank Williams in the days when he was generally considered 'Wanker Williams', an outsider with no chance to make good, can remember how it felt for Emerson to climb down off his mountain and to try to make good in a changing and by then wholly different world. Unfortunately, ill luck, in his case compounded by ill judgement, dogs the unsuccessful, and the only way into the sport, for some who should never be in it, is around the less successful teams. There, a little money will buy you a good deal of swank. Because of his fame, his history and his continued presence in the sport, as well as the strength of his personality, Emerson remained a figure; but also the shadows lengthened about him and few who worked with him in those years have much good to say about their relationships with him or with his team. Then, too, there are the marginals who somehow seep into the paddock, and one of my unhappiest memories of Emerson's decline has to do with the opening of the season which in those years invariably began with the Argentine and the Brazilian grands prix.

The whole F1 family would stay at the Sheraton in Buenos Aires and the Hilton in São Paulo while, between races, a majority of the drivers would take a week's break at Guaruja on the Brazilian coast near Santos, an hour or so away from the smog-filled city of São Paulo. As Emerson and his family had a house on the beach in Guaruja and as, like all Brazilians, Emerson, his lovely wife Maria Helena and his whole family were extremely hospitable, that house became a natural venue for a bunch of cronies and hangers-on whom Emerson, with more good nature than judgement, would invite to stay with him. Naturally, that something less than attractive fringe also found its way to the beach house. In F1, such people are tolerated by some: either because they are good company or because they provide 'services', whether these be the producing of Mercedes cars which are then flogged off at a profit or the procuring of girls. They are flash people who have money to throw about, and not all the money they throw about is honest money.

I do not think those were happy times in Emerson's marriage and they certainly did not enhance his general image in the sport. They offended some of the more straight-laced among the constructors – people who might have been more inclined to help the Fittipaldis if they kept better company – and generally put a question mark over the Fittipaldi team: how it was surviving, with whose backing, by what means. Rudimentary Mafiosi, such as Franco Ambrosio, who was shortly to be a founding member of Jackie Oliver's and Alan Rees's Arrows team, an egregious former self-styled gun-runner and mercenary later gaoled for escaping up Holland Park Avenue throwing bags of cocaine out the windows of his car, floated around on the edge of those early South American season-openers, the former offering fantastic deals (on which he rarely delivered) and the latter procuring the kind of girls that racing drivers can relax with. It was hardly a wholesome scene.

If Emerson had had the finance to develop a team properly, if his brother had been a better manager and if Emerson himself had not become frustrated as a driver by his car's constant failures and retirements, if, in short, he had got his act together, he would quite possibly have made a first-class constructor and been hailed as a Brazilian Ferrari or Chapman. In fact, he had all the mannerisms of the major proponents of the sport but few of their skills. Very good at setting up cars, he was less fortunate in his choice of engineers and, when he had good ones, did not know how to leave well enough alone. By driving his own cars when he was past his peak as a driver, he lost out on the development that could have been contributed by a second opinion. By running a marginal operation that staggered from week to week, he was unable to put together a long-term plan for success.

The best account of Emerson's last year in F1 is in Keke's memoir of his two years with Fittipaldi. It is a bitter tale of unfilled promises, cash shortage and Emerson's inability to allow others who knew more than himself to perform their functions properly. It makes a sorry epitaph to a great career, ended Emerson's F1 ambitions, wound up breaking up his marriage, alienated the public, caused dissent in his own family and forced Emerson into retirement.

Later, Emerson was to continue racing in other forms, in the US Cart championship and elsewhere: the bug was still in him, success came occasionally, but the spirit seemed to have gone out of the man. He was happier than he had been during the seven bad years between 1976 and 1982, still self-assured but now far more reasonable. The final verdict has to be that the underlying intelligence of the man, for all his shrewdness, combativity and skill in a car, was insufficient to match an ambition that was almost forced upon him by his milieu, by his family and by his status as a Brazilian national hero.

Niki Lauda

There was an early view of Niki Lauda – affectionately known as 'the Rat' to much of the F1 family – which thought of him as an automaton. Whatever the business at hand was, he got on with it, rather as if you poured Draino into a sink. Detergents don't discriminate between tasks and Niki was so good at what he was put to doing that this notion stuck, especially when his Ferrari was doing so well that victory seemed almost automatic.

There was a still earlier view which said that he was an arrogant little brat and that what he liked best was having fun, preferably at the expense of others.

Then there is the post-Nürburgring view of Niki which apotheosized him: the way the press and the media treated him, you would have thought Richard Wagner was about to consider fitting him into Valhalla and Charlton Heston play him as El Cid. The man who the media said could do no right, because he wouldn't give straight answers and most of all enjoyed mocking the stupidity of the press, suddenly became the man who could do no wrong.

I would have thought Niki could take all these views of himself with a grain of salt. They are all partly true and they all make up the totality of a man whom I think very few people – perhaps least of all Niki himself – really understand. Either he is as simple and as straightforward as he would like us to believe, or he is, as many who have been around him think, so infinitely and deviously smart that, like a fox, he just can't be captured.

Where all these views would concur is in saying that on the track Niki was as much the natural successor to Jackie Stewart as Alain Prost is the natural successor to Lauda. About his effectiveness in a car, any car, there is very little doubt. About his mastery of the mysteries of driving strategy and deriving the best out of the materials at hand, there is unanimous consent. If Niki the man slips through this net of approbation, much of the fault must rest with his own capacity to mythologize, his utter disrespect for those who seek to read his mind and the kinds of people he has always kept about him, like court jesters, to keep his market value high.

The last is important. Niki is an Austrian and, at that, an Austrian in the full sense of the word, and Austrians, at least after the collapse of their empire in 1918, are a little bit aslant to the world. As an Austrian, Niki is divided against himself, and there are not just two Nikis but several dozen of them. The job of keeping them together has been entrusted to a series of 'confidants' who write his books, churn out his articles, furnish his quotes, capture his image and sweeten the sour, and when I once asked Niki why he wouldn't ever do a serious – and in consequence, a truthful – book about himself, he replied, why should he? The only thing such books were good for, he added, was starting the fire back home: he kept a pile handy by the hearth.

I don't just think Niki doesn't want to be known, I know it. I had a long talk once with the very bright lady who accompanied him in his early days, a lady of charm and accomplishment and infinitely more mature than Niki was. She said she wouldn't know who Niki really was. He was a child, he was a *Mensch*; he was a massive egotist, he was generous; he was foolhardy and petrified; he loved company and loathed it; he was ambitious and careless; he was smart but stupid. Whatever he was, she found him charming and exasperating at the same time and no, she didn't think her relationship would last because you can't keep mercury in your hand, not for long.

The point of all of this is that Niki is an excellent self-publicist and a determined mystifier. He has 'written' far more books than any other driver in the history of the sport; he has given an infinite number of 'in depth' interviews; he has been the subject of as much and as adulatory film footage as the Fellini-like Enzo Ferrari, and while everything he says seems absolutely straight, nothing he says is without a sharp edge to it. The sharp edge of what Niki thinks: about racing, about people, about socialism, about Austria, business, the world. The trouble being that what Niki thinks, beyond the basics of his craft, changes from day to day. The transparent 'honesty' with which he will say good and bad about the people he's worked with and around has always to be taken as having a 'point of view'; that 'point of view' is governed by what Niki is looking for at any particular moment.

Some of this undoubtedly derives from Niki's background, which is proper to the point of pedantry and very much old Austria. Just take the ambiguous sentences at the beginning of Niki's latest book, *To Hell and Back*: 'In Austria, the Laudas are a "good" family. At any rate they were.' It is not a historical statement; but is it the declaration of a creed? That whatever the Laudas were, they are not, in Niki's hands, the same? Certainly nothing about Niki is particularly reverent: the coldness of his family (their 'twenty-room garret' in Vienna), the autocratic 'old' Lauda, his grandfather, his school-and-garage days (hopeless), the various 'borrowings' by which he wangled his cars, all that passes in a breeze. What he is saying is that he always wanted to drive, his family was against it and he defied them and did it.

But the way he did it was with the same connections he defied, and to get into serious racing in his early days, he got a bank to give him credit and a sponsor to give him some backing: though he hadn't, of his own, a sou in the world. What the young Niki did have was expectations, which the bank recognized. He also had expectations of himself. He started out with March in F2, where Ronnie Peterson was a budding star – 'they therefore,' writes Niki, 'did not feel the need for anyone particularly good in the Number Two slot.' That cost Niki 20,000 borrowed quid. That was 1971. By 1972, he needed a fresh injection of capital and he wanted to get into F1. The price at March this time was £100,000. The managing director of the bank that had advanced the first £20,000 was willing, the board, influenced by Niki's grandfather, wasn't. So Niki went to another bank and raised the hundred grand. 1972 gave him thirty starts: in F1, F2, Touring and Endurance. The last three worked passably; the March car he had was a fiasco. Niki knew it, Peterson long refused to believe it and March (in the person of Robin Herd) soldiered on too long. 'The experience was certainly salutary,' wrote Niki, adding that what he learned was that he should trust his own judgement, that engineers get carried away and some drivers don't understand their cars.

Still, 1972 left him bankrupt: financially and in terms of a drive for 1973.

'Rescue' appeared in the form of Lou Stanley of BRM. Except that Stanley, too, wanted money. A further £80,000 was extracted from the Austrian coffers, repayable in three instalments. Only the first would Niki have the slightest chance of repaying. Did 1973 respond to his plans to leapfrog into the elite who would be actually *paid* to drive? BRM was in decline, the best Niki could do was one fifth place in Zolder. But after Monaco, a real miracle did occur: Stanley said to forget the rest of the payments to the team – as long as he agreed to stay two seasons more. Niki signed. With his debts, what choice did he have?

Ah, but Maranello has heard of him. Enzo Ferrari has watched him in Monaco, where in the superannuated BRM he had held on to third place for a third of the race, and then at Zandvoort. The offer came, there was still a contract to be abrogated, but Lauda is Lauda: what he wants, he gets. And at this point, finally, Niki's career takes off.

Niki has 'written' a whole book on what it is like to drive for Ferrari. It is not a particularly good book and Niki despises it, but it does have some home truths in it. One of them is that for all Enzo Ferrari's mythomania – and God knows he loves the pomp and circumstance of his legend and exploits it in his dealings with the outside world – the *Ingegnere* knows his stuff and can be perfectly straight when he wants to. The main fact about Ferrari is that he is *old*. Because he is old, he is a legend. He's a link with the past. He is old and sad because he lost his son. He is old and sad and weak because while the sport dominates his thinking, he no longer dominates the sport, and his thinking, for many years now, has not really dominated the Ferrari sporting division at Maranello.

That is because as a racing team, Ferrari is like Britain before the Norman Conquest: a bunch of fiefdoms, with all sorts of lesser people shoving against each other for power in a small factory where there isn't any ultimate power to be had: at least not until the Grand Old Man goes.

Niki was lucky when he began at Ferrari in that he had a powerful intermediary in Luca Montezemolo, a gentleman in the Italian style, enormously suave, even-tempered, civilized and amiable. Luca is now in charge of Italy's arrangements for the 1990 World Cup. A better choice there could not be. But Ferrari, even then, was not just Luca. The other major force was Mauro Forghieri, the Ferrari engineer, of whom Niki writes that 'he has the psychological finesse of a sand viper' and that 'when the Ferrari went well and all was perfect, he considered me a very good driver, perhaps the best. When things went wrong, I was an idiot.' Whether or not Niki ever said any such thing, since his books are ghost-written without any great elaboration from Niki, who says he never reads them, the facts are true. Forghieri, technically, was a fine engineer; as a human being, he was mercurial, unpredictable, self-contradictory and irascible.

Niki's years at Ferrari were a set of ups and downs. More ups than downs on the track, more downs than ups within the team. We have several times talked about this period of his life, which Freud himself would find hard to fathom, and I think the answer to the manic-depressive cycle lies in the fact that Niki is Niki. He's not the sort of a man whom you can change by external circumstances, for I honestly think he puts very little value on externals. For instance, though he has always been supremely competent at wrestling the best contracts out of his teams, I don't think his real interest lay in the money itself, but in the definition of himself as the best in the world and therefore entitled to the best treatment and the most money.

The record shows that in 1974, his first year at Ferrari, Niki's success was modest. Regazzoni came second to Fittipaldi in the championship, and Niki followed in fourth place behind Jody Scheckter of Tyrrell. What happened to him that year is typical of what has often happened at Ferrari: questions of detail. These are the hardest things for ambitious drivers to live with. Little bits fall off the car, some trifling part has been improperly milled, a mechanic makes a mistake. In the best teams, this sort of thing rarely happens, but if it does, a collective effort is made to put it right. At Ferrari, the only effort to put things right is either to find the scapegoat or to cover up the mistake and deny it ever happened.

That year, Niki had his chances: he dominated the race in South Africa and the car went sick four laps from the end; he had Monaco in his gift, the same defect did him in; at the Nürburgring, his mechanics rolled his race tyres over debris. Not all the faults are Ferrari's. Niki got himself into a series of accidents, some from ill judgement, some from overanxiety, some from inexperience. And in this respect, it should be recalled that the man I later compared to the mechanical rabbit who runs on rails at a greyhound track was far from being the smooth, meticulous driver he later became.

In 1975, he began the European season with the 31ST, which was simply the best car on the track that year. Niki had nine pole positions in fourteen races, but nine out of eleven in the new car. He notched up five victories and was simply unstoppable. I watched him go round and, as it was my first year in the sport, I thought – so this is what F1 is like, eh? It just seemed that the Ferrari superiority was such that racing must be terribly boring for all the rest of the drivers. What I didn't know then was the amount of work Niki had put into not only creating, testing and developing that car, but also dragging an unwilling and divided racing team in his wake. By the end of that season, when he won his first championship by a large margin, I had little doubt who had achieved the triumph: Niki is no braggard, but in the first of many longish talks, he explained to me that his nature was such that he really just couldn't stand the second-rate; and if you saw the second-rate around you, you had a clear choice – either you cleared out and found yourself the first-rate or you simply demanded that second-rate people became first-rate. He had chosen, he said, the latter path, and what was more, it was obviously so. I have seldom, before or since, seen a man spend so much time with his car, be so obsessive about it, put so much work into it, understand it so well and be so unable to divert his attention from it for so much as a minute.

As Niki rightly points out, that year proved something to the whole of F1. Technical development, intensive development, research and rigorous attention to every detail were what paid off. At the same time, he wryly noted, success helped 'create a Ferrari crisis, because it could never be bettered, and the tremendous success brought new problems'. That is equally true.

I noted a new aspect to Niki at the end of 1975, which he concluded with a fine victory at Watkins Glen. That was that all the fame in the world meant bloody all to him. His ego was and is such that the outside world can neither add to nor subtract from it. He was in love with Marlene, had left the lovely Mariella and was determined to keep his private life private. Otherwise? 'I revise my market value, naturally . . . Otherwise nothing was changed as a result of being world champion, absolutely nothing . . . My know-how has reached the summit of effort, and surpassed it. Any further increase of the star image is nothing but a nuisance . . . I don't want to be a magazine hero. I want to be known for my driving, not as a society man or a lover or God knows what.'

Probably this was damned difficult for the people at Ferrari to understand and Niki was always capable of being the supreme turn-off. He was simply his own man and had no intention of playing Ferrari or any other games. But from Ferrari's point of view, this must have seemed like grave disrespect: if one legend runs a company, it has an inbuilt interest in creating accompanying, subsidiary legends.

It was at this point, with Ferrari flushed with success, and as usual – like an Italian after a filling bowl of pasta – somnolent in regard to the future, that Montezemolo went back to Fiat and a successor had to be found. Daniele Audetto was out of the same mould as Luca, but his job was now infinitely more delicate and difficult. Daniele might be running the team for 1976, but Niki and Clay Regazzoni had very much the upper hand. Niki's statement is cut-throat in its clarity: 'If he [Daniele] is to give the orders, he must make the right decisions: right for me, for the team, for success.' Kindly note the order. 'If he makes the wrong decision,' continues

Niki, 'he becomes my opponent . . . Not for nothing is water polo an Italian expression to describe business life: the fouls are done with the feet under the water where the umpire cannot see them.'

Here, a few words about Niki's strained relations with Italy and Italians. The truth is that what Italians do well – live, survive and enjoy – Niki is not interested in, and what they do equally well – knife, subvert, rage, seduce, charm, infuriate, bureaucratize – are all things Niki cannot stand. For him, there is not enough room in life for anything but one-to-one relationships and then as now, Niki has always been better in such relationships than in the goings-on of a board or a team. Then, too, Niki has a low opinion of the media. He can be hugely intelligent when he thinks they can be of assistance to him, but most of the time he knows they're a poorish and raffish lot, living off their own enthusiasms and frustrations. If he feels that about the media in general, he feels it particularly about the Italian press. On whom I think the world ought to take a little pity. Italy has three daily sporting newspapers. They cover sport completely and well. But they are paid, like the tabloids in England, to titillate their public. And nothing in Italy – except perhaps the national football team – so titillates the Italian public as Ferrari. With an obligation, daily, to fill a whole page of the paper on motor racing, and on race weekends, three or four, their poor, harried reporters are frequently forced to invent what they cannot find out. And since Niki – though he always did his duty – was ever notably surly with the press, what they invented about him caused Niki little joy.

The 1976 season was, anyway, going to be an exceedingly difficult one for Niki. The old car went well at the start of the season, but attention to detail was wanting. Nonetheless, Niki soon built on an overwhelming lead in the championship, though a first crisis came at Long Beach when Audetto suggested that Clay Regazzoni ought to have his day in the sun. Niki objected, but Clay did win – because Niki's car failed him. Then, before Spain, Niki managed to overturn a tractor on himself. He could have been killed; he escaped with cracked ribs and bad bruising. The Italian press had a field day: Niki should be replaced. Regazzoni was the true Ferrari star. It all came back to that greatest of Italian national defects, which is less an attitude of xenophobia than a reflection of its people's belief that Italy is God's country and Italians God's chosen. Australians are not so different. Nor, for that matter, are Brits.

Well, Niki was not an Italian. He might drive for Italians, but he couldn't be made of the right stuff. As Niki puts it, 'you can drive

The eyes, the tartan, are unmistakable: Jackie Stewart, the man who changed the sport

Above: *Juan Manuel Fangio, five times world champion*

Below: *Ascari, Maserati, Zandvoort, 1953*

Above: *Farina at Monza for Ferrari in 1953*

Fangio in 1956: 45 years old, still on top

like a god, say nothing but nice things in Italian and always eat spaghetti, it doesn't do the slightest good, you are still a swine...' And Audetto was urging Niki to rest, let Clay take care of Spain. Lauda again declined.

The man who put Niki together again after that little mishap was one Willy Dungl, a masseur-cum-dietician who became Niki's physical guru for years to come and made Niki into the fitness freak he became.

The intra-family dispute with Clay continued. Niki acknowledges that they were never friends; he also has kind words to say about Clay being a good, steady driver and so on. That is more or less what he has to say. Frankly, it is hard to imagine two people more temperamentally opposed. In his racing days, Clay was both a crazy and a hard man. He caused more suffering among his fellow drivers than any other man I ever saw race and the only man who could possibly come closer to him as a road-hog, even when his own position was hopeless, was Riccardo Patrese, a far more refined driver than Clay in every other respect. As a technician, he was grossly inferior to Lauda. To continue to advance Rega's claims against Lauda's, as Daniele did, was inexplicable in racing terms. In Ferrari terms, it wasn't, and Niki should have smelled earlier that yet another Ferrari plot was under way, and without Montezemolo, his flanks were unprotected.

Matters came to a climax over Brands Hatch and its aftermath (a subject fully treated in the chapter on Hunt). This time, it is God himself who descends from his empyrea. Enzo, the Jove of the motor-racing world, who may get all the statistics and results and data from the circuit but hasn't been on the inside of modern racing on the track since prehistoric days, announces to the world that Lauda isn't taking care of his car, he neglects his work, he's got himself married and buggers off home and more of the same. The ensuing scene back at Maranello, when Niki confronts God Almighty, makes funny reading. Whether it makes good history or not is another matter. Audetto, who was present in the later stages, once denied to me that it transpired entirely as Niki says. I doubt it too; it is simply too good comic opera to be true. But what is undoubtedly true about the account is Enzo Ferrari's rage, which is formidable. Because what Niki was doing – the subject was Niki's contract and terms for 1977 – was putting himself on the same level as Enzo. In Enzo's mind, there is no one else at his level, so that any such pretensions are just *lèse majesté*, and *lèse majesté*, we know, is just a step up from insolence, and who does this little Austrian think he is? Only someone as lofty and as besotted with himself as Ferrari could conclude the negotiations by saying, OK, Jew, you win.

After that pleasant scene, which ended with Niki getting a substantial increase in his pay, fate struck again: at the Nürburgring on 1 August. The Ring was a place Niki knew well, and he knew the place was unsafe. Niki had an ambition to drive it perfectly. Why the Ring? Because it was in those days simply the most difficult, challenging and interesting circuit around. If his own tally is correct, 1976 was his eighteenth actual race on that wooded, long and perilous track in the Eiffel Mountains. He'd already had his fair share of accidents there. The difference between the early days and 1976 was that cars were going a lot faster – Lauda himself had been the first to break the magical seven-minute lap in 1975 – and that very little had been done to make the track safer. Jackie Stewart had started the protests and the action to force the sporting authorities to do something, Niki had kept up the pressure. As he has written, 'I steeled myself to drive that fast lap in 1975 although my brain kept telling me it was sheer stupidity. The antithesis between the modern-day racing car and the Stone Age circuit was such that I knew every driver was taking his life in his hands in the most ludicrous degree.'

At a drivers' meeting in the spring of 1976, Niki had proposed the Ring be boycotted. He was voted down. He accepted the decision. He had been merely stating 'a professional opinion'. Whatever, when he arrived at the Ring, Niki was pilloried in the sporting press for his opposition to a great track in which all the other champions had raced: if he was so craven-hearted, they said, he shouldn't be racing.

The actual accident, Niki doesn't remember. He remembers before, especially some idiot handing him a photo of his friend Jochen Rindt's grave through the window of his car, and he remembers after, the sound of a chopper as he's wafted off to hospital, but not the accident itself. Mercifully. He watched a film taken by a fifteen-year-old-boy later, at home in Salzburg. The film showed his Ferrari jerking right (Ferrari never carried out an inquiry, but Niki's chief mechanic at the time conjectured a snapped rear left tie-rod), crashing through the chicken wire into the embankment – it was one of several dozen such places at the Ring and spectators were few – bouncing back onto the track, its petrol tank flying through the air. The Ferrari was on the ideal line for the bend, Brett Lunger came through, struck it and pushed it a hundred yards down the track where it burst into flames. The marshals, who were not exactly close by, could do little: they had no fire-proof clothing. The first drivers through – Guy Edwards, Lunger, the bearded Harald Ertl – leaped from their cars and tried to rescue Niki, but it was the old Ferrari driver, Arturo Merzario, a tiny figure usually decked out in a cowboy hat, who simply waded into the flames and undid Niki's harness: not a second too soon.

The damage was double: the exposure to the flames had been long enough to cause severe burns to his face, head and hands; worse, he had been forced, as the flames consumed the oxygen, to inhale volatile fuel and smoke, both of which critically affected his lungs and blood.

Fortunately, though all memory of the accident had been erased, Niki was not unconscious for very long, therefore his mind had a chance to work. On the one side was the pain and a great big black hole into which he wanted to sink – it was so restful down there – and on the other there were the surgeon, the nurses and his wife Marlene talking to him constantly, trying to get him to react, to fight back. It's something that Niki plays down in his book, but I know from others who were in touch with him at the time, that the mental effort and courage required were tremendous. And inordinately fatiguing. It was four days (during which he was given the last rites) before his doctors gave him a chance to live through. After that, it was all willpower and the result was an extraordinary recovery. Niki's phlegm about the whole incident can be summed up in what must be the driver's quote of the decade: 'There is no point in having a complex about losing half an ear.'

He came back at Monza, five weeks later. He wore a cap on his head ('I even capitalized on my semi-baldness by signing with Parmalat to wear a cap with their name on it') and my memory is of a certain artificial constraint on the part of many in paddock and pit-lane in approaching him. Whatever Niki says, the accident had put him apart and it was, then – for later his scars became part of his persona – difficult to look at him. One knew he didn't want pity, yet he received it.

There is no doubt the accident at the Nürburgring cost Niki a second successive championship. James Hunt was able to capitalize on his absence and even when he came back to racing, Niki was hampered in his driving by the healing of his scars, particularly about his eyes. And the fear of what had happened in Germany still lived with him. He played the hard man and pretended he was beyond fear, but that was nonsense.

If restoring himself to full driving fitness was one thing, Ferrari was no help on the psychological front. They really didn't know what to do about Niki and, like all people who are doubtful and afraid, they reacted defensively. They gave themselves back-up by putting Carlos Reutemann into the team. If Regazzoni was little help to Lauda within Ferrari, Reutemann was even less. In the first place, Niki couldn't stand him personally – and this had to do with a clash of personalities, the Argentine being in every respect the antithesis of Niki – and in the second, the Ferrari tactic was quite clear: if Niki doesn't recover, we get rid of him.

Still, as the season drew to a close in Japan, Niki led the championship by three points. The majority of drivers – by Niki's account, or a minority, if you believe James Hunt – had already decided they would not race in the appalling conditions at the Fuji track. The exceptions to the general feeling among drivers were, however, important ones. Hunt, who lay second in the championship, said he would race if the officials decided the race should start, and Clay Regazzoni, his Ferrari team-mate, said he would anyway. Inside Ferrari, Niki's decision was again made to seem that of a man intent on going it alone.

Anyway, the fact is that if it hadn't rained in Japan, if he hadn't withdrawn from the race after a few laps and waited until the weather improved, he, not James Hunt, would have been champion. I spent some time with him after he drove back into the pit-lane and he was very categorical about his decision: 'It is simply not worth it,' he said. 'If conditions are not safe, drivers should not be asked to drive.'

They weren't asked: they were told. That is the way of F1. But Niki, again, was his own man. I admired him for his decision then, I admired him for not thinking being world champion was worth the risk, and I admire him still for maintaining a moral stance.

But at Ferrari, they were enraged. Lauda the coward, screamed the Italian press. The Grand Old Man offered Niki a contract as team-manager when he got back to Europe. Niki smelled the rat and said unless his driving contract were honoured, he would move to McLaren. No one had – at least officially – offered him the job, though he knew Hogan of Marlboro would be glad to have him, but the bluff worked. He was asked to leave Ferrari's rather funereal office while a major argument took place; when he was invited back in, he was told Reutemann would be the team's Number One driver.

As things work out in F1, contracts to that effect or not – and Reutemann was to have his troubles with Alan Jones on that score later – the Number One position in any team is pragmatically judged on results, and though Niki did not make a brilliant start to the 1977 season, he did re-establish his hegemony within the Ferrari team by the South African Grand Prix. But the 1977 Ferrari was by now outmoded and no longer had the same competitive edge. Niki won in South Africa, Germany and Holland; he came in second six times and beat Jody Scheckter to the championship by 17 points; Reutemann was fourth, 30 points off the pace behind Andretti.

Fed up with Ferrari, Lauda secretly signed for Brabham at Zandvoort. Ferrari made a generous offer for the following season, but Niki told him, 'I don't want to stay, that's all there is to it.' With the championship wrapped up, he declined to start in Canada and Japan and was replaced by Gilles Villeneuve.

The move to Bernard Ecclestone's Brabham was to a team which had a lot going for it – it was owned by the man who was consolidating his hold on F1 and had an outstanding engineer in Gordon Murray – and one serious defect. It had a very poor engine indeed, the twelve-cylinder Alfa Romeo. It was plagued by trifling mechanical problems and its chief technician, the charming *bon vivant* Carlo Chiti, seemed overwhelmed by its problems. As Niki relates it, Chiti spent more time looking after two score stray dogs that roamed through the Alfa factory than he did making sure his engines actually ran. Anyway, 1978 was the year of the Lotus, and Mario Andretti ran away with the championship.

The 1979 season was even worse: Niki's four points were only double those he had earned in his first F1 year seven seasons before. The season came down to Montreal and Brabham was trying out the new version of the famous Cotsworth engine instead of its disastrous Alfa Romeos. After months of negotiation, Lauda had wrested a $2-million-a-year contract from Ecclestone – no mean feat in itself. Gordon Murray's new design looked splendid (it was to become steadily more successful in the following years). It was Niki who had lost heart.

It was a rainy day, a bad day in the heart. Niki just quit shortly after practice started. He told Ecclestone he didn't want to drive any more, he wanted out. And Ecclestone, being the man he is, that is, a creature who understands straight talk and who despises hypocrites, understood at once.

As it happens, I left the circuit with Niki. He was a completely changed and infinitely more relaxed man, patient and courteous and easy. He made his reasons absolutely clear. He had always said he would retire when he no longer enjoyed his racing and he no longer did. His reasons for no longer enjoying it had nothing to do with his accident, now well past him, or with the failure of the Brabham venture; it was within himself. He had looked out the window of his hotel that morning, seen the rain, thought of the day that lay ahead of him and none of it any more seemed worthwhile. He was suffering from third-degree ennui, and that was all there was to it. He loved flying, he loved his home on Ibiza, he loved his wife and child, he no longer loved racing. Was he weary? Yes, he was weary of exploiting and of being exploited. He wanted privacy and not the struggles of circuit and paddock. He wanted to be a different kind of man doing a different kind of thing. What could one do but applaud his decision?

I doubt that anyone really thought it would last. Racing is in the blood, and while a driver still thinks he can do it, at or near the top, he is always going to be tempted. In the interim, Niki had created his own airline, Lauda Air, but it wasn't going all that well. He had also maintained his F1 contacts: principally with Ron Dennis, who had bought McLaren out from Teddy Mayer, though here again, the hand behind the scenes really belonged to Marlboro's John Hogan. The result was that after two years out of racing, Niki asked Ron Dennis to give him a private test – mainly to assure himself that he had not lost his skill and that he could face the new world of F1 wing cars, quicker and much more road-adhering than the old generation. He was a little out of shape (or a lot, if you take into account Niki's manic standards) but the money Dennis and Marlboro offered (the rumoured figure is $5 million) was an inducement. Willi Dungl was still around making Niki work out and adjusting his psyche and Niki knew, if he wanted to, he could make his comeback. Which he did, smiling, at a McLaren press conference.

No sooner back than at the very first race of the 1982 season, at Kyalami, controversy broke out again. As it happened, the morning that the drivers decided to go on strike, I was up early at Kyalami. I saw the drivers holding a conference in a bus in the lower reaches of the car park and decided to mosey down to see what was going on. Didier Pironi told me they were about to leave the circuit for a hotel to meet in private where they could not be coerced by their bosses and, as it happens, along with a half-dozen other early colleagues, my car was well placed to follow the bus as it drove off. An altercation took place at the entrance to the circuit when the irascible John McDonald sought to block the bus with his car – the idea of drivers striking and being independent of their owners struck him as positively mediaeval – but was resolved by a little gentle persuasion and a show of force by an angry Jacques Laffite. The bus took off for downtown Jo'burg, followed by our small convoy of about three cars, though in the ensuing hour, every reporter in F1 was shuttling back and forth between the drivers' hotel and the circuit, where the angry bosses and the choleric Jean-Marie Balestre, president of FISA, met in angry conclave.

The ostensible issue was simple. At the beginning of the year, the drivers make application for their super-licence, a recently introduced, sensible measure designed to make it more difficult for the totally unqualified to buy themselves drives. When applications that year were made, Lauda and others were smart enough to realize that the licences had been so designed as to tie them to their teams, a move cleverly designed by certain constructors to lower the price war among drivers and to prevent desertions in the ranks. The hidden agenda, which has never been properly discussed, was an attempt by American superagent Mark McCormack to muscle into the world of F1 via Didier Pironi, then president of the drivers' association.

Niki was a leader of the strike: not merely by seniority but because he was a natural leader and because Pironi was out at the circuit doing the negotiating. As it happened, speaking a number of languages, I had more access to the room in which the drivers were locked up than most, and I filed a long despatch to *The Times* about the issues in the strike and the feeling among the drivers. It was a despatch which *The Times* never printed: its sports editor was out to dinner, as usual, and the subeditor who got the copy missed a major scoop through ignorance.

The problems the drivers faced were two. First, their own solidarity was questionable. Drivers are noted egotists and pride themselves on being hard men who are in a given place to race and the devil take the hindmost. That was certainly the attitude of the ineffable Rosberg, to cite but one superego. Then, as in any strike, solidarity tends to erode as time goes by. The younger drivers were obviously under heavy pressure from their teams: they had spent years getting into the sport and they were being threatened with dismissal. Second, the pressure exerted by the team-owners and the sporting authorities was exceptionally violent. Some, like McDonald, were willing to risk physical contact. Others, like Frank Williams and Ron Dennis, were simply scornful and mocking. The French teams had their own problems because Balestre was French. The Italians were divided and tried to mediate. Overall, Ecclestone and Balestre both seemed to have lost their minds. Their first tactic was to say they would take away the licence of any striker; their second was to say all striking drivers were in breach of contract and fire them. At this remove, the whole incident seems insane, but at the time it only proved once again what any driver has always known, that the constructors as a class are hard-nosed men with egos every bit as big as their drivers' and that there isn't enough concern among them for driver welfare or safety to fuel a heart for a minute. Some constructors may, on affable evenings and in the afterglow of victory, admit that drivers are human beings; most of them consider them as nothing better than servants. It is the lower class of constructor, the McDonalds and the Jackie Olivers, who are, and were in Jo'burg, the most intractable.

Eventually, the drivers 'won' their case. That is, all firings and dire threats were forgotten and they raced. In fact, FISA took its revenge in the form of a $5,000 fine and, in some teams, the constructors took other forms of revenge that were no less petty.

Once again, however unwillingly, Niki was in the limelight. It was he who held the troops together in their communal dormitory, and it was he who led them out the next morning. On other fronts, too, Niki, was proving a leader, the sort of senior driver whose participation in a team was greater than that of a mere employee, and it is to the merit of Ron Dennis and McLaren that Lauda was allowed to play a wider role. Here, for instance, there is no doubt that Niki was of substantial help in closing the deal which brought McLaren the hugely successful TAG/Porsche engine, developed by Porsche but financed and sponsored by Mansour Ojjeh, the son of the head of Techniques d'Avant Garde, a French high-tech company with a substantial role in the development of weaponry.

Because F1, in the wake of Renault, was shifting towards the turbo engine and because McLaren was beginning to develop the TAG/Porsche engine, 1982 was something of a transitional year at the team and both Niki and his team-mate John Watson suffered in the results table, Watson actually finishing ahead of Niki in the championship, the first time he had ever been upstaged within his own team. The year belonged to Keke Rosberg at Williams – though Ferrari's Didier Pironi might well have won the championship had it not been for his grave accident in the rain at Hockenheim. Williams had soundness and reliability going for them; the rest of the field was extremely well balanced.

In both 1982 and 1983, in fact, Niki seemed curiously abstracted from the business on the circuit. Not that he drove any less well, but there seemed to be an unusual number of niggling little problems, a certain tension in the team; there was Watson's departure, Prost's arrival; there was tension between designer John Barnard, a man of considerable force and conviction as to his own genius, and Ron Dennis, who had worked his way up the ranks in FI and was in a somewhat Olympian mood. I felt Niki was trying to be as much an elder statesman as a driver and though to say he was perfunctory in his driving would be an exaggeration, it was clear that he was looking to the future, and the development of the new engine, rather than to the present.

The engine came on stream in the middle of the 1983 season, and right away one could note that Niki was optimistic. In his usual thrusting manner, he fought inside McLaren to get the engine put to use as soon as possible, knowing full well that engine development on a bench or in testing is very different to developing an engine that will be competitive under the stress of FI racing. Barnard was as uncompromising as Lauda: he wanted the engine in a brand-new car, and that would not be ready until the 1984 season. Niki had his way – in part – and the engine was tried out in the last four races of 1983: with mixed results.

The entry of Alain Prost into the McLaren equation galvanized the whole team, and Niki as well. Prost had come cheap – virtually free for the first year – and Niki had re-signed for a very large sum indeed. Prost could be said to represent the next generation of drivers and Niki the past. Prost was every bit as good at intra-team politics as Niki; he was his equal in testing and perhaps slightly his superior (as would be proper for a younger driver) in combative driving. Knowing both men as well as I did, I was one of the few who did not think there would be any major friction between them – both men were far too smart for that – but I did think Niki would find himself struggling for a primacy which he had long taken for granted. I also knew that, when challenged, Niki would rise to the occasion.

In fact, the next year, 1984, was to be a memorable one in motor racing, distinguished by an extraordinary battle fought by the two men with all the means at their disposal, but always honestly and intelligently, on the circuit.

If Niki had sought to impress Prost with a victory at the very start of the season, the ploy didn't work: an improperly soldered battery cable put him out of action and it was Prost who impressed. As Niki said at the time, his Number One position (an unofficial title, though Prost had made it clear to me, as to others, that he considered his first season at McLaren to be very much a learning process) was under threat, and that was not a situation Niki appreciated. At

Kyalami, Niki won handily, but Prost still finished second: the TAG/ Porsche engine was beginning to show its superiority. Michele Alboreto won the next race, at Zolder, and neither Prost nor Lauda finished in the points. Then, at Imola, Niki again failed to finish – he was, I recall, disgusted with himself and with the engine, which was still having some teething problems – and Prost won. Early days yet, but Prost already had 24 points to Niki's nine.

The French Grand Prix that year was at Dijon, high on a plateau over the city and a race that, for one reason or another, had always favoured the French. Patrick Tambay, driving the Renault, seized pole position, Elio de Angelis was second on the grid for Lotus. The McLarens had not been brilliant in practice, and Niki started ninth. Niki somehow felt this was a make-or-break race for him; his pride was dented, his dander up. After a while, Niki worked his way up through the field until only Tambay and Prost were ahead of him; then Prost had to abandon the race with a loose wheel, a stupid mechanical mistake, which put Niki on Tambay's tail. Lapping Laffite, Tambay got back easily, but Niki had to go airborne over the kerb to avoid an accident. Watching the race, it was obvious that Niki was driving with a sort of ill-controlled fury: instead of the steady, irreproachable Niki, here was a man who was fighting for his life. Right below the press box he tried to get past Tambay and I could swear his wheels weren't more than inches from the pit-wall as he tried, and failed, to get by. Then Tambay, perhaps unaccustomed to such pressure, made a tiny mistake, slipping a little wide, and Niki got past him. But Niki's tyres were going fast: worn by all his attempts to get past Tambay. Niki ducked into the pits, changed tyres and came out twenty seconds behind Tambay. He caught up two laps before the end, Tambay's brakes failed and Niki was home. That restored the balance in the team, but Monaco was next, a race for which Lauda has a particular aversion.

For the sixth consecutive time that year, Prost had qualified ahead of Lauda. At Monaco, that is particularly vital and by then Niki knew in his heart that in the majority of cases he was probably going to start behind Alain. In the paddock, he said, 'I must be getting old.' And there was some truth in that. Qualifying is a young man's job, it requires a huge burst of adrenalin; also, except at Monaco, it is far less significant than it seems. Niki was ever a patient, careful driver and not being on pole never bothered him, because what mattered was the race. What did bother him was that in his duel within McLaren with Prost, the Frenchman, six years his junior, always started with an advantage. That meant that he had places to make up before he could challenge his principal rival, and in making up places, especially at Monaco, there is always an element of risk.

Rain fell at Monaco – providentially for Prost, who was being pushed to the extreme by the young Ayrton Senna, and would certainly have been overtaken one lap later. In fact, there was a widespread suspicion that the decision to stop the race at the halfway mark, when conditions were actually lightening, had been taken to favour the darling of France. Half points were awarded (less than half the race having been completed) and Prost's lead over Lauda increased: 29.5 points to 18.

By this time, I think the fact that Prost was not only good, but *better* in the results department, was the least of Niki's worries. 'Prost no problem,' he said that weekend, and I think he meant it. He knew that Alain was a fair fighter and that he was only doing what every driver does, taking advantage of his superiority in performance.

If Alain wasn't the problem, what was? Well, the answer was obvious to anyone in the paddock. The problem was Ron Dennis and in a way, this clash between the two men is a microcosm of life in F1 and deserves a brief aside. To start with, no matter how the public may consider it, F1 is a sport governed by human relations. F1 is a family. People live together and work together. They are rich people, independent people, egotistical people and often extraordinarily unperceptive people. The sport itself and the money, shelter them from the kind of rough-and-ready exchange that brings ordinary people back from the brink of conflict and leads them to see their adversaries as *people*. Then there is a natural antagonism between drivers and bosses. Jackie Stewart stated that when he contributed to 'professionalizing' the sport; drivers continued in his wake, creating an adversarial relationship between those who drove and risked their lives and those who lived, on sponsor money, high on the hog and risked little but their reputations. Constructors resent the celebrity of drivers; drivers resent the anonymity and distance of constructors.

But between Lauda and Ron Dennis there was a further gulf. For all his qualities, which are many, in those days Dennis still had a huge chip on his shoulder. He had come up from the bottom and made it to the top: no one was to forget that he was at the top and everyone was supposed to forget where he had come from and how he had got where he was. Niki, on the other hand, was a patrician born. There was no social or any other kind of insecurity in the man. Ron Dennis's McLaren, TAG/Porsche, Lauda, Prost, Hogan and

Marlboro – that was the top. It had money, fame and everything that goes with it, the biggest motor-home, the best-oiled publicity machine, you name it. In my view, it went slightly to Dennis's head in one way and to Niki's in another. To Dennis's in the sense that he thought he could act as team-boss without regard for Niki; to Niki's in that he thought his personal world outweighed Dennis's and the team's.

The original bitterness was over the way Niki had pointed a gun at McLaren's head and taken the team for a great deal of money. The results of the first two years really did not warrant such astronomical sums and Dennis knew that the following year he would have to pay Prost a sum equal to his evident worth. That meant Niki would have to take a cut. This Niki was not inclined to accept.

The two men had it out. Dennis reproached Niki with 'aloofness' and an 'egocentric attitude'. That, coming from one of the biggest egos in the paddock, was a bit much. Next came an accusation, which Niki reports as follows, with Dennis saying, 'If you pay somebody such an amazing amount of money, you can surely expect a little friendship in exchange.' That got to Niki. Niki has very few close friends, and none of them, to my knowledge, are in F_1. And, responding as a patrician, what could he say to a man who confused friendship with money? Thus, when Dennis offered him exactly half what he had been making, Lauda thought he'd had a touch of sun.

From that moment on, that relationship settled into a form of sullen resentment that lasted throughout Niki's season. Niki went fishing for another drive, and thought he had one at Renault; but the big-manufacturer politics of that season and Gerard Larrousse's increasing weakness therein, sabotaged that: Niki was kept dangling, offered the drive and then dropped. Dennis, in revenge, said he had been 'talking' to Keke Rosberg.

Meanwhile, on the circuit, the season continued; so did McLaren's domination, so did Prost's rise. In Canada, Niki narrowly lost out to Nelson Piquet and Prost trailed in third; on Detroit's bumpy street circuit, which Niki liked no better than he liked Monaco, Piquet scored a double. Only five cars finished and Prost was fourth among them, well back. Coming up to the first ever and only race in Dallas, a race run on a track that was breaking up and in the most intense heat imaginable, neither McLaren scored in a race that was brilliantly won by Keke Rosberg. Back in Europe, Niki made a fine come-back at Brands Hatch, winning the race handsomely; Prost was forced to retire. That put the two drivers on fairly even terms, Niki having 33 points and Prost 36.5. At Hockenheim, the roles were reversed and for all Lauda's efforts, he finished just behind Prost.

It was at the Österreichring that Ron Dennis chose to put his foot in his mouth with Niki. He said that unless Niki gave in and raced on the terms offered, he was going to go with Keke the following year. At the same time, it was becoming obvious that between his two drivers, Dennis was favouring Prost. The differences were tiny, nonetheless significant. It's the sort of thing it is easy to observe if you stand around in the garage during practice or generally stick around a team, watching who gets the first briefing, who is paying more attention to whom.

The Zeltweg race was, after all, on Niki's home territory, and when Prost spun off on a patch of oil, the race took on a new perspective for Niki: he found himself in the lead, with Piquet behind him and no threat with badly worn tyres. With fifteen laps to go, the race was his: if he could make it to the end. Suddenly, there was a big bang and Niki lost all power. Coasting a bit, fiddling with his gears, he found that third gear worked. Fourth didn't, but fifth did. A driver like Niki knows how to improvise. But having only two working gears was going to cut his lap times. In the end, Piquet was out-bluffed. Not knowing how much was wrong with Niki's car, he thought Niki was only letting up and could apply the power whenever he wanted to. So Lauda won and for the first time he led the championship: 48 to 45.5 for Prost. And he said to me, pugnaciously, 'That ought to show Ron.'

At Zandvoort, Prost was on pole and destroyed the opposition with an impeccable race. Niki was second. Prost's lead was a half point. We all knew we were into an end-of-season of extraordinary interest, despite the fact that Niki conquered Monza in style and Prost again failed to finish. It seemed that everything in the championship really hung on the reliability of each driver's car. When both worked, it was down to the skills of the two drivers and there seemed very little to distinguish them. Prost was always ahead on the grid; Lauda was always quickly up through the field. Prost was more open, more 'brilliant'; Lauda was safer, surer, more conservative. But otherwise – if both cars were given equal care – what could distinguish them?

The next race, the Grand Prix d'Europe, was taking place on the newly rebuilt Nürburgring, much shorter than the old, infinitely safer, but also less interesting. Time was running out. Niki had not yet signed with McLaren; he had been dumped by Renault; he was on his own. As he admitted, 'The tension got to me.' Not for the first time, John Hogan at Marlboro played his skilful middleman's role. Niki re-signed, for better terms than Dennis had offered, but less than he had wanted. Both men's pride was assuaged and one could sense that a corner had been turned, that the two last races of the season would be run with strict fairness and impartiality.

On the day, Prost was unbeatable. On a new ultra-smooth track, and in a race which began with a multi-car shunt at the start, he drove an absolutely perfect race, while Niki got himself held up in traffic by the inexperienced Mauro Baldi and could do no better than finish fourth.

One race remained, and that too was on a new and unknown track: at Estoril in Portugal. Lauda led the championship by 2.5 points, not exactly a comforting margin, especially when Prost again qualified ahead of Lauda: not just ahead, but five rows ahead of him. Pursued by the press, both men hid themselves as well as they could. I played a round of golf in a group which included Prost and Mansell. Prost seemed utterly at ease with the pressure being put on him. Niki still thought Ron Dennis was giving Prost the better service. Prost moved out of the team hotel for quiet, Niki stayed and fretted, with only Willi Dungl to keep him in moral and physical shape.

When it came to practice, the weather was appalling, with low clouds streaming in from the sea and rain falling constantly. Though Niki's car had a series of defects, his low placing was also the result of his own mistakes.

The night before the race, Dungl massages Niki to sleep. Prost has the runs. Running into him in the paddock early on Sunday morning, I sense all is not well with him; he is nervous, he bites his nails, he runs his hands through his thick hair, he keeps scampering through the paddock to the hideous toilets, he is off his feed. In the warm-up, Niki is three tenths of a second faster than Prost, but he doesn't like his engine and gets it changed. Marlene, whom we never see at the circuit, is sitting in the Marlboro motor-home, a talisman.

Niki starts with one advantage. A second place will give him the championship. Prost has to finish four points ahead of Lauda to be champion (having more victories; it would have been three if Monaco had not been curtailed by rain, but then, if rain had not fallen, Prost would not have won in Monaco). Niki also has, he has written since, 'an indescribable feeling of power. I have never felt as strong as this in my whole life.' Still, with all the experience Niki has, he knows that the tiniest defect in his car could lose him the championship; any mistake on his own part and his title is gone. So he decides to be cautious and for the first few laps, he just sits and waits. Piquet is in the lead and Nelson and Niki are as near friends as any two drivers are; Niki can count on Piquet doing Prost no favours.

Then suddenly he sees Piquet go into a spin and doesn't get back into the field for a long time. 'I have the kind of feeling,' Niki writes, 'you have when your only friend has suddenly disappeared.' Niki eats up a few places and then finds himself at the back of a bunch of five cars behind Prost, who is running second. Niki is behind Johansson and he can't get past: Stefan's Toleman is faster on the straights and the track has few other places for overtaking. Johansson is driving the race of his life and he knows he is in charge of the championship, even if it's not going to be his. Niki thinks his engine isn't giving enough power; he boosts his turbo pressure from 2 bars up to 2.5 and that is taking a hell of a risk with his fuel consumption.

Finally, Johansson makes a mistake: he brakes too late and Niki is unable to avoid having his wing clip his own rear wheel as he goes past. No apparent damage, because Niki is now reeling in car after car and when he overtakes Senna, he thinks he's in second place. But he isn't. Mansell is in front of him and behind Prost, who is now in the lead. One more position, Niki thinks, and the championship is mine, whatever happens to Prost. But Mansell is no less than thirty-nine seconds up on him, which means he has to make up at least a second a lap and preferably more. Everyone watching knows what is at stake. The French in the press box, for whom Prost is not just an idol but their feed-bag, are on the edge of their seats watching the monitors as they show Niki closing in on Nigel. The process is relentless, until . . . Niki comes up on a tightly bunched group of lapped drivers. Berger moves over promptly for his fellow Austrian; the rest all want to be heroes. Niki loses six seconds to the sort of ill manners to which even the greatest drivers are subject.

When Niki finally breaks through the crowd, he finds a Lotus in front of him. He thinks it must be de Angelis, because surely Mansell is further ahead. It isn't, it's Nigel and Nigel has a bad brake problem. A grateful Niki coasts towards the finish, with Nelson, a lap down, riding pillion behind him, as though to push him across the line if he runs out of fuel.

There was no danger: the crowd would have blown his car across if it could have. It had been a hard year, the public felt Lauda had been ill done by, and everyone felt that they were seeing the apotheosis of one of the great drivers and the first signs of greatness in his natural successor, Alain Prost. Least of all did Alain begrudge Lauda his third title. He said, 'I am younger, I have the time.'

There is a postscript to this valedictory. One can say that Niki continued to drive on for McLaren in 1985. One can also say that with his third championship he had thrown in the towel. He and his Ibiza neighbour, Keke Rosberg, were both fed up with the sport, and things were going badly for both of them. Keke was having a totally unsatisfactory time at Williams and Lauda the miseries at McLaren. Both were no doubt reflecting on their families and their good lives and the absurdity of the Monaco circuit. They were in Monaco, the home of poseurs, and when Keke said he was fed up, Niki could say, 'That makes two of us.' He wrote, 'That very day, everything had struck me as totally mad . . . I was in the wrong place and in the wrong job. This had to be ridiculous, zooming round here like so many trained monkeys, 1000 hp on this circuit? Madness. For the first time in my career, I was assailed by doubt.'

Well, doubt is something that strikes drivers when they have reached, and imperceptibly slipped past, the apex of their careers. Is it worth tempting fate? Keke was to try another year, slipping into McLaren in Lauda's wake, because it is always worthwhile *if you think you can win*. Niki was convinced he couldn't. So far, nothing had gone right for him. Little things were wrong. Endless little things. Brakes, the on-board computer, pistons, the electrics, the rear axle, a differential, a loose wheel, a turbo. Of course part of it was that McLaren were placing their bets on Prost. That was reasonable. He was well ahead in the championship race. They did not screw up Niki's car deliberately, but they probably thought the wind had gone out of his sails. 'The plain fact is,' Niki noted, 'that I am caught up in an insane series of setbacks which are oppressive in their consistency and which seem to . . . prey on my mind. Ten cases of "bad luck" in a row is something I wouldn't accept from any driver in the world. I would tell him he had to be at fault somewhere along the line.'

Once it goes, it goes quickly. Everyone notices it.

By the Nürburgring, Niki had told Ron Dennis he wouldn't be racing the following year. Ron asked for secrecy so that he could sign another driver without its being known that he was truly needy. It was one of the less well-kept secrets in the paddock. Anyone who knew Niki knew, in spite of his denials, that he was at the end of his rope. The only question was when he would announce his retirement. Rosberg was signed and Niki chose Austria.

I remember the occasion well. We all heard Niki was going to give a press conference on the Saturday morning.

It was one of the least gracious occasions I recall in my years in motor racing. Niki's speech was short and succinct and perfectly clear. He wanted to live, he'd put in long years, he'd been champion three times, it no longer excited him to race, this was it, goodbye and thanks.

Then Ron Dennis got up and said it was all John Barnard's work and McLaren's and they were bloody geniuses and Niki . . . Well, he didn't mention Niki, he didn't congratulate him, embrace him, he didn't hand him so much as a crumb. I walked out, numb and disgusted. What a way to end, I thought. A big ego so utterly ungracious and another big ego, Niki's, that had to swallow that kind of shit. It was too much a paradigm of what the sport had become to be forgotten. It was like the star chefs, like the film directors who think they make films single-handed, it was a world of overblown egos in which someone like Dennis – and, goddamn it, he had known some tribulations in his day! – could forget or, worse, overlook the common decencies of humanity. The rest of us there were moved by Niki. We were *glad* he was getting out. Now, while the going was good. We were glad we'd probably be seeing him again some time, unlike some who hadn't got out while the going was good. And someone had just stubbed a cigarette out in Niki's cake.

James Hunt

The reason I called James Hunt 'Master James', a sobriquet which his sponsors, Texaco, took up and plastered (without payment!) on billboards all over the country, was that he appeared to be exactly that, a rather well-brought-up young man, properly educated, well-mannered (when I gave him the name, though not in some of his more flamboyant later incarnations!) and thoroughly at home in the establishment circles in which he moved. When I first knew him, he also did not seem quite grown up enough to be called 'Mr Hunt' or 'James Hunt, Esq.'. Everyone called him just 'James', including not only the denizens of the sport but all the periphery of Fı life, discotheques, tennis courts, night clubs, fancy hotels, good restaurants, etc., and I saw no reason to do otherwise. Certainly, he was the world's familiar, as well as familiar with the world.

It was in that respect that James differed most radically from the other drivers I was getting to know. Though mischief or simply tomfoolery played a large part in his life, he was certainly not track-mischievous in the way Niki Lauda was. At Regine's, where Jody Scheckter would have been as out of place as a hyena at a symphony concert, James was thoroughly at home. Ronnie Peterson, off-track, was a model of milk-drinking virtue and not unlike a whole set of happy-family cards; James was no model of deportment anywhere, least of all in his marital and other personal relations. Carlos Alberto Reutemann, that cunning, solitary ace from Argentina, worried about his racing twenty-four hours a day; James seemed to give it scarcely a thought – technically, as a contributor to development he was something less than a devoted genius (but on the track he had extraordinarily good reflexes and a lot of savvy). Fittipaldi was arrogant, James debonair.

Some of his difference obviously came from the milieu from which he came and the milieux – there were a half dozen of them – in which he moved. He and Niki had started out together in Robin Herd's and Max Mosley's March team. Good friends from the start, as well as matchless needlers of each other and trigger-happy competitors, they put together such a record of collisions and accidents and general brouhaha that by the time I reached the F1 scene, both were considered as 'wild men' who needed some settling down. Niki got his training in fortitude and temperance when he moved to Ferrari, where they do not like drivers to be so adventuresome as to wreck cars; James took a year longer to learn his lesson, at McLaren. There he became a world champion in a year filled with controversy and difficulty and there he learned that he neither really liked being world champion (it was inhibiting) nor really driving fast cars as fast as he was expected to (they were thoroughly frightening).

The milieu in which I met James in 1975 was that of the florid young Lord Alexander Hesketh, undoubtedly the last figure of unbridled fun ever to have competed in what is now a grimmish, strictly money-oriented sport. What Hesketh was (besides being the heir to a grocery fortune, with a mother of enormous talent and charm and a rather large estate near Towcester) was simply ebullient and fun. He went into motor racing for the fun of it and it seems unlikely that he ever took it as seriously as others thought it should be taken. Not that Alexander was anyone's fool. He simply did not want to be solemn. He had grown up in the splendid sixties, had been born with a silver spoon in his mouth, enjoyed whatever he did to the hilt and was enough of a gentleman never to look back. The delicious Rob Walker who, in a journalistic disguise, was and is still around in the sport, must be the only other man I ever met in F1 who while at the heart of the sport never took it with the grim tenacity with which the more parvenu consider the business of winning and losing.

Besides that endearing characteristic, and like his eccentric mother (a friend to S. J. Perelman, the great humorist) Alexander had ample funds of wit. He may have been called 'Bubbles' because of his corpulence, his high spirits and his weakness for champagne, but he knew who he was and considered the whole business of being in F1, and being taken seriously in it, as something of a lark. He was the sort of man who, when caught riding up in a lift in Rio's rather staid and old-fashioned Copacabana Palace Hotel with a lady whose skin was some forty shades darker than Alexander's own pink and cream, told a desk clerk who remonstrated that 'ladies' were not allowed in guest bedrooms, 'What do you mean by "ladies"? This is my sister.'

James was in every respect the kind of driver Alexander would get along with and that their enterprise did not finish so very far from winning, and failed to win not a few times only through misfortune or the injustice of fate, speaks creditably of an underlying seriousness that they rarely allowed to show. The externals were champagne, extravagant marquees, immaculate helicopters, the best suites at the best hotels, the best restaurants, the handsomest girls, the best company, the most ease and the most fun possible; behind the scenes, real work was done, not least by Master James and the March engineers who, then as now, were no slouches.

James had several other aspects to his life which set him apart from many of his colleagues. First was his upbringing and education – at Cheam and Wellington College. The son of a stockbroker and part of a large and easy-going family, James was brought up with more options than most. The fact that he was an outstanding, if not completely graceful athlete, that he played anything with a racquet commendably well – I remember battling him at tennis in the oppressive heat of Guaruja to an 8–8 deadlock before we both gave up to avoid heat prostration – that he is a better than average golfer and could just as well have played football or cricket and enjoyed all sports, made him less exclusively obsessive about racing. Then there is the fact that he remains, even within the constraints of his later career as a commentator alongside Murray Walker on the Beeb, remarkably open and frank in his judgements, both of himself and of others. Where most drivers pussyfoot when talking about their colleagues, James was always ready with a sound analysis: or, for that matter, with a personal prejudice. Finally, though all drivers are at heart egotists and publicity-seekers (it is part of the game), James always played his life right out in the open: sex life, life style and all.

I happen to think that behind much of that flamboyance in his earlier years there was a fund of timidity and reticence. Where James might well have preferred to be a private man, it was quite clear that circumstances would not allow him to become one. He carried on his life in the full glare of publicity as though to say to one and all: 'this is the way you want to read me, well, so be it.' Underneath all that razzmatazz, the girls sneaked aboard the *Queen Mary* in Long Beach or into his room in Guaruja, there was a man of some sensitivity who felt that both fame and sexual prowess had somehow been thrust upon him; I think he found both hard to resist, and it must be acknowledged that a chauvinistic British press, his looks, his celebrity and his companions made it hard for him to do anything else than accept the role thrust upon him.

The very first time I met him, we lunched in downtown Barcelona with his first wife, Susy. It was Susy who took up most of the lunchtime conversation, partly because I probably didn't know enough about the sport to talk about it sensibly to James. Susy was a long, tall, romantic girl who had grown up – lonely, she said – on a farm in Rhodesia. Most of her talk was about music, about Chopin ballades in the moonlight; she was trailing a gossamer childhood behind herself and James was clearly infatuated by it. Knowing Susy with James, it is hard not to believe that inside Hunt there was every bit as much affection and sensitivity as there was extrovertedness and snook-cocking. It is, however, a side of himself that I suspect James did much to conceal in those early years. I think the toughening and, if you like, the coarsening of his nature had much to do with his own insecurities, his fears, his shyness and his realization that he was somewhat out of place among the more gung-ho and simple-minded types who make up the bulk of racing drivers.

Hunt's beginnings were supposed to take him, as his parents wanted, to medical school. Whether he would have made it with his fairly anaemic academic record at Wellington is another matter. The fact is that he went to a race meeting at Silverstone in 1965 and decided right then and there that what he wanted most was to be a racing driver.

His way into the sport was typical of the drivers of his generation: not having any money of his own, and his parents being both unwilling and unable to finance a career on which they must have looked with some distaste, Hunt had to start where he could: in the event, with a stripped-down Mini in which he learned the rudiments of the sport. From thence he progressed into Formula Ford, with an Alexis that he bought on the never-never. He didn't do badly in F. Ford, but F3 beckoned soon enough, a step which his biographer Eion Young rightly says proved a rite of passage from racing as a hobby to racing as a profession.

In F3, he started with a two-year-old Brabham BT21 and ended with the Grovewood Trophy. The general opinion around the paddock when I first started in motor racing was that James had early shown himself to be a driver of exceptional reflexes and considerable competitive temperament. The latter quality was to remain with him throughout his career, for whatever else his faults may have been, no one ever slighted James's desire to win: to win at anything and everything, from backgammon through girls to any sport he ever played.

By the end of 1969 his success had been just sufficient for him to collect some sponsorship for 1970, when he raced in a Lotus 59. James has always recalled this as a happy period in his racing career: F3 was friendly, money was short, but everyone mucked in together and drivers were friends, not just gigantic slot-machines into which money was to be poured. It was a period of penury – such that James and his team spent one night in Pau furtively thieving back the petrol that had been stolen from their car and eventually hitchhiking back home via Le Havre, with no food on the way – and it brought out in James qualities of tenacity that he hadn't really suspected in himself. He learned his trade and was reasonably competitive in an old car for someone who had no money for either equipment or spares.

In 1970, his hard times continued: not for the first or last time in his career, he found himself in trouble with the authorities, being disqualified twice, once when he was winning and once when he was in second place. Because he had only two wins to his name that year, James decided to struggle on in F3 in 1971 while other drivers of his generation, such as Fittipaldi, Lauda and Pace, moved up. But his 1971 season was ruined by an uncompetitive March 713 and by the beginnings of his reputation as Hunt-the-Shunt, including a spectacular accident at Zandvoort which looked far worse than it actually turned out to be. His troubles in 1971, however, were not just the March and his propensity for accidents: the fact was that he was now an experienced F3 driver, known to be quick, but by the nature of the formula was racing against a lot of people who were just beginners and knew far less than he did about the sport. As a result, he was, when involved with other drivers in a confined space, somewhat excessively temerary and suffered for it; given a good lead and a clear field, he showed his worth.

He stuck to March in 1972, but quit the team in Monaco after a first-lap accident in qualifying. As he says of himself at that juncture in his career, his quitting in Monaco was 'the climax to a situation which had existed all year, stemming . . . basically from a lack of interest and enthusiasm'. He did what he could to motivate himself in adverse circumstances, but finally decided he would be better off racing on his own.

It was then that first contact was made with the egregious Hesketh, who provided an F3 car, a Dastle, in which 'Bubbles' Horsley and Hunt raced for part of the 1972 season. It was a gamble of sorts on both sides. Hunt was acquiring something of a bad reputation: both for being accident-prone and for being excessively forthright. The pair of them added a fair number of crashes to the record that year and when both Hunt and Horsley crashed at Brands Hatch (Hunt made it a double by crashing his Mini on the way home!) Hesketh dropped out of F3.

Picking up the pieces of his career, Hunt managed to move into F2 at the end of the year. Hesketh backed him, Horsley (intelligently) moved into team-managing and Hunt began to finish in the points. The March 912 in which Hunt drove proved competitive and some reasonable results enabled the Hesketh team to stagger through the year. For Hesketh, now committed to racing and to Hunt's career – with a generosity unparalleled in F1 – it seemed as sensible to take Hunt straight up into F1, and Hunt duly made his debut at a non-championship race at Brands Hatch early in 1973, there earning, in a used Surtees TS9B, a third place just behind Denny Hulme – and Hulme was, let it be noted, driving the McLaren M23, a far more advanced car.

The die was cast, then and there, and Hunt and Hesketh and company hit Monaco in style: yacht in the harbour, helicopter to hand and a March 731 to drive. To the general surprise, the March – it was worked on by Harvey Postlethwaite, now at Ferrari and one of a handful of the really bright ones – proved an effective foil for Hunt's driving style: Hunt qualified ninth and was running sixth when his engine gave up the ghost. His first F1 point came in France, a fourth place followed at Silverstone, a third at Zandvoort, a sixth in Canada and a fine second behind Ronnie Peterson at Watkins Glen. Fourteen points put Master James eighth in the championship and Hesketh made of him a public figure, a British hope at a time when Graham Hill, Mike Hailwood and others were fading from the scene and Jackie Stewart was about to retire.

In 1973, Lord Hesketh had been able to race – as against party – for quite a reasonable sum. 1974 was to prove a different story. My own opinion is that the causes for the increased budget were two. First and foremost, going to the races had gone to the team's collective head and with Master James as a media star – and few have known how to manipulate the press with such skill, to make so many journos think they were 'particular' friends or to understand the voracity of Fleet Street's sports editors' avidity for upbeat Brit stories – the Hesketh operation became something of a Back Britain campaign, with patriotism overcoming business common sense. Secondly, with a car that was not far off competitive standards, the costs of taking that next step upwards rose sharply.

Results in 1974 were not in keeping with aspirations. The new 308 offered a lot of frustrating retirements. Hunt admits that he is not a 'natural' developer of a car: he would test because he had to, but his temperament was far more adapted to racing. Still, though 1974 provided only 15 points for Hunt, it did offer him his first F1 victory, in a non-championship race at Silverstone.

The year 1975 was in all respects better for the Hesketh team. The car's reliability increased immeasurably and Hunt finished eight of the fourteen races and scored a total of 33 points. The high point of the season was the team's first championship victory at Zandvoort in Holland. The race had started on a wet track – it is almost never dry for a whole weekend in Holland – and Hunt's victory resulted from the finest sort of judgement about when to come in and change his wet tyres to slicks. It is the kind of judgement that Hunt had in generous portions, and something that makes him, even today, a capable judge of the more refined points of racing on television. Lauda and Regazzoni had had their turn in the lead when Hunt ducked into the pits; once he had changed his tyres, however, there was no holding Hunt. Pressed very hard by Lauda in the final laps – 'leading a race was a brand-new experience for me,' he admitted at the time – he simply clung to his lead by driving as hard as he could. The boost in his own confidence was tremendous and I recall James feeling, quite rightly, that he had now proved his right to be included among the top drivers. The last lesson, quite simply, the lesson of Zandvoort, was how to keep his head while under pressure.

But if Hunt had now set his mark on the F1 scene and matured, at Team Hesketh matters were quite different. A new car, the 308C, was introduced and, like many new cars, didn't succeed right away, and the end of the season was a struggle on the racing front. But neither the car nor the team was the real problem. The real problem was money. Lord Hesketh had poured his own fortune into the team and it was in his nature to run the whole show. He wanted it to be his personal team. It was made up of friends, of people he enjoyed being with, and he didn't want to become like the other teams with their heavy commercial involvements. As a result, he consistently neglected the search for sponsorship and, when in desperation he got around to looking for it, it was too late. At the end of the 1975 season, he threw in the towel – though Hesketh, under Horsley, was to stagger on for two more years, with indifferent results.

This faced Hunt with a professional dilemma. Having finished fourth in the 1975 championship behind Lauda, Fittipaldi and Reutemann, he was now an 'established' driver. But where could he get the best possible drive? To keep his F1 empire going, and because he was also fundamentally a patriot, Brabham's Bernard Ecclestone offered

Hunt a drive in a Cosworth-powered Brabham, while Reutemann and Pace would use the new BT45s with the Alfa Romeo engines. Though Hunt was grateful, this was hardly an ideal solution. Another possibility was Lotus, but Lotus's Colin Chapman was notoriously stingy to his drivers. As Hunt puts it, far straighter than anyone else has ever dared do, 'They seemed to be of the opinion that their drivers shouldn't be paid. The meeting with Lotus comprehensively wasted three hours of my life. They didn't even buy me lunch – we went out to lunch, but we didn't get any.'

Fairly standard stuff for Lotus, but not exactly what Master James was used to!

Actually, to anyone close to the motor-racing scene at the end of 1975, it was fairly obvious where James would wind up. The man in charge of Marlboro in F1 was John Hogan. Wooed from being European marketing director of Coca-Cola, Hogan was then, and remains now, the architect of F1's promotional side, if only because Marlboro controls so great a proportion of the F1 budget: through direct sponsorship of its teams, through individual contracts with drivers, through sponsorship of races, through general advertising, through supporting the press, through the general glamorizing of the sport. Hogan not only controlled vast funds – subject of course to the complaisance of his superiors, a number of whom were also deeply interested in marketing – but he is also an extremely intelligent, able, shrewd, engaging and, if desperately shy, perceptive Australian. I would think that his knowledge of the inner workings of F1 is second only to that of Bernard Ecclestone, and even that is doubtful. The two men share confidences, for they both have equal vested interests in the sport. But Hogan is the sharper of the two when it comes to understanding (and manipulating) drivers. Certainly I thought at the time that Hunt would end up sponsored by Marlboro and driving a McLaren.

The one problem was Emerson Fittipaldi, who spent the latter part of 1975 in something of a dither. McLaren boss Teddy Mayer as much as admitted at the end of 1975 that he thought Emerson wanted to move – or that he was in personal trouble of one kind and another – but the official news reached Hunt before it got to the team, and got to Hunt through Domingos Piedade, an eccentric figure close to the cheerful groupie Googie Zanon, a wealthy (textiles) Italian aristocrat whose support has been crucial to many drivers at critical points in their career, then 'manager' to Emerson and now to Ayrton Senna – a fringe career from which Domingos, hugely personable, but also often more a talker than a doer, has made a more than reasonable living.

In fact, as soon as Domingos told James, James renewed his long-standing contact with Teddy Mayer, had a brief conversation with Hogan and that was it. That year, Hunt came cheaply. The contract resolved his own financial difficulties and gave him a very competitive car. Later, after his championship, the relation was to make him rich.

In entering the world of Marlboro McLaren, Hunt was shifting from a privateer's caravanserai into a highly professional, completely race-minded team. It was a radical change in style as well as manner. Gordon Coppuck, who was to build two McLarens of great distinction – the M23 and the M26 – was quiet, immensely competitive (he had been a motorbike driver of distinction) and utterly absorbed in solving the engineering and design problems associated with F1 racing. Gordon is a purist. He acknowledges that F1 is the cutting end of technology and yet his solutions have always been simple, economical and remarkably 'easy' in their handling. In that sense, he is no 'revolutionary', but rather a deep student of solutions, with a solid capacity for the kind of apparently trivial details that make all the difference between winning and losing, between safety and risk. He and Hunt – who had always been deeply interested in driver safety – worked in excellent cooperation. Over the years, James had become more sensitive and careful in his handling of machinery. He provided Gordon with excellent feedback from the track and by now he rarely got into trouble on the circuit.

His relationship with Alastair Caldwell, his team-manager, was also one of extreme friendliness. As for team-boss Teddy Mayer, he knew that he had a winning combination going and didn't interfere as much as he does when things are going less well.

The question in Hunt's mind, when I saw him at the beginning of the 1976 season, was whether changing teams and style was going to make a substantial difference in his way of life: in his informality, his private life, his sense of his own personal liberty. McLaren was a pretty buttoned-up place (it still is), keen on uniforms, regularity, cleanliness, smartness. None of these are Hunt trademarks. With Marlboro's backing, McLaren made the right decision: Hunt could continue to be himself. It was his own insistence – 'Life,' he wrote in his authorized biography, 'is too short to be bound by regulations when it isn't absolutely necessary.' He wanted 'to do what I want to do whenever I can'. Fair enough. Marlboro and McLaren gained infinitely more publicity and a far better return on their money in terms of free advertising by letting James run loose. Hence the inevitable scruffy T-shirt (or naked torso), the jeans and the high-jinks.

In all respects, 1976 was an extraordinary year for Master James and for motor racing. Hunt more than earned his championship: he earned it against the envy of some and the bloody-mindedness of others. From beginning to end of the season, nothing was clear: neither his championship possibilities nor whether the fates would conspire to deprive him of it.

To start with, though his new car was an excellent and reliable machine, it lacked that complete superiority over its competitors which would have made it – as the Lotus, say, did for Mario Andretti – a necessary world-beater.

Secondly, the championship itself was especially rich in first-class drivers: Ferrari, his chief rivals, had Niki Lauda and Clay Regazzoni as its main drivers (with Reutemann filling in for the grievously injured Lauda at Monza), and Lauda, far more than Hunt, was at the very peak of his form, the peak of Lauda's form being, together with Alain Prost's, the summit of racing artistry. Even if Lauda had been James's only opponent, there was no way in which at the beginning of the season James could foresee the possibility of a championship. But Ferrari, on paper at least, was not the only opposition. Brabham had come quite close to the championship in 1975, and in Reutemann and Pace it had two first-line drivers of the highest quality. Nor was Lotus a negligible factor: it had taken a severe dip in 1975, but anyone knowing Chapman had to know that Lotus declines were generally followed by Lotus ascensions; with Andretti and Peterson driving against him, Hunt was starting the season in a star-studded field. Even Tyrrell, with Scheckter and Depailler, was still hunting with the leaders.

Thirdly, something James could not know when the season began, 1976 was going to be one of the most contentious seasons, politically and administratively, that I have ever known in the sport, and there were several times in the year when it really looked as though the fates were conspiring to make it impossible for Hunt to win.

Fourthly, one could not describe James's home life as entirely perfect background for a racing championship. His marriage with the lovely Susy, designed to give him stability, peace and quiet – things that I believe James actually, despite occasional appearances to the contrary, cherishes – had broken up. With his characteristic candour, James accepts his share of the blame and, knowing Susy, I think his estimation valid. 'I thought marriage was what I wanted,' he has written, 'but in fact it wasn't. I really wanted to go racing on my own.' The travelling, the exigencies of the business, the constant promotional activity, prolonged absences, his own mercurial nature, made life difficult for Susy if she stayed at home and not much better if she accompanied James on the circuit, something she never much liked to do. It was the kind of life that 'was making life miserable in the extreme for her and since I felt responsible for her it was making me miserable too. So we . . . agreed to split up and then Richard Burton came along and solved all the problems . . . We all ended up happy, anyway, which is more than I can say for most marriages.'

OK. Fair enough comment. But no marriage ends without mountainous difficulties and no marriage that ends with one's wife marrying Richard Burton, in the full glare of publicity, both James's and Richard's, is going to be easy. Susy's affectionate and gentle nature eased it on the one side, James's common sense and recognition of Susy's value to his life made it easier on his. Burton, too, contributed: a wayward genius, too much of a drinker for his own good, Richard did in this instance behave like the very bright and perceptive gentleman he could be.

But then there was the question of replacing Susy, without James running himself ragged with the thousand-and-one chicks who wanted nothing better than a quick hop in the bed with a world star. That was solved by the delicious Jane Birbeck, a girl as pretty and as fresh as a primrose. Though Jane – scurrilously known as 'hot-pants' – earned her share of notoriety in that year, she was also a creature of considerable balance and judgement, no fool, certainly not just a pretty face. The year was not without James's usual sloping adventures, but behind it there was something solid.

When the 1976 championship year began for Hunt, he was driving a car with which he had no more than a nodding acquaintance. The season began in January in Brazil and prior to that he had had only a couple of rainy test-sessions at Silverstone. Even fitting Hunt's body into the old made-for-Fittipaldi M23 was no easy job.

The venue was the old Interlagos circuit in São Paulo, a bumpy, quick and tiring circuit whose main high-speed curves faced the opposite direction from most tracks, causing many drivers severe neck-strain from the opposite G-forces. Friday was spent squeezing Hunt into the car; Saturday morning an engine blew; Saturday afternoon, Hunt earned himself pole position. Alongside him on the front row was Nikki Lauda.

As Hunt saw the situation on that first Sunday in a new team, he could not be certain about his own capabilities. So far, he'd been driving in a one-car team and in that situation, there is no way of knowing who is quick. Is it the driver, or is it the car? In São Paulo, he was about to find out, but a complex series of engine mishaps put him out of the race. Nonetheless, he had proved he could stay up with the leaders, and he went to South Africa in March in good spirits. The Kyalami Ranch was very much the sort of place where James liked relaxing: you might have to wait two hours for your dinner, but never a moment for the sun, and James is a basker, the deckchair his habitat. His car was thoroughly competitive, he won pole position again, and this time – after a hard end-of-race charge after Lauda's Ferrari – Hunt finished second and his team-mate Jochen Mass third.

But Niki was still on a roll. He was the reigning world champion and he'd won the first two races of the season. Hunt had the greatest respect for his capacity as a driver; on the other hand, as Hunt said at the time, the difference between Niki's Ferrari and the McLaren was really negligible. I think that James knew in his heart that Niki was a more complete driver than himself and I remember him saying back then that while he was taking himself more seriously every race that went by, he knew that, compared to Niki, he was still the less 'thoughtful' and the more 'instinctive' driver. What he admired in Niki was his capacity to wrest the best out of whatever situation he was in: that, James said, was the mark of the champion.

The word 'championship', however, no matter how much he may have been thinking about it privately, I did not hear from him until much later in the year, when the scales began to tip in his favour.

The next race was at Long Beach in California, billed as the US Grand Prix West, and though it ran through some streets, its relationship to Monaco, much hyped in the local press, was pretty tenuous. The Long Beach of those days was just emerging from the sleaze of being a naval base; its downtown was full of porn-movie houses, run-down discount shops and 'boutiques' for the geriatric, who formed a large part of its population. The track itself, which contained a wicked ninety-degree right-hand turn with a steep gradient to follow, was much less varied and taxing than Monaco. Running well in the race, just behind Regazzoni, first Hunt's engine faded for three seconds, stranding him behind Depailler, and then two laps later, when he was trying to overtake Depailler on the outside, Depailler moved over and blew Hunt into the wall.

I well remember Hunt standing by the side of the track and waving his fist at the feisty little Frenchman when he next came by. The incident was much discussed and analysed, the question being whether Hunt's car was even with Depailler's at the crucial juncture or not. It's the sort of fruitless post-mortem that bridge-players do but the point of the incident is that it showed the extent to which Hunt's temper could affect his judgement, for in motor racing, as Nigel Mansell was to find out a decade later, to lose one's cool harms only oneself. Clay won that race, with Lauda second, so that in three races, Niki had accumulated 24 points and Hunt exactly a quarter of that.

Spain, which came next, was a most unusual race in many respects. It was at Jarama that we first saw Derek Gardner's revolutionary six-wheeled car and it was there, too, that a few silly millimetres deprived Hunt of his first victory of the season, achieved against stern opposition from his team-mate Jochen Mass and a Niki Lauda who had been quite seriously injured in a tractor accident back in Austria and was therefore not entirely fit.

The millimetres, eighteen, were in the width of Hunt's McLaren and the facts were not disputed by team-boss Teddy Mayer. As I wrote at the time, though the error may appear small, any error is significant given the close tolerances of F1 cars. As there is every advantage to a team cheating, I thought it right that the sporting authorities had stomped on McLaren for an avoidable mistake, and I retain that view. Nonetheless, at the time, having a win taken away hurt Hunt badly: his reaction was one of numbness and defeat. To the public, especially the British public, fed by its rabid tabloid press, it seemed an absurd technicality; further, given the power of Ferrari within the sporting authorities, there was a widespread belief that there was a plot against Master James and to hand the championship to Lauda, who was awarded the race while Hunt was disqualified.

Mayer immediately protested the decision, saying the extra width could have been of no possible advantage to Hunt, a view with which I disagreed then and still disagree now, for a sporting rule is a sporting rule. To widen a car eighteen millimetres is equivalent to widening goal posts by half a foot; to violate the rules is always to seek an advantage. In mid-summer, however, FISA reversed its decision, Hunt's victory and points were restored and the team merely fined. I do not think this reversal did much to uphold the seriousness or credibility of the sporting authorities; it did, however, solve certain in-house problems and – until Monza – lower the temperature in the great debate about Ferrari 'influence'.

Coming to Belgium in mid-May, Hunt's championship seemed fairly hopeless: Lauda had (though temporarily) increased his championship points to 33 and Hunt was still stuck on six. It was the beginning of a frustrating period for Hunt and his mood swings were on the downturn. His normal raggedness became positively disreputable and he spent much of his time sulking inside the McLaren motor-home: the joy had gone out of his life. Not because the decision in Spain weighed on him, but because while Niki's Ferrari continued to perform with unfailing reliability, his own car, due to minute adjustments to accommodate new regulations, was turning into a pig: proof once again that even the tiniest changes in a car can gravely affect its performance and that it is the smallest defects that are the hardest to detect.

At Zolder, Hunt's transmission seized up and he retired, while Niki scored another victory. For Hunt, an added discomfort was that his team-mate Mass was now ahead of him on points. At Monaco, a race which Hunt does not greatly admire – since the race is meaningless if one is not well up on the grid at the start and passing is well-nigh impossible – he qualified well back on the grid, spun in frustration and then had his engine blow on him. Result: zero. The winner, Niki Lauda.

At this point, even the most ardent admirers of Master James would have written the championship off. Niki had 51 points, Hunt 6, Mass 10. Anderstorp in Sweden improved the situation not at all: the team was, in Hunt's words, 'tearing its hair out', and with reason, for 'the car was still evil'. Scheckter and Depailler made it a double for the Tyrrell six-wheeler (which was later to be banned, like many another intelligent innovation), Niki came third and Hunt limped in fifth, nearly a minute off the pace. That gave Niki an apparently unbeatable lead: he had 55 points, Hunt eight. There were nine races left, but the odds on Hunt you could get in the betting shops were astronomical.

France was to be a turning point in what is rightly called a 'miracle year'. There were two more turning points, probably more significant, to come. But history will record that McLaren solved its problem (by setting up the car as they had for Spain), Hunt was on pole alongside Niki, Niki led the race for eight laps until his engine blew, Hunt then led it but was put under heavy pressure by Depailler, was suffering from the dry heaves inside his helmet and somehow survived to win a race from which Niki garnered nothing.

That was not all. First and most importantly, confidence was restored at McLaren. This was quite tangible and I remember the mood of the victory party that night: James was at his most exuberant, Teddy Mayer was all smiles and squeaks, the whole team was on a new high. They had known all along they had a good, competitive car; a single mistake had mired them for three races; it was now solved and they could build for the future.

The next day there was further good news when McLaren went to Paris for the hearing of their appeal over the Spanish race. Hunt's points were restored and Niki lost three, so that the position was now one which could be contemplated with some equanimity: Niki had dropped down to 52 points and Hunt leapfrogged up to 26. The Italian press and the Ferrari team were furious, their fury only slightly lessened by the fact that Niki's championship cushion still seemed ample.

In England for the British Grand Prix at Brands Hatch, I had a long conversation with James, of which I recall principally that it was about fate. He was saying that the gods had so far been unkind, that they might turn kind, but that what the gods did for him was secondary to what they might do for Niki, a remark that turned out to be prophetic. Hunt meant that no matter how well he now did, Niki had to do considerably less well than he had done so far if he, James, was going to have any chance to catch him. As he says in his autobiography, 'I had to take every race as it came and just try to win it because whatever happened to Niki and the Ferrari was not relevant to me at that point. There was nothing I could do about it.' Only fate could.

At Silverstone, Hunt was the national hero. Not that he had only supporters – for there were many who thought he was, and behaved like, a spoiled brat – but because Britain was thirsting for sporting heroes (as it was to do again with Nigel Mansell a decade later) and the British circuit should by rights have favoured his chances.

The grid positions were reversed at Brands Hatch, Niki having taken pole, but that was strictly secondary to the appalling accident that took place just after the start at Paddock Bend, with its fierce ensuing drop. James's own description of the accident is worth repeating, if only because it shows how much (and how little) racing drivers really observe in a multi-car shunt:

I'd made my usual lousy start, Niki had made a reasonable one and Clay [Regazzoni] had made a super start. He went up on the left of me, sliced back in front of my car and dived at the inside of

Monaco, 1956. Hawthorn's Ferrari goes by the Gasometer.
Inset: Hawthorn and Moss

Above: *The Cooper-Bristol inaugurated at Goodwood in 1952. Hawthorn wears his customary bow tie*

Below: *The quiet Scot – the legendary Jim Clark*

Above: *The first American champion, Phil Hill, 1961*

Above: *John Surtees in 1961, three years to go before his title*

Below: *Surtees testing his new Ferrari at Monza, 1963*

Above: *Sleek but unsuccessful: Surtees in the Vanwall, 1961*

Below: *Silverstone, 1964. Brabham's Climax has just gone by Graham Hill's BRM on the last lap*

Niki from way too far back . . . I was able to enjoy it for I suppose
a half a second . . . two Ferrari drivers take each other off the road.
But it quickly became obvious I was in it too. I got on the brakes
because there was no way through. Then all hell broke loose. I was
into Regazzoni's car which was sliding backwards and my rear
wheels climbed over his. My car was in the air, flying . . .

Hunt was able to continue for a while but his car was severely
damaged and the race was stopped. That decision was the second
major controversy of Hunt's extraordinary year: this time not just
Ferrari but many others felt that the race had been stopped to give
Hunt time to repair his car, an argument given plausibility by the
fact that Lauda had made his way out of the trouble and was clearly
leading the race when it stopped. I confess that I felt that way at the
time: the track was, despite the massive pile-up, clear.

That was only the beginning of the controversy. For next the
stewards decided that only those drivers who had completed the first
lap would be allowed to re-start. At the time, I was on the tarmac,
where Hunt, with the offending Regazzoni, whose fault it had all
been, behind him, sat in his repaired race car, which he had abandoned
around Druids – *not* having completed a lap. Both the crowd and
Hunt reacted with extraordinary vigour and I remember Hunt saying
he'd start no matter what, the elegant Daniele Audetto holding a
desperate argument with the stewards, who were insisting that no
one would be allowed to start in his spare car, which Ferrari's
Regazzoni was clearly seeking to do. An hour had passed, the crowd
was in a grumbly mood, the pit-lane a scene of chaos.

Eventually, it was ruled that if, when the race was stopped, a driver
was still running, he could re-start in his original car. Lauda made
the better start and led for about half the race, but Hunt's car, suffering
from severe understeer, was catching up fast. On lap forty-five, he
finally got past Lauda (who was having trouble with his gear linkage)
going up Druids and the crowd went wild. Niki had a big cushion
on the third-place car, eased off and placed second.

For James, it was a moment of triumph. But it was not going to
last for long. Protests were lodged by Tyrrell, Fittipaldi's Copersucar
team and, most urgently, by Ferrari. There was an immediate inquiry
at which evidence was given that Hunt had been running when the
race was stopped, but not really racing. Given the division of evidence,
the stewards offered the three protesting teams the chance to withdraw their objections to Hunt's victory. Two did, Ferrari didn't. Hunt

says in his autobiography that he thinks Audetto didn't withdraw his protest because he couldn't do so without consulting the old primadonna of Maranello. It is generous of him to give Daniele an out. But the fact is that a Hunt victory was not on the Ferrari books: if they had ceded – after a re-start which looked as though it favoured Hunt – they would have been lynched in Italy, where only a Ferrari is allowed to win. So the Ferrari protest was upheld, an appeal lodged and Hunt's result nullified. Niki picked up an extra nine points, James got nothing. Score: Niki 61, James 26.

Now fate was about to take a hand in the outcome of the championship, for at the next race, at the Nürburgring – a great track, in its old version, for its challenges but a wooded retreat for Germanic savages, drunks and the wettest clouds of Europe – Niki came very close to death. Ironically, it was a track which Lauda had always opposed on safety grounds and there had been much discussion about the Ring's lack of safeguards and medical access (the track is so long, 22 kilometres, that marshals and safety equipment were not only widely scattered but often whole stretches of the track, such as that where Niki's car went off, could not be seen from any marshal's post). The drivers had finally agreed to race: more or less coerced by their bosses (including McLaren), 99 per cent of whom care rather less about safety than they should.

Once again, the race was held in two stages, the first being handsomely led by Hunt's team-mate Jochen Mass. Hunt needed the win, but how could anyone stop Jochen on his home track? Before the final decision could be taken, Niki had his accident and the race was re-started. The rain had stopped and Hunt had a relatively easy time of it to win.

Like many people at the end of the race – even in that world of wild rumour which is F1 – Master James had underestimated the extent of Niki's injuries. To his credit, he excoriated the lack of safety at the circuit, had the highest praise for the drivers who pulled Niki out of his burning car and did not even think in terms of his now enhanced championship chances, not only because he thought Niki would be back in Austria, but because he was honest enough to know that without the accident and Jochen having to re-start, he might himself have placed no better than third. Still, in the next few days as the news began to filter in from Niki's hospital that Niki had been given the last rites, that he had inhaled burning fuel and damaged his lungs, that his face had been appallingly burned, the facts did begin to sink in. A week after the Nürburgring, I think anyone would have been hard put to imagine that Niki could possibly return to racing. James's victory gave him 35 points to Lauda's 61, his car was clearly among the best, he had matured greatly as a driver, he was on a good roll himself: the championship seemed to be there for his taking.

There is in fact a fine line in Hunt's book in which he describes his reaction, on getting to Austria – Niki's home circuit – and learning that Niki was a very sick man indeed. James says simply that 'it was suddenly very important to me that he should live'. We talked about Niki in Austria and from that conversation I realized that the two drivers were reverse medals of each other and that if you could combine the two, you would probably have the perfect driver. To my mind, Niki was technically and mechanically the better driver; he was willing to make the absolute best of even the most minimal chance. Hunt, on the other hand, was – that year at least – a driver more utterly dedicated to victory in the Churchillian sense: he wanted the unconditional surrender of the rest of the field. Furthermore, James had something that Niki never had, at least a smattering of general culture, and there is no doubt that appreciating some of the finer things of life is no impediment, but an adjunct, to success in many fields, sport no less than others.

What happened in Austria, however, and in Monza two weeks later, simply confirmed the sheer awfulness of the Ferrari camp and their myriad sycophants. With Niki still on his bed of pain, but perhaps beginning to turn his iron will towards recovery, Ferrari did everything they could to try to get the Austrian Grand Prix cancelled. They said first they would never race again, then that they were withdrawing for the season, then that it was unpatriotic of the Austrians to run a grand prix while their hero was near to death. It was all the usual Maranello balderdash and came down, basically, to the inflated notions Ferrari had of his own importance. True, they were furious about Spain and England, but much more to the point, as redoubtable in-fighters, they were determined to do whatever lay in their power to ensure victory for themselves, by fair means or foul.

Despite Ferrari, the race went on, and a memorable race it was, with thunder-clouds overhead, a wonderful high-speed circuit to urge drivers on and a hugely combative field in which Hunt, who held pole position, went into an early lead, was swept aside by John Watson in a Penske, with Ronnie Peterson in his March coming up almost right alongside the leaders, eventually overtaking both. Then for a lap Jody Scheckter took his six-wheeled Tyrrell into the lead; then Gunnar Nilsson joined the fray. Hunt, with his car damaged by a piece of debris from Scheckter's eventual crash, finished fourth: not the best result for his championship hopes.

Hunt's fine victory at Zandvoort, which I remember as one of his most controlled and patient races, also marked Hunt's twenty-ninth birthday. He won by a whisker from Regazzoni with Niki still absent, so that the score, going into Monza, was 61 to 47, with four races left in a hugely dramatic season.

Niki's comeback at Monza was, as anyone will remember, one of the most moving occasions motor racing has ever witnessed and the way Lauda pulled it off – both on the personal level, in facing his disfigurement, then much more extreme than now, and at the professional, getting back into the car which had nearly destroyed him and finishing fourth – remains the most outstanding moral and physical achievement I have ever seen in motor racing and an example to all.

Hunt was unlucky at Monza. Once again, Ferrari did all it could to hamper his chances, to upset his equilibrium, to seek to guarantee their own success. They protested the octane rating of the McLaren's fuel and managed to get James relegated to a lowly position on the grid. Monza, after all, was in Italy. Countless times, before Longines took up the electronic timing of practice, Ferrari had managed to surprise every one else's chronometers with their 'times': they had a rabid press and rabid fans behind them and the Monza authorities, besides being among the least efficient on the circuit, were also the most pliant.

Starting twelfth, Hunt got caught in a battle with Tom Pryce and went off the track and into a sand trap. Finis to the race, but not to the incidents which marred his season. First the marshals wouldn't even let Hunt get back into the car to try to get himself going again; then, on the long walk back to the pits, Hunt, head hung, had to face the most vituperative barrage of noise and insult I have ever heard. I walked back behind him for the last several hundred yards, and was shocked at the sheer, mindless, bestial ferocity of the crowd. Niki's three hard-earned points made the score 64 to 47 and the race was no sooner ended than the Ferrari dirty-tricks brigade was at work again in Paris, wrapping up their exclusion of Hunt from the podium at Brands Hatch. Hunt was understandably bitter. As he has written, 'it was an exploitation of the rules by Ferrari that hurt everybody. It hurt us, it hurt them and it hurt the sport. It was another nail in the coffin of the FIA governing body.'

Worse, the decision briefly poisoned relations between Niki and

James, which until then had been well within the bounds of friendly competition. When Niki said the Paris decision had been the right one, one knows two things about Niki that explain his position: first that any Ferrari driver has to speak through both sides of his mouth, and second, that even were that not so, there is nothing Niki likes as much as winding someone else up. What Hunt took as high serious-ness, I took as a typical Lauda sideswipe, the fox laughing at the huntsman.

The Mosport track where they next met was perhaps the most awful track I have ever seen. Unkempt, ill-favoured, ugly, it was also hugely run-down and dangerous. It was a poor place for bad tempers. James's book rather rewrites history when he says that he wanted Niki to think he'd been psyched out. The truth is simpler: Hunt was in top form and Niki wasn't. After the race, the two men met and sensibly buried the hatchet. Since Hunt won and Niki dropped out with suspension troubles, Hunt was now within reach of Lauda. Watkins Glen was a race Hunt and McLaren expected to win, Japan was an unknown. The gap between them, with those two races remaining, was down to eight points.

The Glen was really a race between Jody Scheckter and Hunt. Lauda was never really in it. After much hard work – Hunt castigates himself for driving the first third of the race like a 'grandmother' – Hunt eventually got by Jody when Scheckter was held up by a back-marker. Next it was Hunt's turn to be confused by the Australian Warwick Brown, who was driving his first race and who, practically without gears, was going as near zero as possible in the middle of the chicane. Snatching at his gears, Hunt missed, Jody caught up with him and blew past. So once again, getting past Jody was essential. Hunt knew he had the faster car; what he needed was the opportunity. It came again as James slipstreamed Jody at the chicane, ever so close to the edge of real peril, and pulled away from the start line. With Niki well back and holding an honourable third place on a circuit unsuited to the Ferraris, only three points separated champion and aspirant as the F1 family headed for Japan.

Japan will always be memorable for two things: for Niki's moral courage and for Hunt's perseverence in adversity. Eion Young wrote at the time that Lauda had become human, and thus vulnerable, that victory was no longer his consuming goal, and he is right: one comes out of an inferno, as Niki had, with a renewed appreciation of the value of life.

The morning of the race, Fuji obscured under a bank of moist clouds, fog drifting over the track, the circuit itself full of huge puddles which men with brooms sought vainly to sweep, a whole season was in the hands of a malignant fate. Drivers are an odd lot, and even in these absurd and hugely dangerous conditions, there will always be those who want to race. Few of them are to be found in the top echelons of racing. Which is fortunate. At the top, drivers know what is involved. There are difficult conditions in which it is possible to race honourably; there are absurd conditions in which one may race honourably if slowly; and there are conditions in which it is impossible to race. Fuji was such a race. Yet Fuji held the world championship.

We were all out early. It was cold, damp, clammy. The two men who were fighting for the title met privately. Hunt, an honourable man, said he thought they should race another day. Niki thought so, too. But Hunt said that if the race were officially started and the cars lined up on the grid, he would have no choice but to race. He would not race hard – no more than Lauda did he wish to risk his life – but he would race. He could not agree with those drivers who were considering refusing to drive, and they weren't – at least in those days – a majority. The drivers were deeply divided. We moved among them, asking them what they thought. We got a lot of different answers. I well remember Alan Jones referring contemptuously to the elements and the obstacle they represented. Alan was the sort of driver who would have gone out on an ice-skating rink.There were crazies like Vittorio Brambilla: when I asked him if he raced in conditions like this, what about his wife and kids? Vittorio shrugged. He said he was paid to drive and drive he would. Some were rinky-dink experts on the wet, like Hans Stuck; he was one who thought the conditions actually favoured him.

Behind the drivers lay the real power-brokers, the people who owned the drivers. Not one of them, to my recollection, gave a second thought to the risks involved. They, after all, did not have to drive in them. And there was all that television waiting to watch. The sporting authorities, who could easily have postponed the race, tergiversated: as much by habit as from reason. The Japanese were new to F1. Something like their national honour was at stake. It was they, in growing darkness, who took the decision to race.

As the cars lined up on the grid, Andretti on pole, Hunt alongside him, Pete Lyons wrote a wonderful paragraph which said it all: the mechanics drilling holes in Hunt's visor so that he could see in the mist.

Niki gave up after two laps. With his visibility problems aggravated by the scar tissue around his eyes, he couldn't see; he thought it was just stupid to race under these conditions; the world championship wasn't worth the risk involved. And when a man like Niki said that as he climbed out of his car, no one present doubted his courage.

Conditions improved, but Hunt, in the lead, began slowing down. In the McLaren pits, it was plain that something was very wrong. Depailler went by Hunt as though Master James were standing still. With ten laps to go, he fell back with a puncture and Andretti inherited the lead, with Hunt second. Hunt's steadily deflating tyre held up until the last corner before the pits; in he came for a tyre change. When he went out again, he lay sixth. Or so said the signals on the pit wall. Sixth was not enough. He needed to finish at least third to wrest the title from Niki. He himself was, as he later said, in a sort of blind rage: at the fates, at his tyres, at Fuji, at everything. He went past Regazzoni and Jones in his Surtees almost without knowing it. On the last lap, we watched three cars coming towards the chequered flag almost side by side: Andretti, Depailler and Hunt. First, second and third. Few realized that Depailler and Hunt were both a lap down on Andretti.

The melee was extraordinary, because it took some time for Hunt to realize that he was world champion. He wanted *proof*, he said. And only when he got it did he accept that his day had arrived.

Who took the braver decision? Niki to withdraw? Hunt to go out after his pit-stop and storm through, whatever the odds?

Champions have to continue racing after their championships. It is in the year following that they can command the fees for appearances, endorsements and so on that will allow them to live a life of ease in their eventual retirement.

Hunt's championship was a narrow squeak, achieved in a car that was far from being all-triumphant; it was achieved by Hunt's merits and by Lauda's misfortune. It was hardly likely to be repeated in 1977, when Niki returned to form with a vengeance and ran off with the championship by a huge margin, leaving Master James stranded in fifth place. And once decline has set in, it is hard to reverse. Niki moved to Brabham and produced good results but no wonders there; Hunt stayed with a McLaren in serious decline and was able to do even less in 1978 than in 1977: he and team-mate Tambay totalled a mere 16 points between them.

There are many reasons one could argue for this descent into retirement. One of them would undoubtedly be Hunt's physical condition. There is no doubt in my mind that the many years spent wrestling indifferent cars around the track, trying to make up for what Lauda calls the 'evil' that dwells in all of them, must take its toll. Hunt is a big man and a strong one, and while at his peak, he stayed in remarkable physical condition for someone who put so great a strain on himself. He worked out regularly, jogged, played tennis and squash, swam and generally kept fit. That was especially true of his championship year, when so much was at stake.

In a way, smaller men do better at driving under F1 conditions. Races take less out of them, the G-forces involved seem to affect them less. Neither Stewart, Lauda nor Prost, to mention the three most successful in the modern era, are large men. In many ways, it is easier for smaller men to keep fit; they are less subject to variations in weight and musculature. Further, someone as competitive as Master James in as many fields puts additional strains on himself, particularly on his joints.

Then there is the cumulative effect of accidents, small and large. Master James had his fair share, if not slightly more; they undoubtedly marked him.

Success brings its own problems and there is no doubt in my mind whatever that the Hunt we saw in 1977 was no longer the Hunt of 1976. The demands of F1 at the top are very nearly as ascetic as those imposed on jockeys. Abstinence, abstemiousness and a carefully controlled diet keep them in one piece. In none of these departments was Master James particularly careful. He was a muncher and sometimes a devourer.

Then there is the matter of sex and lifestyle, on which subject I recall a curious interview between Stirling Moss and Hunt in which Hunt says something like, 'Luckily, I never made no-sex a rule before a race. I never thought that it had to be a "rule".' I think that's rather cute, coming from someone who led, before, during and after a race weekend, the kind of life that would exhaust most even if they did not, additionally, have to engage in one of the most physically demanding sports in the world. If James had any rules whatever during the years of his ascent, I never observed them. I know that whether it was trying to dig him up for some doubles at Kyalami or just dropping in on him aboard the *Queen Mary*, I always called up first to make sure he was not otherwise engaged, and I can recall many times when James appeared at the track looking benign but far from fresh.

Success has another effect, which is that of slackening effort. The difficulty of winning a championship, the strain and gamble it

involves, are so great that if a driver does not carry through to the
following year sufficient momentum and he does not have the same
advantage – of car, team, etc. – that he had the previous year, the
results are often disappointing. This was as true of Hunt as it was of
Jones, Rosberg, Scheckter or Andretti, all great champions, but
one-time champions. And there is, whatever one might think, a very
great difference between the driver who wins the championship once
and those who go on to win it twice or three times. The difference is
part luck and part circumstance; but it is also in the driver's mind.

Motivation of course plays its part and in Hunt's case, lamentably,
it was quite clear that the overriding motivation was waning fast. He
had his house in Spain, his ease, his investments; when immediate
success did not come his way, it led to disaffection. Neither Jochen
Mass nor Patrick Tambay did much to push him towards fresh
championships; his Number One status in the team was assured
without effort, and I have often been led to wonder what would have
happened if Teddy Mayer had been smart enough to hire a young
hot-shot to give Master James a needed shot in the arm.

But what I saw when we went to Spain in 1978 and I had a long,
relaxed talk with James in the patio of our common hotel, actually
frightened me. In the first place, his appearance had changed: what
had been youthful good looks had changed into a sort of equine
distress. His face had lengthened and hardened; the lines on his face
were deeply etched. True, he was quite relaxed and, as always, full
of bonhomie, but somehow he seemed to be looking with far greater
intensity towards the past than the present. He said, as all drivers
say, that when he ceased to enjoy racing, he would stop; he did not
say that he had stopped enjoying it, it was simply evident. So that,
when cornered, he admitted that over the year he had become affected
by simple, inexplicable bouts of fear. He hated the car and he hated
himself in it; he hated what it could do to him and what it had done
to him.

Some of this fear he controlled, and had controlled for some time,
by smoking the odd joint. It relaxed him and drove the nightmares
away. After all, Niki did too on occasion – until it brought Niki a
recurrence of the Nürburgring nightmare and he never touched
another joint in his life. At the time, I was far from alone in wondering
if he had not wandered further down that path than he knew, whether
the playboy and gilded youth had not taken over from the redoubtable
fighter. James denied it categorically, but the fact is that after a small
part of another season in Walter Wolf's car, Master James gave up

the sport with relief. By the end, I think it had become quite intolerable to him. Then, the moment he had given it up, the old Hunt returned. Therein surely lies the proof.

Mario Andretti

'Now there is one of nature's gentlemen,' someone had told me at Monaco in 1975 when I first met Mario. With his broad, beaming face, an eternal smile which you'd think could never contain an ounce of malice, his burly body, Italian charm and American friendliness, he was what Americans call a 'natural'. I can't say we really got to talk properly until we played tennis together at Kyalami in 1976, just before he took up his Lotus drive, but it was evident from the first that he was of sound mind and body and somehow radically different from any other driver I've met before or since, and if I were pressed to say why that is so, it has to be because of his utter imperturbability. With Mario, you felt that if you were walking through the wilds and a bear came bellowing from behind a tree, Mario would seize its paw, shake it vigorously and tell it a good story.

I put a lot of Mario's cool, his unflappable nature, his congeniality, down to America: to a sort of wide-eyed gratitude that life had offered him an opportunity to survive and become a star. His temperament, in fact, was rather more a golfer's than a racing driver's and I can't be sure that the likes of Arnold Palmer and other big sportsmen who'd made good in the States weren't in some way role models for the young Mario. In some ways, he was so sleepy and relaxed that you wondered how he ever got the adrenalin up to race.

At Kyalami Ranch, he'd have a blade of grass in his mouth like a kid on a picnic, he'd never think of holding court or taking himself so seriously (as later champions did) that you wanted to needle him. If you strolled up to him and started a conversation – on anything – he was anecdotal, pleasant and often revealing. He had mind coordination more than body coordination. He knew exactly what he wanted, how to get it and how to exploit it. He was just as straight about what he didn't want, what he wouldn't do and what he couldn't be bothered to do.

One of the sport's most natural drivers – no one, ever, participated in more forms of motor sport, for as long or even remotely as successfully – he favoured, as a simple man, those things which gave him simple pleasures. Winning gave him pleasure. Not winning didn't.

If he saw he wasn't going to win, he just moved on: no matter what the temptations and the beguilements offered.

In his early days, he must have been hell to tie down. It was obvious he was good, it was obvious he should be in F1, but somehow he dallied and twiddled and procrastinated and didn't get around to it seriously until he was thirty-six years old and then it took him only three years to become champion.

But what Mario liked to talk about most often – aside from the intricacies of the sport, its management and its personalities, all of whom fascinated him, and its machines, which absorbed much of his mind – was his past, his 'folks', his kids, his life and how funny it was that he should have wound up where he was.

It was all part of a private mythology that Mario had worked up to fit the American Success Story, and quite wonderful it was. Mario was one of twin brothers, born on 28 February 1940, at the beginning of a lousy war which no one wanted. His brother Aldo wanted to race just as much as Mario but – due to a couple of accidents – never did as well. His place of birth, Montona near Trieste, was one day just handed over to the Communists and became a part of Yugoslavia. As a result, Mario is no admirer of socialism in any form – though, quite untypically of racing drivers, he has some serious thoughts about politics.

His father was a farm administrator, and that went, too, when they were offered the chance to leave Yugoslavia. Mario described himself to me as a hungry kid, adding that maybe those early experiences had left him with a permanent sense of insecurity. Maybe that is why – unlike some drivers with a more refined sense of a balance sheet – it was Mario's practice always to travel and live first class. That might help undo memories of living in or around Lucca in a displaced persons' camp when they left Trieste; a little cosseted security makes up for the times when there were seventeen families in one room.

He went on at some length, complete with the appropriate gestures and noises, on his experiences as a car jockey in a parking garage: other people's cars were part of his early training as a driver and, like every Italian kid his age, he had had a burning admiration for grand prix racing and the great heroes of his day, especially Alberto Ascari.

In one of the most touching passages, he recalled coming up to America on his emigrant ship in 1955, his father and brother and he standing by the rail, feeling this sense of opportunity, this relief that the bad times were over, that a new world was out there waiting to be conquered. Being Mario, that brought to mind his mother crying back in the camps because there wasn't enough food to put on the table, and that led to considerations of the importance of the family in his life, of the value of tradition, thoughts of how Italian he was as well as American, of the kind of clean life America had offered, of his gratitude, of his feeling for his father who'd made this giant move at such cost to himself, who had suffered so long and who now saw some chance for his kids of bettering themselves.

If it hadn't been Mario, you'd have thought it was schmaltz; with Mario, it was peppered with self-irony, with seriousness, punctuated with laughter, with suddenly remembered incidents.

There was always that about Mario, that if he hadn't been one hell of a racing driver, you still would have wanted to talk to him; and that, although he was one hell of a racing driver, you still preferred to talk to him about other matters. You knew he was smart about cars; he was savvy about life too. Nor has he ever changed. Moping around Meadowlands last year when Mario's son was racing and the old man was too and the whole scene was as unglamorous as the Jersey flatlands can be, the burgers blazing on wet barbecues, Karl Haas's cigar smouldering briefly in the foreground, it was as if Mario had brought a whole world of his own into the paddock, a world he'd always had, that was completely self-sufficient and had a cleaner, friendlier air. And his son Mike was just as nice as he was.

Mario and his brother both did some racing while still in Italy: in miniature, underpowered versions of grand prix cars called Formula Junior. Otherwise, Mario's apprenticeship was served in all sorts of bangers on Pennsylvania tracks near Nazareth, where the family settled in 1955 when Mario was fifteen. The relevance of this early experience, in Hudson Hornets and the like, is that Mario was always mechanical. That was what he did for a living and it stayed with him all his life. It is also one of the big dividing lines between champions and the rest. Champions understand cars. They have to. Their performances and their lives depend on that knowledge. You can be a hot-shot driver and very quick and gutsy, but it does no one any good if all you can do when your car isn't performing is pull into the pits and say the car's a pig. You have to know why. Mario always did.

Another thing that distinguished Mario back in the very earliest days was that he always wanted to win at *everything*. Before he was twenty (an age at which most F1 drivers today are already well established in the regular line of ascent towards F1), Mario was racing several times a week – sometimes five races in a day – in whatever cars he could get his hands on: jalopies, sprints, three-quarter midgets, midgets.

As Nigel Roebuck points out in his book with Mario, 'on 21 June 1964, Jackie Stewart (born seven months before Mario) would have been racing Ken Tyrrell's F3 Cooper somewhere and James Hunt playing tennis at Wellington College. Mario . . . was at Langhorne for his first championship race on the dirt.' That sums up Mario's early days in a nutshell. Langhorne was an impossible, fiercely danger-ous dirt track, practically round, full of ruts, hot and unprotected, but Mario – as he often liked to point out – hadn't been born with a silver spoon in his mouth; he couldn't afford the fare to Europe; meanwhile, while dreaming of his grand prix heroes, he'd just have to be better than anybody else at what was available. Langhorne was it just then, and the race was won by one A. J. Foyt, not by Mario, who came in ninth in his Windmill Truckers Special: for $637, to be split with the owners, and with hands like hamburgers.

There are two people Mario always said had the deepest influence on his life in motor sport. One was obviously Colin Chapman. The other was a man called Clint Brawner who in his own field of American racing was just about as big a winner as Ferrari or Chapman in F1: over fifty wins in eighteen years. To hear Mario talk about him, Brawner was one of those woolly American health freaks: suffering from chronic asthma he spent half his time talking about pollen counts and his symptoms. Later on, Brawner was to go down hill, working on low-grade cars for low-grade drivers, but back then Brawner was the tops and he gave Mario his first nibble at the big time. Not only that, but they struck up a partnership which produced thirty championship races in six seasons.

Brawner recalls the young Mario as being 'real hard-working and ambitious' and tuned in to the cars as if they were human beings. He remembers telling his wife he was tired of working with 'old guys' and thought he'd try a 'new kid. It turned out to be a good choice.'

USAC was fine and Mario was a star there, but to be a real star in America, you have to win Indianapolis, and that was one place, Mario recalls, where he had a really lean time of it. Often favoured to win, he was just as often out of the race before the pace car finished its lap. In fact, he only won it once, and that was after a bad accident when a hub sheared on a brand-new Lotus 64. Strapped into his back-up car, a Hawk, Mario qualified second and won the race going away.

The Indianapolis 500 is one of those races with a special mystique about it and if you talked to Mario about that one victory, he would admit the sheer joy of victory, 'going from chump to champ' in three hours, he called it in his autobiography. But he would also say as a race it was nothing special: as a race it was 'out of all proportion to the fame and fortune' and needed 'no more ability than any other place'. Typically honest, he admits his win wasn't one of his more brilliant races.

Push him a bit and under Mario the American driver you'll always find the Italian kid who wanted to make good in grand prix racing. Indy is a one-off; to be a world champion in F1 it takes putting all the marbles together over a whole season. Anyone could get Mario to talk endlessly about the difference between American racing and the worldwide top formula. He never knocked his origins in American racing, but also he knew damned well that technologically America was behind and that in America you could do spectacular things but in grand prix racing you needed savvy, experience, strategy; you had to have the smarts. The two couldn't be compared: it just took so much more to be really good in F1.

Mario's first outing was in a Lotus 49 at Monza in 1968. He was twenty-eight and at the top of the profession in America, a place where he had commitments, a secure job, money coming in, young kids, a home, a life style. As it turned out, Mario wasn't allowed to race at Monza because he'd driven a dirt-track race within the previous twenty-four hours, and it wasn't until Watkins Glen at the end of 1968 that he first drove in a F1 race. New to the car, the circuit and the formula, Mario took pole position ahead of the eventual winner, Jackie Stewart, Graham Hill, John Surtees, Dan Gurney, Jo Siffert and Bruce McLaren, four champions and two others of no indifferent talent. He had three further drives for Lotus in 1969: in South Africa he was sixth on the grid and dropped out with damaged gears; on his first Nürburgring, he qualified twelfth and fell victim to a shunt on the first lap — one of his very rare accidents, for Mario has a finely honed sense of doing things the safe way. Back at the Glen, he qualified a lowly thirteenth and his rear suspension went on lap four. By Lotus standards of the day, it was a poor year all around. Jackie Stewart won the championship, Graham Hill broke both his legs at the Glen and aerofoils became common, though banned at Monaco.

He put in a year, or rather five races, with Andy Granatelli's STP team — Granatelli being a lifelong friend and Mario's fellow opera buff, *Aida*, *Rigoletto*, the kind of music Mario says fits his ear — but the heavy clumsy March 701 of those days was no great success, despite a remarkable win in Spain. The times were changing, and fast. The old crew were giving way to younger, more 'professional' drivers. Graham Hill was on the wane – though he raced until 1975 when he was killed in a plane crash, he scored only 11 points in the seventies. The year 1970 was the great Bruce McLaren's last in racing and he died on 2 June testing a Can-Am car. Jochen Rindt, the sport's only posthumous champion, was killed in his Lotus practising at Monza, and at the end of the season, the affable, tough and brilliant Jack Brabham was to announce his retirement. Jo Siffert was to go the next year in a non-championship race at Brands Hatch.

Mario's results in 1970 included a retirement at Kyalami, third place at Jarama, another at the Nürburgring and an accident in Austria. In between times, among the many kinds of racing in which Mario indulged his taste for speed – and his need for money – there had been a bunch of sports-car races for Ferrari, generally teamed up with Ickx, the team-leader. The connection led to an invitation to drive in F1 for Ferrari, an arrangement which in those years seems to have been a rather casual affair. Certainly it appears so to Mario who's given to saying things such as 'Yeah, I had a couple of years back then with Ferrari . . .' Mario's lack of awe towards that highly operatic team of great divas and sweltering foot-soldiers in the chorus is something I always found highly refreshing. He's the only man I've met who doesn't fall obsequiously to his knees and bow in the direction of Maranello when the name of Enzo Ferrari is mentioned.

Mind you, perhaps Ferrari should have taken more notice of Mario a lot earlier, but 1971 and 1972 were indifferent Ferrari years. I personally never rated Ickx as a driver or as a human being and Regazzoni, though a great step upwards from the slick gigolo type that Ickx liked to play, like a second-rate understudy for Jean-Paul Belmondo, always struck me as stronger on brawn and stubbornness than on brain. The car, with everybody saying their piece simultaneously back in Maranello, was a weakish compromise.

The fault, however, was not all Ferrari's. Mario himself was of a divided mind. As he notes in his autobiography, he was torn between the conflicting demands of American and F1 racing: 'I recall saying to Peter Revson at the time that I really envied the hell out of him.' Why? Because Revson just did a small number of American races and spent the rest of the time on the F1 circuit. And why didn't Mario follow his example? Mario says it was because of his commitments to the Firestone Tyre Company, who had 'their own guys in Europe'.

Left: *Jackie Stewart – first of the modern champions*

Above: *Niki Lauda – returning from the wars, 1976*

Below: *Emerson Fittipaldi – 1980, after things had gone downhill*

Above: *Fangio at Reims in the Lancia-Ferrari, 1956*

Left: *Fangio in his Mercedes at Monaco, 1955*

Above: *Jim Clark getting some help in 1963*

Left: *The great five-time champion in a Maserati at Aintree, 1957*

Above: *Graham Hill gets four wheels off the ground*

Above: *Mario Andretti going up the hill at Jarama, 1979*

Below: *Jackie Stewart between championships in his 1972 Tyrrell*

Above: *Niki Lauda – 'the rat' – thoughtful as ever*

Left: *The unforgettable Jim Clark at Zandvoort, 1967*

Below: *The background is Detroit's 'Ren-Cen'; the foreground is hogged by Keke Rosberg*

Above: *Fittipaldi in his first year as driver/boss at Copersucar, 1976*

Above: *Lauda on the way to victory at Monaco, 1976*

Left: *Nelson Piquet in the Brabham at Long Beach, 1981*

Below: *Alain Prost on home-ground at Le Castellet, 1985*

Above: *Mario, Mr Nice Guy*

Above: *Looking positively smart, Master James Hunt in retirement*

Below: *Jody Scheckter in his Tyrrell days*

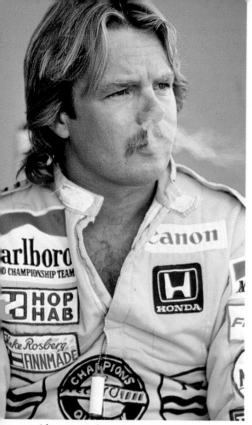

Above: *Keke, never without smoke, 1985*
Below: *Alan Jones – ebullient, tough, Australian!*

Above: *Nelson – 1987 was his third championship, but the season had its complications*

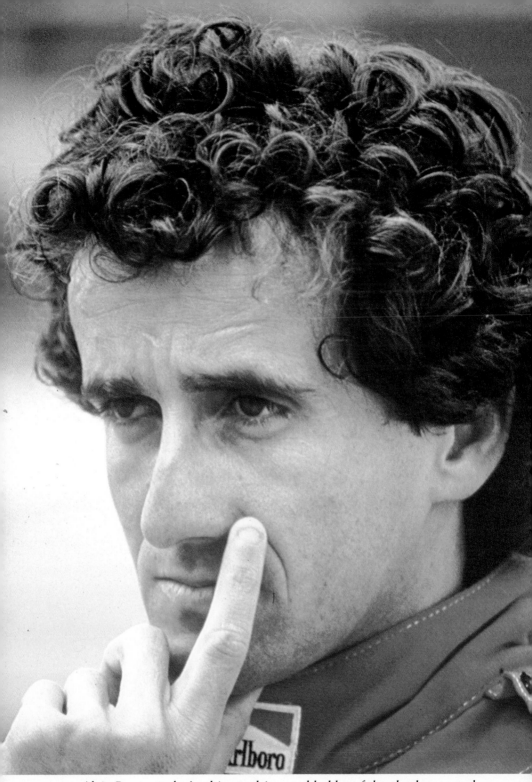

Alain Prost – today's ultimate driver and holder of the absolute record for victories – 28!

It was, Mario says, 'time to be practical. There isn't much security in this business and the Firestone contract represented a lot to me.'

I remember discussing this with Mario on the way back from Brazil once, and I don't think that's the sole reason. It may indeed have something to do with the thoroughly ambivalent American attitude towards F1 racing, for there is a golden rule in American sporting life: if it ain't American, it ain't real. That's why Americans spurn soccer for their own (wonderful but still local) game. The same is true of motor racing. By and large, despite the many attempts made to persuade Americans that F1 is the top of motor sport, the Yanks remain unconvinced. Long Beach, which succeeded Watkins Glen as an American F1 venue, eventually gave up the world formula for the more local Cart. Detroit, which remains on the calendar, often seems much more a social event than a real race. New York and Dallas both failed to get off the ground, either financially or politically.

Mario's living, like that of many drivers, depends on their fame. As an American, what could Mario, and Mario's sponsors, derive from F1? Have American sponsors – apart from multinationals, like the tyre or tobacco companies, or Ford – really taken to F1? Mario and I agreed during that long flight that part of the trouble had to be media coverage. In America, if the media aren't interested in something, it won't get covered, and the media won't be interested unless the public is. A law of American life says that the world is a market, and markets are what you cater to. You don't educate or create a market; you simply pander to an existing one. Hence America's trade troubles throughout the world: the nation produces what America wants but not much of anything anyone else wants.

Without a base, then, Mario had only his private ambitions to fulfil, and it was to be some years before he did. Not that there weren't offers for Mario's services, but they weren't very convincing. The ineffable Louis Stanley, operating from his suite in the Dorchester, launched new but already outmoded cars with monotonous regularity; Stanley gave Mario 'his sales talk', but Mario could spot a loser a mile off. So that in 1974, after a year out of F1 racing, he did the one logical thing remaining; he sought to persuade Americans to get into F1. In USAC and F5000, Mario was driving for the Vel's Parnelli Jones team. Their chief designer was Maurice Philippe, designer of the Lotus 72 then, and now for a number of years Ken Tyrrell's designer. Philippe produced his new car for the last two races of 1974, in Canada and at Watkins Glen, where it qualified third.

It seemed the future was not without promise, and a European base was set up with the amiable Andrew Ferguson as team-manager. Like many other such dreams, this one did not work out and the reason would seem to be that same old American resistance to working seriously in F1 – it happened with Roger Penske, it happened with Parnelli as it was later to happen with Karl Haas.

'Parnelli never really got into it,' Mario says. 'Vel [Miletich] was keen on the programme, but neither he nor I got any psychological support from Parnelli.'

There were other reasons, too. F1 by 1975 was a radically changed sport technically. It seemed hardly a week went by without a new 'breakthrough' in the technological aspects of the sport; costs were inflating; teams couldn't be run without proper (i.e. large) budgets. 'They used their failure to get sponsorship as an excuse to get out,' says Mario with understandable bitterness, and what hurt him most was that they strung him along until well into 1976, despite the fact that he could easily have had another drive. The end was curt and unpleasant: Mario not only lost his F1 deal but also backed out of racing for Parnelli in America.

At this point begins Mario's love affair with Lotus and theirs with him. In a way, it has to be put down to mutual dependence. Mario needed an F1 drive; Lotus needed someone with Mario's skills in development, his instinctive understanding of machines. 1975 had been one of the most disastrous ever at Lotus. The once dominant Lotus 72 had lost its edge; Chapman was developing the 77 and had abandoned the 76.

Here I must admit to a certain prejudice, in that much as I admired Chapman's engineering brilliance – it was intuitive, radical, lateral-thinking and extremely sharp – I did not share, then or now, the belief that Colin was a constructor in the class of Enzo Ferrari, nor did I feel any faith in him as a man or a leader of men. The Chapman I knew and observed over a decade and more seemed to me never to have outgrown his background, his appetites, his ambitions or his selfishness. He often struck me as the kind of wide boy one found in England right after the war, people who made deals of the spivvier sort and didn't care who went down as long as they went up.

If there was one thing Chapman couldn't stand, it was criticism or interference in his affairs. As a result, at least off the track and in business, he had about him only sycophants. At one time it was quite obvious that his main sponsor, Essex Petroleum, run by the flamboyant American ex-decorator and former Brussels bus-boy, David Thieme, was in some sort of dire trouble and that this trouble was bound to affect Team Lotus as it did; Chapman knew I was looking into the complex affairs of Thieme and Thieme's long-standing relations with Lotus. As a result, he once stopped his car as I was walking up the track in Monaco, opened his door and said, 'Hop in.' Thanking him for giving me a lift, I sat down in the passenger seat and waited for Chapman to get moving. He did. He got about fifty yards up the road, stopped, turned towards me and said, 'I hear you're looking into my affairs. Don't!' At that point, he leaned across me, opened the door on my side, and shoved me out of his car.

I understood the threat and resented the bully-boy who made it. Not so much because of the menace in his voice and manner, but because it caused me to lose what little respect I had for him. It was simply the action of a stupid man who hadn't considered the consequences of his action. When, not too long afterwards, an emissary came to ask me how much money I wanted not to look too closely into Thieme's affairs, I knew what many an 'investigative' journalist knows: for some people, there are no rules, no codes they do not think they can break.

This was long before the De Lorean affair began to cast its long shadow over Chapman's empire, but the two incidents served to keep me on my toes.

The other matter which Chapman could not accept was any charge that his cars had been 'dangerous', despite the fact that an inordinately large number of people had been killed or injured in his cars. On one visit to Chapman in Norfolk, he told me that it was true he always worked 'to the most minimal margins' and that he 'subordinated everything to creating the fastest possible car'. My own opinion then was that this was a characteristic sentiment. Chapman not only wanted to win; he had to win. At a time when FISA, the sport's organizing body, helped by the drivers' own association, had belatedly begun to pay some attention to safety in a notably risky sport, Chapman's remarks showed a callousness towards his drivers – and by implication, towards other human beings – that I found it hard to admire.

The late and lovely Ronnie Peterson, one of the sport's true gentle-men, and in 1976 about to become, after a disastrous season, Mario's team-mate, said laconically that Chapman's creation of 'marginal' cars – that is, of cars stripped of weight and precaution – was 'something you just had to accept'. But then Ronnie, in his own phlegmatic way, could live with it better than most: his skills as a driver were so refined, his reflexes so quick, that he could handle even the trickiest cars.

Still, when Mario embarked on his four-year career with Chapman, I was not the only one who felt a certain apprehension. Mario was vastly experienced, he was certainly no coward, but he was also, in his later days, a very 'correct' driver and a very prudent one. Characteristically, he explained that he thought he could 'handle' that sort of problem.

The way he did so was by contributing greatly to the development of the new Lotus. Still, when he arrived at Interlagos in São Paulo, a very fast and difficult track with a bumpy, deteriorating surface, Mario records that 'that Lotus was really frightening. I don't think I scare easily, but I sure as hell scared myself that weekend. It was twitchy like a go-kart.' In fact, in the race, he and Ronnie bashed into each other on the sixth lap.

Still, the point is Mario needed Chapman and had faith in him. There is also no doubt that Chapman needed Mario. One part of the need was obvious: Mario was a first-class driver and extraordinarily savvy in development work. Another, less obvious factor, seldom mentioned, was that Chapman was planning a major expansion of Lotus (his road cars and not his race cars) in America, and Mario was to be, for him, an important marketing tool.

The 1976 season started with Mario and Peterson in the 77, but the 78, which promised great things, was already in the works. Apart from a few lesser results, the high point came at Fuji in Japan – the race that saw James Hunt crowned champion when Niki Lauda, his nearest rival, still recovering from his terrible and incendiary accident at the Nürburgring, withdrew from the race on the second lap because, as Niki said, 'only a fool would race in these conditions' – when Mario was on pole and won the race magisterially. It was Mario's first F1 win in five years.

The 78, which appeared at the beginning of the 1977 season, was one of Chapman's greatest and most revolutionary contributions to motor racing and the concept which it employed (the so-called Venturi effect, by which the air was channelled under rather than over the car, thus giving it infinitely superior down-force and road-holding ability) set the standard for many years to come. As Mario was to say at the time, though the 78 was obviously a 'fantastic' car in concept, it was going to take a while to work all the bugs out of it:

the braking system was twitchy, the steering too flexible and it was, due to its side-pods, slow on the straights.

The first two weekends of the 1977 season were for Mario anyway marred by accidents: in Argentina the nose-mounted fire extinguisher exploded, and in Brazil he found himself sitting in a pool of petrol and got out of the car while it was still moving just as his cockpit went up in flames. Rolling in the grass, he doused his fiery overalls and luckily suffered no severe injury. South Africa was marred by the fatal accident to Tom Pryce when a marshal ran across the track: a memorable moment when a dead man's car kept running down the straight. At Long Beach, Mario notched up another victory and by Spain, the new car was beginning to show its real value: Mario was on pole position, led the race from beginning to end and put the opposition into disarray.

Throughout 1977, Mario's team-mate at Lotus, Peterson having moved over to Tyrrell, was Ronnie's fellow Swede, the hugely talented and much-missed Gunnar Nilsson. After 1976 and a disastrous Lotus season (a mere 29 points), Ronnie had thought he could do better at Tyrrell, though once again fate was to forestall his ambitions. But Nilsson was something of a phenomenon: he was brave, audacious but controlled on the circuit, quiet, affable and engaging off it. As Mario tells it, 'there was no outward sign of any big problem, except that I used to think he got tired very easily for a guy his age'. A big problem there meant cancer, from which Gunnar was to die in October the following year. It was Gunnar who won brilliantly in the rain in Belgium: his only victory, but certainly not the only one he would have scored had he lived to go on racing.

Engine failures cost Mario a number of races that he was leading and at Silverstone he had an unpleasant run-in with Hunt, putting Hunt off the track, which caused a lot of bad blood in the hugely provincial and chauvinistic British press, which backs a Brit no matter what. My memory is that Mario was dead right, that Hunt was (correctly) hogging the insides of the curves and that Mario had no choice but to go outside, at which point Hunt just moved over on him. When it comes to racing etiquette and forthright language, Mario has few equals. He says he told Hunt, when the latter came barging into the Lotus motor-home in protest, that if Hunt 'didn't know I was alongside him, he was like a horse with blinkers on'. A particularly apt image, since Master James's hotter moments increased the equine nature of his features.

As the season moved on, the Lotus continued to improve, but its engine remained unreliable and Mario began to have doubts about Lotus. We talked about it at the time (since journos are often good sources of information for drivers) and it was quite clear there was only one place Mario could even think of going: Ferrari. I stated my objections: first, there was still Lauda there and with Niki in the Number One seat, Mario couldn't possibly accept that. But what if Niki left? Had I heard any rumours to that effect? Sure I had. One of Niki's tactics in that elaborate form of board game called 'driver negotiations' (i.e. how does a driver get the best car and the most money?) was always to talk to a lot of teams, hinting, not so subtly, that 'if the package was right', he could be seduced. Not just Niki did this, but every smart driver does. I knew that Niki had not been happy at Ferrari, that he found the pressure of the Italian press and of Italians in general something abhorrent, that he didn't like being attacked in that country's three sporting dailies as a failure, and that he found the byzantine intricacies of Ferrari's Maranello a bit hard to take. I also happened to know that Brabham's Bernard Ecclestone wanted him badly. There was movement that year among all the teams and Pace's death in March not only upset Brabham plans but also caused Ecclestone, who was very attached to Carlos, both as a man and as a driver, considerable grief.

Well, of course, if Niki left, Mario said back then, he'd have to give that a good long look. I said, 'Wouldn't you find exactly the same problems Niki did?' Mario smiled in that offhand way of his and said he didn't think he would. I took that to mean, quite correctly, that he was a different sort of animal from Niki. That's true and, indeed, it was tribute to Mario that though, like all drivers, he always adjusted the world about him to his own advantage, he also got along supremely well within any team.

A second problem that might have caused Mario to leave Lotus was money. Though in some ways Colin was quite close to his drivers – closer to some than to others – he was, in financial matters, something of a cheese-parer and though his sponsors were generally reasonably generous, even at the height of Lotus's reputation he neither enjoyed the kind of largesse available to some teams nor, with his many other commitments and his fairly flamboyant life style, could devote all of what he did receive to his team. Furthermore, he was a stern opponent of 'inflated' driver salaries. Like many other constructors in F1, Chapman thought drivers were good, bad or indifferent tools to do a job: if they did the job well, so much the better, and if they didn't, the fault was theirs. Whatever, they were all replaceable.

As a result, Mario was earning considerably less at Lotus than he could have commanded in any major team, and certainly less than Ferrari was offering him, which was in the neighbourhood of $2 million, a fairish fee for those days. There was no doubt in my mind at the time that Ferrari wanted him and that negotiations had reached a fairly advanced point: perhaps exactly the point Mario wanted, the point where he could go to Chapman and say that he'd like to stay at Lotus but that Chapman had to be able to match Ferrari's money.

In the event, Chapman did, having also, Mario reports, made sure that Mario understood the kinds of problems he might encounter at Ferrari. The deal was signed at the Monza driver bazaar, and at the next race, at Watkins Glen, a new difficulty arose, when Mario learned that Colin Chapman was dispensing with Gunnar Nilsson and that Ronnie Peterson was returning to the team.

Ronnie's return was to cause all sorts of problems in Mario's championship year of 1978. Mario was always very clear on the subject, and I also talked at length with Peterson during the following year. Mario's position was that two stars in one team was one too many. He liked Ronnie, he admired Ronnie, but he thought, rightly in the event, that having two principal drivers in one team was an invitation to trouble.

Chapman's position was unequivocal. Two factors – besides Nilsson's growing illness – had influenced his decision to bring Ronnie back. First, he wanted a double-pronged attack. He needed the championship to restore Lotus's fortunes. This was both a matter of pride and of business sense at a time when he was making a major export drive towards America. Secondly, he knew Mario's skills as a preparer of cars were second to none. 'His personal contribution to the development of the 79,' Chapman has written, 'was immense. Without him it would have been a different car.'

Where Chapman perhaps got it wrong was in underestimating Ronnie's ambition, his ruthless quality of self-appraisal, the total superiority of the Lotus which made it equally possible for either driver to win the championship, Ronnie's far more exuberant and attacking style and the pent-up frustrations of Ronnie's own career. Ronnie had been in F1 since 1971, he was recognized as one of the sport's quickest ever drivers, he had given Lotus four years of loyal service during relatively lean years and he thought he thoroughly deserved the reward when Lotus came good.

Mario, however, had a contract with Chapman and that contract had stipulated, as at Mario's insistence it always did, that he was to be the team's Number One driver. 'I mean, that was unequivocal,' wrote Mario at the end of the 1978 season.

I felt it was my due. And Ronnie signed as Number Two, which he well understood and accepted. I knew he was an honourable guy. The man was a Number One driver, nothing else. It seemed ridiculous to me that a guy with his experience and ability should have to accept the restrictions of a Number Two. The agreement was that if both cars were running at the front with no problems, then I was to win. Ronnie accepted that when he signed his contract.

In the many conversations I had with Ronnie that year, I never heard Ronnie deny it; nor did I ever know him to be disloyal. What I do know is that whatever Mario says ('I don't think he was too unhappy about it') or Colin thought ('The atmosphere within the team was the happiest I can remember'), that was not the way Ronnie saw it. Throughout the year, until Ronnie's awful accident at Monza, the two men raced very much on even terms. Mario got the preferred equipment and Ronnie made up for it in sheer aggression. Until Ronnie's death, as a result of his injuries at the start of the race – I was among the first at the scene and recall vividly the exsanguine look on Ronnie's face and the mangle of his legs – they were separated by a mere 13 points: the final margin between them, because Mario scored no further points that season.

Nothing takes anything away from Mario's championship, which was solidly built and solidly achieved by his own and the car's merits. What Ronnie might have achieved, had he been allowed to race on completely even terms, is a matter of pure speculation. What is, however, very clear in my recollection is Ronnie's bitterness. He knew Mario was the Number One and he knew why Mario was Number One: it was a matter of business. I think it is also fair to say, in retrospect, that Ronnie undoubtedly thought – and the proof is there in the figures – that he was fully Mario's equal on the track. One image sticks in my mind from Brands Hatch that year, a race at which Ronnie, who was then lying just about level with Mario, had taken a notable pole position. I was on the grass below the paddock when Ronnie's car pulled off the road with a completely inexplicable failure: inexplicable in that Ronnie could find no reason why his car, which had been going so well, should suddenly come to a halt. I remember saying, ironically, 'Sugar in the petrol?' and Ronnie shrugging and saying, 'What do you expect? Mario has to win, doesn't he?' It wasn't meant disloyally; it was just a statement of his frustrations. His anger was fully under control, but his pride in his own craftsmanship was disturbed beyond recovery, and though he was on the front row again in Holland at the next race, I know that by Monza he realized he had been defeated by forces beyond his control. To the extent of his death, I don't believe.

Mario went on to win the next race at the Glen and the championship by a handsome margin, with Ronnie posthumously second. The next year, he raced again for Lotus, only the Lotus was a less good Lotus, the Ferrari was a lot better car, his team-mate Carlos Reutemann finished consistently ahead of him and some of the smiles had gone out of Mario. He continued to do a workmanlike job, but the pleasure had gone out of it and he finished joint tenth. 1980 was even worse. Elio de Angelis was his team-mate and he garnered such points as a deeply disappointing Lotus offered, winding up with a single point. The next year he moved over to the Alfa team, but could score only three points in a car whose engines rarely survived a race. In 1982 he was an occasional driver in the Williams car when injuries created an opening, but the dominant Mario had disappeared back to America.

By then he was forty-two years old, he was tired of the strains of F1 racing, his kids were grown up and beginning to race themselves, his business interests (and, by now, his reputation) were all in the USA and, as he said phlegmatically at Las Vegas after his last race in F1, 'I just don't see any reason to continue any more. I am an American, this is my home, it doesn't do me any good commercially to race in a formula the people back home don't understand. Why should I go on?'

The question was a rhetorical one. Mario of course went on racing in America. He's still racing in America. And probably they'll have to crowbar him out of the sport before he quits on his own, he's that enamoured of the business of driving cars fast. In F1 he'll be remembered more as Mr Nice than as a great driver: he won his championship in a car that probably a half-dozen drivers would have driven equally competently and successfully, and in that one year lost the one man who could really push him to greater excellence, Ronnie Peterson. After that, he never had a competitive drive again, and without that, no driver can prove his real quality. But I think that by the end of his career, Mario knew that he belonged to another time and another place. F1 is no place for the ageing. The smart ones drop out, the less smart linger on and eventually the sport gets them. In America, Mario knew nothing but success and when I last saw him with Karl Haas at the Meadowlands, a world away from F1, he was still a happy man, still at ease with himself and without regrets.

When I asked him once whether his F1 career had really mattered to him that much, he answered characteristically that of course it had, but that he enjoyed racing in any form, and of all the forms of racing he enjoyed winning best: 'I win more over here,' he said, adding with a characteristic grin, 'and it's easier.'

I think what he meant was that it was easier on the man. Not easier on the driver. In America he had planted roots. His kids were grown up and racing. It was his home. And a true gentleman he remains to this day: ever sunny, ever a pleasure to be with.

Jody Scheckter

We were in what remains of the old Olympic Stadium in Barcelona, up in the narrow, green mazes of the Montjuich Park, a few hundred yards away from the corner where, the next day, Rolf Stommelen went off, killing five spectators. Eion Young, then as now a rubicund, cheerful New Zealander, had taken me in hand, for I was new to racing. He introduced me first to 'Uncle Ken' – Ken Tyrrell – who was then not so far off his great days of triumph with Jackie Stewart as he is now. As is his wont, Ken talked about the 'rubbish' I was writing about the sport, then about football and cricket, which rival his love of motor sport. The 'rubbish' is Ken's way of being friendly: he is a great winder-up and piss-taker, a man who thrives on argument, on being sure he is right and the rest of the world wrong. Nora, his wife with the sexy Scots accent, was in the background and Jody was sitting on a camp-chair in front of the motor-home with Pam. It was a fine, warm spring day in 1975.

At the time, Jody sported a set of enormous, unkempt sideboards, several chips on each shoulder, a strong South African accent and a reputation as something of a hothead. His problem wasn't really that, but a strange form of inarticulacy. What made him seem gruff and aggressive was that there was no skill and no honey in his talk; he said more or less what he wanted to say, but often it got lost.

Drivers are chary in talking about each other, but it had already been made plain to me by a number of drivers that Jody was supposed to be 'thick'. That is, in a world which contained Hunt cavorting in the best restaurants and clubs with ultra-sophisticated girls, that old smoothie Carlos Alberto Reutemann, the flamboyant Niki Lauda with a solid Austrian family (and money) in his background, a charming death-seeker like Patrick Depailler, and the gigolo-like figure of Jackie Ickx, Jody stood out like a sore thumb. He was the country bumpkin come to town and the Formula One family, as I dubbed them (I now think of them as a travelling boarding school complete with headmaster Bernie Ecclestone, masters, nannies, old boys and new boys rather than as a 'circus' as F1 was then known), took a dimmish view of him.

The likelihood is that this had something to do with Jody's South African background, the fact that he was the only Jewish driver on the circuit (a fact that we were asked to conceal, in an age of terrorism, for obvious reasons), that his origins were fairly prole and that he didn't play the sort of games most drivers played. Not that his ego was any smaller than theirs, but he expressed it in a different way.

Whatever, Jody was something of an outsider, and I remember walking away from that first meeting with him thinking not at all that he was unintelligent, but that he was fundamentally lacking in self-knowledge. He had the brains: he didn't know where they were, what they meant, or how to use them. Which is why, the first time I was asked to give a thumbnail sketch of Jody, I wrote that he was 'dangerously undereducated'. It was a damning sentence which Jody came up to me in Monaco to ask about: what the hell had I meant by that? he asked, scratching his wiry and unruly hair. I said, I thought he ought to be able to figure it out for himself. He said he couldn't and it sounded like an insult. I said it wasn't an insult, but an appraisal.

The underlying point of that remark was that, at the time, people like Jody, who raced and thought about little else, seemed to me perforce 'undereducated'. They couldn't be stupid, because there is no way anyone can drive an F1 car and be stupid, but it could be that they were so slavishly devoted to a single activity – and that activity was necessarily brief in duration – that they couldn't create a life for themselves. A real life. Here they were trundling backwards and forwards across oceans, dwelling in luxury hotels, risking their lives, being bored in between races and doing bloody all with themselves. I mean, did they ever read a book? Just comic books, Jody answered, and the sporting 'comics'. And when I said, how was it then that he'd seen the *Sunday Times* piece (in those days the paper was not the *News of the World* it is rapidly becoming), he grinned. Not so dumb.

A lot of what Jody was suffering from in those days did come from his background and he was far from being alone among drivers in having neglected to develop his abilities to the full. As many other drivers will admit – and some of them proclaim with pride – motor racing is such a consuming activity and getting into it when young requires so much energy that there simply isn't room for anyone else. Jody's dad, after all, ran a pair of garages that happened to build go-karts: show something like that to a kid like Jody aged eleven and you've lost him for life. It is typical of Jody that his father said he could have a kart of his own if he did well in his exams; obviously he didn't expect him to, but found Jody coming out top.

Like that other South African who made good in F1, Gordon Murray, then the Brabham designer and now working with McLaren, Jody liked to talk about his early days in South Africa. It was not unlike Alan Jones talking about Australia. They were stories imbued with the sun, with adventure – crazy adventure – with a kind of freedom that this older continent never has and never will know: open spaces, broad skies, deserted roads on which to perform deeds of derring-do. Motorbikes seemed to have been his first love: he raced them, fiddled with them, worked up an engineering apprenticeship in his father's garage and, inevitably, graduated to his first car. Since his father had a Renault dealership, that was a Renault 8.

His wife Pam told me she'd sit up half the night with Jody while he worked on that car, coffee and sandwiches to hand, every inch the devoted woman who somehow thought she wouldn't become a racing widow and, in fact – since Jody's family ties were, for a racing driver's, inordinately strong – never really did. In his rather limping autobiography, Jody said that his great advantage in his early racing days was a profound ignorance of regulations. An ironic statement for the man who was to become the gaolhouse lawyer for F1 drivers and be one of the main moving forces in seeking regulation changes to improve racing safety! The fact remains that he was black-flagged in his first national race for 'dangerous driving'; it was a habit which was to remain with him well into his F1 career. Not that Jody drove any more dangerously, when I first saw him race, than any other F1 driver. It was just that he was naturally impetuous, contemptuous of the opposition, absolutely determined, not self-aware enough to know the risks he was running and totally uncunning. Whatever he did, he did visibly: the devil take the hindmost.

Still, he ended 1970 as the leading South African driver and the prize was money and air tickets to London. All of twenty-one and with his military service behind him, Jody was ready to take on a wider world.

He wound up in London at Andy Marriott's apartment. Marriott was and is a cherub, a journalist and PR man who in those early days, before F1 was the all-professional, all-commercial sport it is now, was, like many of his colleagues – and indeed, many of the people who now own or run teams – as much a part of the motor-racing scene as any driver. These were people who ate, lived and slept motor racing, dossing down where they could, helping each other out, borrowing from each other; they were overgrown schoolboys with a mechanical passion, a fire that survives in some but was certainly not part of the scene around me when I first met Jody four years later in 1975. Racing was then a small and intimate world. It was no less competitive but it was certainly more open, and in many ways Jody belonged throughout his own career to that early world. The growing sophistication of the sport didn't really rub off on him. Or maybe the rough diamond was an image that he carefully cultivated for his own purposes.

Since racing, or, strictly speaking, getting into racing in any serious way, is all about connections, Jody soon teamed up with a group of people who were going to be of substantial importance to his career. Stuart Turner, whom I know as one of the funniest after-dinner speakers in England, as well as a devoted part of the Ford family, smoothed Jody's way into Formula Ford, his first attack on single-seater racing. Nick Brittan, who Jody swears had hair back then, was the other vital element, because Nick – who later wrote (until he fell foul of Jean-Marie Balestre of FISA for writing about Balestre's wartime past) undoubtedly the only genuinely funny and well-informed column, Private Ear, in the motoring press, a field remark-able for its boyish enthusiasms and utter lack of humour or self-irony – was one of the earliest 'agents' in the sport. A former driver and a smoothie, Nick – who is now a property mogul of sorts in Australia – appreciated that there was money to be made in racing: it was only a question of bringing sponsors and drivers together. Because he had wit and charm, because he was wry, untoward and something of a mountebank, Nick obviously got on well with Jody, who has his own streaks of rather slantwise humour.

In those days, Jody lived in Colchester, worked as a bracket maker at Boreham and started to learn his business on tracks up and down the land: the hairy way. Formula Ford was where an awful lot of good and indifferent but all hugely ambitious drivers forced their way into the sport. As Jody says, 'We were all really pushing our luck too far, but it was the only way to make the grade . . . I was probably better off doing the unexpected and keeping out of harm's way.' Going through the weeds on a curve to get in front of two other cars 'suited the way I drove and the way I thought'. In retrospect, that seems a fairish description of Jody's talents at the time, and part of his make-up in his later apotheoses. His own man, his own driver, very straight and quite without fear.

Formula Three, in a Merlyn, came next: it was the competitive ground on which Jody was to establish his own self-confidence, to gain a minimum of reputation and stake his claim to better things: in short, part of the long apprenticeship which almost everyone who makes it into F1 undergoes. And by the end of 1971, Jody felt he was ready for the bigger time, which in those days meant Formula Two, which Jody rightly described as a kind of kindergarten F1.

His chance came with McLaren. Offered one or two rent-a-drives and a job with John Surtees, he dismissed the first because he couldn't raise the money and hesitated over the second, thinking of the possible personality conflicts, Surtees not being, then or since, one of the easiest men in the world to get along with. When McLaren offered him a three-year contract, Jody jumped at it.

The McLaren of those days was not the super-sophisticated McLaren of today. McLarens raced in F1 – with the New Zealander Denny Hulme, a friend indeed to Jody, and the American Peter Revson, who was later killed in Jody's native South Africa – but they also raced in F2 and in the American Can-Am Series and in USAC. As Jody points out, they had two cars entered in each formula, and consequently Jody quickly found himself a small cog in a big wheel: without much experience and without personal sponsors or a fortune of his own. As though that were not enough, the car which Jody raced in the F2 series was something of a lemon. In Jody's picturesque words: 'I could have driven it round my bedroom fast enough to know we had a problem on our hands.'

He spent the early part of the season suffering the frustrations that all beginners in motor sport feel: they think they are good, they even know they are good, but the car is a dog. Eventually, McLaren being McLaren, a big outfit, the problem got sorted out and Jody scored his first victory at Crystal Palace, beating out Mike Hailwood. That put him on the fringes of the big time – if only because in those far-off days, F1 drivers didn't snub the chance of competing in other formulae and Jody was competing against the likes of the Fittipaldi brothers, Wilson and Emerson, Reutemann, Francois Cevert, Graham Hill and Beltoise.

The fact that the 22-year-old Jody was competing against seasoned F1 drivers kindled in him the obvious ambition: if he could hold his own, more or less, against drivers who drove in the senior formula, why shouldn't he too get a crack at F1?

The chance might have come at the Nürburgring, when Dave Charlton was unable to drive the Lotus he had bought and entered. Jody's contract with McLaren, however, precluded his taking up this option without giving three weeks' notice, so he reluctantly gave up the idea. Almost immediately afterwards, Jody was asked if he would join Lotus as the Number Two driver behind Emerson Fittipaldi. The Lotus of those days was a major force: in 1968, 1970 and in that same 1972, it won the championship. Colin Chapman was the engineer and designer of the hour. The opportunity was great, Jody knew it and would clearly have accepted the offer – if he could have.

It was a classic driver's dilemma. Jody had his contract with McLaren and his offer from Lotus. McLaren pointed out how much they'd done for Jody by taking him on and by giving him his basic training: and Jody pointed out that part of McLaren's reciprocal obligation was to provide him with a car capable of winning – which, after Crystal Palace, it no longer had. No stooge when it comes to that part of bargaining, Jody also pointed out that he ought at least to be given his opportunity in F1: by McLaren, if they objected so strenuously to his racing for Lotus.

Behind the scenes, McLaren's Phil Kerr was incensed. And not without reason. Chapman's offer was typical of the man. Contracts, morals, the niceties of sportsmanship meant less to him than to most, and if F1 was changing rapidly from the old days in which loyalty and friendship still played its part, then Chapman was, in his way, as much an agent of that revolution as Jackie Stewart. In fact, as Kerr pointed out, it was attempted piracy, and when it later happened to him, Chapman would condemn it in forthright terms.

Jody consulted a friend, Denny Hulme. In those days drivers had friends in the sport and weren't simply trying to undo each other. Today, he would probably have done what his manager told him to do and gone for the bigger bucks, whoever offered them. Luckily, Hulme was of the old school. Not only did he think Jody would be better off staying with McLaren, but he pointed out quite forcibly that Number Two driver at Lotus was a nothing job: you put out for Chapman and got nothing back in return, something many drivers, Ronnie Peterson among them, had to learn the hard way.

After he had politely declined Chapman's offer, McLaren repaid Jody's 'loyalty' by offering him a drive in a third car at Watkins Glen at the end of the season, and I doubt greatly that that first experience for Jody was any less exciting than it is for any other driver coming into F1. First of all, the atmosphere in F1 – even in those less hyped days – is vastly different from that in any other motor-sport venue. It's not just that the crowds are bigger and noisier (and up there over

Above: *The great Jack Brabham in triumph, Silverstone, 1960*

Above: *Denny Hulme in 1967 – champions can afford to smile*

Below: *Graham Hill shows off the new Brabham BT34 at Brands, 1971*

Left: *Jochen Rindt in 1969: in 1970 the Austrian became the sport's only posthumous champion*

Two of Stewart's cars at Tyrrell:
Above: *The 1970 March Ford 701*
Below: *The 1973 Tyrrell Ford*

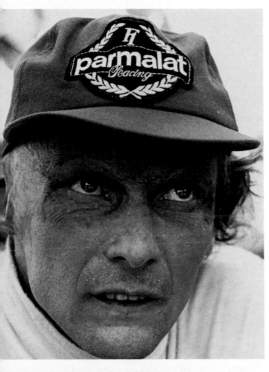

the Finger Lakes in upstate New York, rowdier, much rowdier), it's that F1 is the top of the sport and its drivers are idols. The atmosphere of Watkins Glen is very special indeed. It is a little one-horse town, with one cinema (even then, mostly for porn), a diner or two, a set of motels for summer visitors, and cheerful locals in red-checked jackets and hunting caps who drive pick-up trucks.

Then there is the matter of mixing, more or less as an equal, with the big shots of the sport, who included, on that October weekend · in 1972, Jackie Stewart, Mario Andretti, Graham Hill, a young Niki Lauda, John Surtees, Denny Hulme and Emerson Fittipaldi, to mention just the champions. In that field, Jody acknowledges he was just an anonymous chip, bobbing through the paddock mesmerized and unrecognized.

Before Watkins Glen, Jody had had just a day's practice at Silverstone in the McLaren M19, and he'd been told not to push the car but keep it a good thousand revs lower than the top speeds of which it was capable, so that when he went out in practice at the Glen, as he says, he soon discovered that 'the extra thousand revs that had been denied me at Silverstone were the ones that made all the difference between having a nice cozy ride and scaring the pants off myself'.

As happens to many drivers, his first time out came close to convincing him that he had no business in F1. It took a good while in the pits for Jody to grasp the implications of what he was doing and go out again. But, being an instinctive driver as well as fiercely competitive, Jody soon enough found himself taking the devilish S's flat out: something a lot of drivers don't do. Lacking the special qualifying tyres Goodyear provided for Hulme and Revson, Jody's performance was neither brilliant nor a failure. As rain washed out Saturday practice, he found himself in a thoroughly respectable eighth place on the grid, Jackie Stewart being on pole.

Race day, Jody made a good start and soon found himself running third behind Stewart and Hulme (team-mate Peter Revson had been involved in a first-lap shunt that cost him a minute in the pits). Fittipaldi was on his tail but backed off when his tyres faltered, Cevert went past him and eventually overtook Hulme, but Jody could feel well satisfied with his debut. Until he ran into a wall of rain that appeared – as it usually does at the Glen – out of nowhere. Jody spun off, was quickly joined by Graham Hill and a March, got himself a little illegal assistance from the marshals and took off again. The spin cost him two laps and he finished ninth. A perfectly creditable ninth and with the second fastest lap of the day. You could say the young South African had arrived.

The time between 'arrival' and consecration in F1 is probably the most trying period in a driver's career. He has worked years to learn his trade, he's had his opportunity and in his own eyes he's proved his point, that he's capable of driving among the best. But around him are drivers who've arrived long before him, who have vital stakes in the sport, who have reputations, sponsors, a network of friendships and contacts. They all know the sport better than the new boy. They are the cuckoos in every new arrival's nest.

1973 was going to be no different for Jody. In the first place, there were other new boys about. John Watson, for one. In the second place, the top teams (which in those days, besides Lotus, McLaren, Brabham and Ferrari, still included Tyrrell) were full up with established stars; McLaren, his own employers, retained Hulme and Revson and not only could not afford to continue in F2 but could not run three cars in F1. South Africa, in March, was an obvious exception: it was worth money at the turnstiles to have a local boy in the race, and Jody was it. Third fastest in practice – he and Revson were in the M19's, while Hulme got the brand new M23 – Jody was lying a comfortable second behind Hulme when Clay Regazzoni's BRM spun off the track into Mike Hailwood's stopped Surtees. Clay's car, with him strapped barely conscious inside it, caught fire. With his own overalls flaming, Hailwood pulled Regazzoni out.

The debris from Rega's car must have punctured Hulme's tyres; he stopped in the pits; Jody led the race – on his own home turf. Like so many early dreams, however, his moment of glory soon faded: he led for a skimpy two laps before Stewart outstripped him, Fittipaldi and Peterson overtook him and finally Revson went past all three of them. In Jody's memory, the race was marred by Clay's accident and the contention that Stewart, the eventual winner, had deliberately ignored the marshals' flags after the Regazzoni accident.

In all, Jody put in four more F1 races in 1973: the French and British grands prix in July and Canada and the United States at the end of the season. In a way, the French Grand Prix marked another special step in Jody's style of driving, the development of what might be called his driving personality. Second on the grid in the new and superb M23 between Stewart and Fittipaldi, Jody led the race for forty-one laps before Emerson Fittipaldi caught up with him and started putting on the heat. When Emerson tried to take Jody on the inside coming round the last curve towards the pits, the two cars touched, Jody's flipped up and Emerson's banged into the guard rail.

Emerson, never the politest of men, came back to the garage with some heated words boiling up inside his volcanic mouth. Always irascible, seldom temperate, an ego gone wild and fed by a voracious Brazilian press – not to speak of the goading done by an F1-mad family – Emerson let Jody have it. It was a load of abuse which Jody never forgot and, for that matter, never really forgave. It wasn't just Emerson's appalling manners that got to him – drivers say a lot of things they don't mean in the heat of the moment – but Emerson's *presumption* as reigning world champion that an upstart novice from South Africa, Number Three and spare wheel inside McLaren, had no business offering him a serious challenge.

On the one hand this was yet another example of Fittipaldian arrogance; on the other, it was the beginning of Jody's conviction that he was just as good as anyone else and, in that instance, if Emerson thought his car was that much quicker than his own, why had he waited forty-one laps to make his move? What got to Jody, and stuck with him, was the notion that the sport might contain exactly the sort of 'establishment' that ruled in other sports and that, as a pig-headed maverick from South Africa, the wrong side of the cultural tracks, he had been fighting his way through for some years.

Viewed from that establishment's point of view, neither France nor the British GP at Silverstone was much help to Jody's career. At Silverstone he ran off at Woodcote at 150 m.p.h., spun back onto the track and was the cause of a nine-car pile-up. At Mosport in Canada he crashed with the popular Cevert and at Watkins Glen, where the hugely talented, charming and affable Cevert lost his life, he withdrew with a broken suspension. Five races, three accidents, no finishes.

True, all through the season he'd been busy in other cars winning other races, including the L&M Championship in the United States and some picturesque Can-Am races in which he drove virtually without brakes, but basically Jody was now, in his own mind at least, an F1 driver. The question was, how many other people believed in him? Was he not hard on his cars? A hothead? Not particularly couth or good at the slimy smoothness of PR which was just beginning to take over the sport? Was he not a danger, to himself and others, on the track? Had he matured sufficiently to be a *responsible* driver?

A number of factors made it possible for Jody to join Ken Tyrrell for the 1974 season. First, Phil Kerr at McLaren had told Jody there wouldn't be a drive for him the following year and released him from the final year of his three-year contract. That put Jody on the market. The first offer he got was again from Colin Chapman, who knew that Emerson Fittipaldi was leaving Lotus for McLaren: for the Marlboro McLaren, the beginning of that sponsor's huge investment in F1. There was a nibble from Ferrari, for whom neither Jackie Ickx nor Arturo Merzario had given very positive results. There were offers from Americans who'd seen Jody race in the United States.

Jody would later say that in fact he'd already made up his mind which seat he wanted and it was with Ken Tyrrell. He was certainly, when I first met him, quite clear on the subject, and on the difficulties he faced within the team. He said he felt perfectly confident of his own abilities, but also knew, or was beginning to know, something about his deficiencies as a driver. That is, he knew the ability was there, but somehow circumstances hadn't brought them to the fore.

Ken also had more to offer Jody than just a good drive in a team that with Jackie Stewart had been in solid championship contention for some years. 'Uncle Ken' was known to be an uncompromising competitor and a first-rate, if slightly dogmatic, trainer of drivers. Jody knew he had a fiery temperament; Tyrrell might be able to temper it.

Behind the scenes, events were taking place of which Jody – when he first called Tyrrell from Seattle saying he would like to have a few words with him at Watkins Glen – knew nothing. The most important of these was that Jackie Stewart, the three-time world champion, was going to announce his retirement at the end of the 1973 season. That had opened up a possibility for Jody. Cevert's death at the Glen, which caused Tyrrell to withdraw his cars from the race, provided another.

Stewart's decision made it necessary for Jody and Ken to talk discreetly, for the news was carefully kept secret. In fact, they had adjoining rooms at the Glen Motor Court and Tyrrell offered Jody a drive within three minutes. But it was not until after Cevert's death that Jody knew he was going to be Ken's Number One driver: a doubly hefty responsibility in that he would be succeeding a world champion and also, after a mere six grands prix, be the leading driver in a major team.

On Ken's part, there must have been some hesitations. And also some hard facts to be faced. Tyrrell, despite the support of the giant French Elf group, was, relative to some other teams, severely underfinanced; though the money paid to drivers in 1974 would seem ridiculous today, Jackie Stewart had managed to raise the standards of driver pay, if not to today's astronomical heights, at least to respectability. The leading available drivers were, even before Cevert's death, committed. Lotus had replaced Fittipaldi, who moved to McLaren, by promoting Ronnie Peterson, the amiable Swede who was also, then and later, the quickest driver I have ever seen, and, with Stirling Moss, the only absolutely first-class driver not to win a championship, while Ickx moved over from Ferrari. Fittipaldi and Hulme were at McLaren; Reutemann, the brilliant Brazilian Carlos Pace and John Watson drove for Brabham; Ferrari lined up with Regazzoni, a driver who'd not yet had his chance in a major team, a mischievous, quick and feisty Austrian called Niki Lauda. In the circumstances, the choice of Jody, young, fast and with much to learn, was a sensible one: he could be had relatively cheaply, he was eager, he was aggressive and he was desperately ambitious. The same, with one additional qualifier, could be said of Jody's new team-mate Patrick Depailler.

Where Jody's relations outside his family and team (the two became relatively synonymous) were rudimentary and often sheepish, Depailler had charm in abundance, a quick smile and a way with the girls (too many of them). He was an Ariel, a free spirit. He was also a brave and reckless driver. The extra qualifier is that he had a death-wish. I've seen this in a very few other drivers – notably Gilles Villeneuve – but Depailler is one of the few ever to admit it to me and state it outright. He said, 'If I live too long, if I live beyond the next race, or tomorrow, I don't know what I'd do with myself.' Patrick practised his death a number of times, notably hang-gliding, and finally got what he wanted going out exhausted and red-eyed to practise at Hockenheim.

This odd pair – because Jody was and is thoroughly attached to life, to family and, in his later years, to safety – were what Ken Tyrrell sent into fray in 1974, in the Tyrrell 006 now suddenly uncompetitive (considering that Jackie Stewart had won his third championship in it the year before). Stewart, still around at the beginning of his new career as a consultant to everyone in the universe, helped Jody understand the new circuits, and Tyrrell advised Jody not to worry about poor results, but the early season was still a bitter disappointment. In Argentina he got involved in an accident not of his own making and later dropped out with a blown head gasket; in Brazil, he had endless handling problems, the rains came and he wound up thirteenth; in South Africa his tyres went and he finished eighth. For Tyrrell and his drivers, it was like starting from scratch all over again.

The new start was provided by Derek Gardner's 007. Gardner

had been Tyrrell's chief engineer since Tyrrell's beginnings as an independent constructor. An able, retiring, intelligent, thoughtful man, he had been responsible for the years of success; he was now, despite his noble experiment with a six-wheeler, going to provide the cars for the years of decline. Gardner's 001 and its successors were in fact the first cars of any kind he had designed, his principal engineering interest being gears.

The 007 made its debut at Jarama, which just happened to be the beginning of yet another Ferrari revival, Niki Lauda taking both pole and the race, which began on a wet track which soon dried out. Despite a long pit stop, Jody managed to finish fifth: his tenth grand prix had produced his first championship points. At Nivelles, he added four more; in Monaco, six. At Anderstorp, a frigid circuit surrounded by gloomy pines, dark lakes and sparse amenities, the 007 occupied the front row and Jody finished ahead of Depailler to notch up his first win.

Nonetheless, the lesson of 1974 was the growing strength and reliability of the Ferrari engine: at Zandvoort, it notched up its second double of the season. In France, Jody had to settle for a fourth place: the Implacable Obstacle, Clay Regazzoni, was ahead of him. I've watched Clay when he didn't want to let someone past: he could have been a huge success in American football, because when he blocked, he really blocked.

Silverstone was next, and Niki Lauda again dominated practice: he was to accumulate nine pole positions in that year, a feat he repeated in 1975. Niki took off into the blue beyond of the airport circuit, Jody settled into second and Regazzoni did his usual job of holding up the entire field behind him. Jody admits he would never have caught Niki if the Austrian hadn't had a puncture, and might not have held him off if Niki had been allowed to rejoin the circuit after his pit stop. For some mysterious reason, he wasn't, and Jody racked up his second victory and was now a mere two points behind the championship, the reliable if unbrilliant Emerson Fittipaldi, whose score card looked like this: 0, 1st, 0, 3rd, 1st, 5th, 4th, 3rd, 0, 2nd. With Emmo, if you gave him reliability, he was going to score.

The problem for Jody, who rather impetuously, and against Uncle Ken's advice, thought he already had the championship in his sights, was that the Nürburgring was next, and the Nürburgring – with its fourteen kilometres of ups and downs and roundabouts – did not really favour the 007. Nonetheless, Jody scored a highly creditable second place: behind Regazzoni and ahead of a hard-charging

Reutemann. The creditable part of it comes from the fact that it was Jody's first outing on the Eiffel circuit, which is no joy even when a driver knows it well.

Austria was a dud for the Tyrrells. At Monza, which Ronnie Peterson wrested brilliantly from Fittipaldi, Jody managed a third when most of the field ahead of him collapsed. At Mosport, despite all of Jody's superstitious refusal to play tennis – something he should long have done for purely stylistic reasons! – and his great care walking up and down stairs, his brakes gave way and he crashed. At the last race of the year, in Watkins Glen, to become champion, Jody had to win and neither Fittipaldi nor Regazzoni could finish in the first five. Jody didn't, Emmo did, winning the championship, his second, with a fourth place.

The next year was, apart from a victory in South Africa and a second place in Belgium, a major disappointment. Jody's brother Ian had his outing in a Williams but failed to make his mark and the season was dominated by Lauda, the Tyrrell team slipping to fifth place behind Lord Hesketh's private team where James Hunt was making his fairly spectacular debut as a track and media star.

Jody's hopes revived in 1976: he won in Sweden and finished second no fewer than six times; it was the end of the season that betrayed him. His Tyrrell was losing its competitive edge and he trailed off with a series of lesser placings. Jody was never the sort to feel bitter; he was much too shrewd a man for that. But he did feel the time had come for him to move to fresh pastures and for 1977 and 1978 he raced for Walter Wolf, a Canadian mega-magnate who at the time had made a fortune in oil exploration. Walter's was a private team, backed up by nothing much except determination and Jody's skills. The results were astonishing, and indeed astonished the motor-racing world, which considered the Wolf team a non-starter. Jody was at last on his own and with all the attention focused on him he made his very positive contribution to the Wolf car. He won the opening race in Argentina in style, failed in Brazil, and came second in his native South Africa, just a few lengths behind Lauda. Two thirds followed in Long Beach and Spain and a brilliant win in Monaco just eight tenths of a second behind Lauda put him in the lead in the championship. But bit by bit Niki overhauled him. Jody failed to finish in Belgium and again in Sweden and England. A second place in Germany kept him in the race, but a failure to finish in Austria and Niki's victory at Zandvoort put Niki just about beyond reach. A win in Canada was insufficient to overhaul Lauda and Jody was again frustrated.

He had, however, proven his world class. His initial shyness had gone; he was at ease with himself; he drove with care and when his car was up to it, he scored as consistently as any other driver on the circuit. Coming on that initial and surprising success, the Wolf's second year was a severe disappointment to Jody. He scored a mere 24 points in the year in which Mario Andretti ran away with the title. Walter Wolf, having had his fling, dropped out, and when Reutemann left Ferrari for Lotus, Jody took his place, joining Gilles Villeneuve at Ferrari in what was to be a memorable year and a closely fought championship.

The Ferraris were not particularly good at the beginning of the season; it wasn't until the new car was ready for South Africa that the two got down to the serious business of racing. Villeneuve drew first blood by beating Jody on his home ground; at Long Beach the same one-two dominated the race entirely. In Spain it was a different story, but at Zolder Jody won his first race of the season and Villeneuve failed to finish. The same happened in Monaco and the two were just about level. It was obvious to all that 1979 was going to be a Ferrari season and if there was a difference between the two drivers, it was that Jody was the more seasoned and experienced of the two. He did the majority of the development work; he was a better finisher; he took greater care of his material than Gilles. Never mind, in Italy they loved Gilles; at Ferrari, they worshipped him.

I remember Jody being conscious of the fact that the public gave its esteem to Gilles rather than himself. He was tight-lipped about it, but it hurt. Underneath his rough exterior, there lay a sensitive man. He determined to beat Gilles at Gilles's own game, and on the track. Gilles led for forty-five of the eighty laps at Ricard and Jody was forced to retire: not very auspicious. At Silverstone, it was Gilles's turn to drop out, but Jody could not capitalize on this and finished only fifth. At Hockenheim, Jody added three useful points and Gilles again fell by the wayside, too abusive of his machine, a story repeated in Austria. Villeneuve led for half the race at Zandvoort, but he again failed to keep things together and it was Jody who garnered six points for second place just behind Jones.

Monza was billed in the Italian press as the great showdown; it was in fact a remarkable duel, all the more remarkable for the fact that it was Jody who was the more flamboyant of the two. The message seemed to have reached Gilles that he was supposed to finish races and, suddenly infected with caution, Jody took total command of the race. The crowd might have cheered Gilles throughout, but a Ferrari one-two on home ground was more than they could bear. They swarmed onto the circuit and toasted the two as equals. Jody, as usual, could not quite get in the spirit of things; as soon as he could, he retired back into the paddock, pursued even there. I remember him being rescued from an affectionate lynching by a lone eighteen-year-old policeman with a single dog dying of thirst and lying down on the hot macadam.

Gilles finished ahead of Jody in Montreal and won at Watkins Glen, but Jody's lead was insuperable: even shedding nine points to Gilles's six, he was champion.

But what goes up must come down, and Ferrari, who had been constructors' champion by an enormous margin in 1979, toppled into the abyss in 1980. Gilles got exactly six points and Jody two. That was enough for Jody. Wisely, he retired rather than face another year of such results. Wisely, I say, because Ferrari were little better the next year. They had entered one of their slumps and Jody was well out of it.

It was Master James Hunt who helped me see past Jody's exterior. The two were fast friends – James greatly admired Jody's intelligence, his diligence, the tenacity with which he pursued not just the sport but his outside interests, the consistency with which he tried to improve himself in everything he did – and for some years they both lived in Spain in the most amicable of relationships, one of the few genuine friendships that I can recall in F1. Jody was not a natural for the rough-and-tumble of F1. Profoundly serious and conscious of his own defects, he simply made himself better year by year. Towards the end of his career he became increasingly concerned with the safety of circuits and after he moved to Monaco he became a highly respected head of the drivers' association: unobtrusive, calm, disciplined and shrewd.

I'll give you one more oddity to close with: of all the retired drivers I know – and they're the smart ones, because they're alive – Jody is the one most at ease with his retirement. I don't think he misses motor racing one bit. For me, that counts as something of plus.

Alan Jones

Alan was ever good ink. In fact, no sportsman I've ever met was anywhere near as good. Which only means that he says what he thinks and the devil take the hindmost. There is not an ounce of tact in the man, not a cavil, not much refinement of meaning: he is as he appears to be, slightly larger than life (and slightly larger than he would like to be), aggressive, competitive and very funny in an absolutely open and not quite innocent way. He is the kind of Australian who would, I suspect, have quite shocked Sir Jack Brabham in the old days. Brash. He takes some compassing: like trying to square a circle.

I first saw him in Kyalami trying his hand with three air hostesses and last saw him in Adelaide sitting in a lobby and dreaming of being elsewhere. Somewhere between those two poles, overactivity and overindulgence and downright indolence, is the real man. Born and bred with cars, with a father who 'wasn't the first or last of the big spenders, just a man who'd turned spending into an art', Alan came to England in 1969 with 'exactly fifty quid in my pocket' and a 'certainty that I would one day be world champion'. The motivation lay in his father, who also raced. 'My old man died wondering whether he should have gone to Europe or not . . . I didn't want what happened to my father to happen to me. I didn't want to live under a question mark.'

Many mishaps and adventures along the way, but eventually Alan got himself into F3: down in Brazil, his first taste of high life. Then back to England and what he calls 'the world's first, last and only all-Australian racing team'. He finished 'high enough to get myself noticed a bit, I thought. That was where I was wrong.' In fact, no one called him up and the first opportunity he got was no more than to try out a March. 'There I was,' he reports, 'literally surrounded by rich kids who'd driven up in their brand-new Porsches . . . I knew half of them couldn't drive out of sight on a dark night and I couldn't help the anger and the envy.' His way of life was just very different from theirs. Not just that he hadn't their money; he hadn't their attitudes either. 'I raced for myself . . . I actually resented the other people who were doing what I was doing because they were in my way. Those were simpler-minded days: my philosophy of driving was to get into anything I could and go as fast as I could, and if I smashed a car up, well, I'd think about paying for it later.'

It went on like that for years: the bills were bigger than the income and winters were times spent waiting for telephone calls and drives that never came. In the interim, he worked his boarding-house dodge: rent a big house by driving up in a Rolls, then stick three Antipodeans to a room. It kept him alive and one day the call did come: his old friend Harry Stiller said he was 'as tired of pissing about as you are, so I've done a deal with Hesketh. You're going to race an F1 Hesketh.'

It was, for Alan, a great leap. He drove four races for Lord Hesketh (on whom see the chapter on James Hunt) and four for Graham Hill's Lola Embassy team that year, garnering exactly two points in Germany. His debut, at Barcelona, coincided with mine, and with one of the many drivers 'strikes' over safety that I've observed. Jonesey was never much into meetings or safety. He remembers 'sitting in the Grand Prix Drivers' Association trailer arguing about safety. What had I got myself into? Politics? A debating club? . . . I knew I wasn't in Barcelona to argue about Armco and fencing.' But Stommelen's accident at Barcelona, which caused the near strike, was instrumental in getting Alan his next drive: as Stommelen's replacement in Hill's team. As Alan says, 'it wasn't the happiest period of my life. Butter wouldn't melt in Graham's mouth; he could charm snakes out of the trees . . . A great showman, a great ambassador but a wretched man to work for . . . He wouldn't listen to anyone's advice. He was stubborn and inflexible.'

By the end of 1975, Hill was dead in a plane crash and Jones was back in the perennial soup. Lou Stanley made an offer which Jones felt able to refuse; Surtees made a half-offer which he couldn't refuse. Again, no one else had called up. Worse, the team was just about owned by an American driver called Brett Lunger, a perfectly nice rent-a-driver but no great shakes on the track. But Lunger got the preferential treatment. The TS9 was a 'pretty good little car' but Surtees shared Hill's vice: 'He thought he knew everything there was to know about racing . . . Former drivers always think they know best . . . their driver is just a surrogate for themselves . . . His ego got in the way of the team.' Alan's record for 1976 reflects the difficulties he faced: a total of seven points: one fourth place and two fifths. They were the only points the team scored.

The next year, AJ drove for Don Nichols at Shadow. Don was a tall, goateed, shady fellow with a long and complex past in Japan which was supposed to have involved the CIA. But his team was at least reasonably competitive and for Alan, it was a steady job. 'Nichols and his team were in deep financial trouble and I considered myself lucky, at that stage, to have a good, steady drive. To drive a consistent loser is in some ways better than to have a potentially quick car being ruined by neglect, which was what I had at Surtees.' His tactic was to keep himself visible in the hope something better would turn up and it was in Don's car that Alan scored his first grand prix victory, in Austria: the only victory Shadow ever scored.

At the end of that year, Don Nichols's Shadow team – designs, material and personnel – had been nicked by Jackie Oliver and Alan Rees and Arrows created. Nichols was out of business and Jones would have been out of a job except that he had signed a contract with Ferrari and had the ritual interview with God. One of the unlikelier un-meetings of minds one can imagine. Anyway, Jonesey got screwed by Ferrari, which was about par for the course. Ferrari wanted to boost North American sales, Villeneuve got the job and Alan was out in the cold.

The next lifeline Alan got thrown to him was Frank Williams's. Here, since Frank is now in the big time, it is well to recall that at the time Frank was known as 'Wanker Williams' and that being offered a drive by Frank was not so very different from being offered one by Osella today. As Alan put it eloquently, 'everyone told me I was crazy and taking a big step backwards in my career'.

A few years ago, Frank had this to say about Alan's driving for him:

As the team has matured, so has AJ; he's always been a stable character, settled and determined. With maturity, a good driver becomes quicker and better; it isn't merely that he has more experience, it's also that his mental attitude is much more suited to the task at hand and his intelligence begins to prevail over his instincts ... I soon found out that I had the best driver in the world, the most complete, the most competitive and the most meticulous.

High praise indeed. But 1978, his first year at Williams, was not all that fortunate. Lotus dominated the championship with Andretti and Reutemann won the races for Ferrari that Lotus didn't win. Jones picked up a second place at the Glen, a fourth at Kyalami and a fifth in France. Slim pickings. By the following year, however, Williams had picked up some solid sponsorship and with money, the team started its advance to the top. Alan's team-mate that year was Clay Regazzoni – of whom Alan tells a marvellous story of Clay being taken through the BRM works by Lou Stanley and being told 'with my team and my factory, we will make you world champion', to which Clay answered, 'Fucka the championship, how mucha you pay?' and by then Clay was a much cooler character than in his earlier days.

The combination paid off, if slowly. At Long Beach, Jones picked up a third place; Clay got a second in Monaco; Jones a fourth at Dijon, then Clay won at Silverstone after Jones had led for thirty-nine laps. In Germany, it was Alan's turn to win and with Clay finishing just behind him, that became the first of many Williams one-twos. Alan followed that up with a decisive win over Villeneuve on the ultra-fast circuit of the Österreichring and repeated the feat at Zandvoort. Monza was a washout, but Alan won again in Canada and led the race at the Glen until forced to retire.

For Williams, it was very much a case of from rags to riches. Jones was third in the championship with a total of 43 points (40 only were counted) and Regazzoni fifth with 29. Scheckter was the new champion for Ferrari, but Jones's four victories in a year had definitely put Williams on the map. Now, 1980 could only be a further progression.

What part did Jones play in that progression? That is more difficult to answer. Around the obsessive Frank and the reclusive Patrick Head, the Williams designer, I think of him as the bull in the china shop; at least he kept the pair of them from being so totally introverted as to float away from this earth. Just seeing Alan basking in the sun outside the motor-home, his overalls rolled down to his waist, a sweaty T-shirt showing over his broad chest, somehow seemed to make everyone feel better. He exuded confidence of a special kind and it was impossible not to think you were around a natural winner. Technically, Alan's major contribution was what Frank called his 'honesty'. Amusingly enough, he thought of Alan's 'singularly unobsessive' nature as being a weakness. I disagree. That made each day's racing just a job to be done as well as possible. For Frank, utterly bound up in his team, it must have been difficult to work side by side with someone whose mind was on the car, truth to tell, only when he was actually in it, and I think that aspect of Alan is one of the major differences between AJ and the other champions I have known.

Debriefings, which occur after every session, frankly bored AJ out of his mind: information had to be prised out of him with tongs. And then Frank paid him the ultimate compliment by recognizing where Jones's talent really lay: 'The name of the game is racing, and AJ is brilliant at getting cars across the finish line . . . When AJ is racing he's a different man.'

Jonesey agreed with that verdict: 'Racing,' he said, 'is a form of commitment: once the flag drops, that's it . . . There's something important to me about having my back to the wall.'

A back to the wall. Jones had his share of shunts, but I can't resist quoting him again on the ultimate shunt, on dying, if only because as always he says things that other drivers don't dare to say:

I think it fair to say we're a callous lot about death (though the death of friends drove many champions out of racing). If I were killed tomorrow, Frank would probably say, 'that's too bad; AJ was a bit of a character' . . . but Frank is in the business of motor racing and in his plans, I am a cog. If I go, Frank must replace me . . . It's something we have to live with. All of us. I know it sounds cold, but . . . we are bloody mercenaries and we can't get hysterical every time someone gets killed . . . Every race I do is a calculated risk. But once I get in the car, I've committed myself and the risk no longer plays a part. Analysis stops when the car heads out of the pit-lane.

All very true, all very Jones. Alan is pretty much an absolutist, an anarch. In all the years I knew him he did pretty much as he wanted; he indulged his appetites when and how he felt like it; he played games the way he wanted to, without regard to style; he chased skirts and was chased by them; he drank beer to his heart's content; he didn't exactly get up at the crack of dawn to do lonely five-mile training routines. He seemed to work best when he was just being himself.

That came to the fore in his championship year, 1980. The car he drove was the now famous 07. Introduced some way into the 1979 season, it had taken a while to sort out and then had proved a miraculously good car. As Alan says, 'It was reliable, adaptable, simple and quick, and all those things in greater measure than any other car in F1.' Partnered in 1980 by Reutemann, Jones made a fine start in Buenos Aires: he won pole position and proceeded to dominate the race, which gave the whole team a much-needed boost of confidence. Brazil, on the other hand, was a complete let-down. Alan qualified poorly and was quite lucky to finish third in what Frank calls the 'Economy Run' because Alan drove so sluggishly that he finished with four gallons of fuel in his tanks rather than the usual two pints. Celebration in Argentina may have had something to do with it; myself, I think it was the week off in Guaruja between the races, when Alan enjoyed himself to the hilt and gave racing not a thought.

At Kyalami, he qualified eighth, started brilliantly and then dropped back through the field with his gearbox bearings gone. At the end of the same month, in Long Beach, his old friend Clay Regazzoni went straight into the crash barrier, an accident which left him paralysed for life. Jones's own race was ruined when Giacomelli put him out of the race. It was then, in his own words, 'that I began to sense the threat posed to us by Nelson Piquet'. Nelson in fact now led the race with 18 points to Alan's 13.

When the F1 family returned to Europe, war was breaking out on the political front between Messrs Balestre and Ecclestone; the atmosphere, I remember, was thick with unpleasantness. Jones's humour was not helped when his car broke down and in practice he raced back to the pits to get in Reutemann's; he found the Argentine in it and had to wait. It was the first sign of a growing rivalry between the two men. But though on his last try Alan did take pole position, his race car had a bad case of understeering and he was ultimately lucky to finish second behind Pironi. Next was Monaco, a race Alan admits he cannot abide. 'It's not just the poseurs and their yachts, though they're bad enough . . . it's the race itself, which is just a bloody procession. The truth is that the cars have outgrown the circuit . . . and it is exceedingly boring to drive . . . I'm not alone in thinking it were better it died a natural death.' Alan qualified third, Pironi held him up, but just as he was ready to overtake Pironi's Ferrari, his gearbox blew up. With his mind already set on the title, to score no points at all was a disaster.

Spain was a political battlefield, a showdown between Balestre and FOCA, with the 'loyalist' teams, Italian and French, marshalled by Ferrari, finally refusing to race. I translated the whole meeting in the Spanish Federation's motor-home and I remember the acrimony well. Alan won the race as the three cars in front of him all faltered, but he was not credited with the nine points because Balestre declared the race 'illegal'. 'Not to get the nine points I needed after winning a race was a bitter, disheartening blow . . . I know just as much effort, preparation – mental and physical – and risk went into that race as any other on the calendar. I have neither forgiven nor forgotten.'

As Alan says, 'Knowing that Renault had backed Balestre over Spain and that the French has combined with the Italians to put the season, and my title, into jeopardy, I went to France in a fighting mood. I not only wanted badly to win that race; I wanted my win to be a personal gesture of defiance.' From fourth on the grid, Jones made a good start, raced against Arnoux and Pironi (two Frenchmen!) in the early stages and then began to haul Jacques Laffite (a third!) in bit by bit. He won well and I remember the whole Williams team cavorting up and down the pit-lane for a half-hour after the race, waving their Union Jack in defiance. More importantly, Alan had now settled into the lead of the championship with 28 points to Piquet's 25 and Arnoux's and Pironi's 23.

At Brands, the French came roaring back, qualifying first and second on the grid. The Ligiers luckily had tyre problems, Pironi going right off the track when his came off its rim, and Alan won again. Piquet, however, finished second and remained within six points of Alan. Germany was another disappointment: Alan was on pole position again, he fought Jabouille's Renault on uneven terms for more than twenty laps and could only take the lead when Jabouille's engine blew. Then, with ten laps to go, a puncture sent him into the pits and though Williams changed the tyre in no time at all, he went back on third and stayed there to the end of the race. Piquet finished just behind him, so the race remained tight: Jones 41, Piquet 34.

Austria was expected to favour the French Renaults with their turbo-charged engines, and so it proved. Though René Arnoux's tyres went off, Jabouille persisted and held off Alan by the margin of a second. Alan thought it a race he could have won had the pits informed him earlier of the progress he was making behind Jabouille. Still, the six points were a consolation and Alan's title lead went up to 11 points.

Before the race in Holland was one of the few times I can recall him being slightly twitchy. Obviously, the pressures of being front-runner in the championship were getting to him and, like every other driver, Jones was deeply superstitious. 'I'm going to kill anyone who calls me "champ" before it actually happens,' he growled. He had further reasons for being upset: a nasty shunt when his throttle jammed – one of racing's more unpleasant sensations – had left him feeling bruised. He was on the same row as Piquet when the race started and made one of his best-ever starts to take the lead; then in exactly the same place where he'd had his practice shunt he drifted wide, went off and hit a rut, damaging his skirts. Race and points were gone. Worse yet, Nelson had won and narrowed the gap between them to two points and there were still three races to go.

At Imola, he finished second behind Piquet, putting Nelson back in the lead for the first time in some months. But because of Nelson's consistent finishing earlier in the season, Jones knew Nelson would have to shed some points. Montreal was the key. Nelson *had* to win in Montreal; it showed on him, as he was plainly nervous the morning of final practice. Alan has always contended that on Saturday afternoon, Piquet's car had been souped up with additives. I thought so myself at the time, because for a driver in Piquet's position to find a whole extra second and a half during last practice is a bit unusual. One could even say miraculous.

Then came the start of the race, and a multiple shunt over which multiple accusations were made. Nelson accused Jones of shutting the gate on him; Alan replied that he'd taken up the correct line for the upcoming corner and it was Piquet's business to accept the fact that Alan's wheels were in front: as indeed replays showed they were. The re-start cost Jones a good lead but he again got a good jump on Nelson. Nelson fought back but his engine blew on lap twenty-two and then Alan knew that if he could just nurse the car home, he was champion. To prove the point, which I think is so typical of Alan, he repeated the performance at Watkins Glen.

But the championship was won in Montreal and Alan celebrated in true Jones style: the last I saw of him, he was heading out through the revolving door with the girl his buddy Charlie Crichton-Stuart thought he was dating that night, Alan having thoughtfully had Charlie paged to the telephone so they could sneak out unseen.

Alan raced another season with Williams but this time it was Nelson who won out by the narrowest of margins: one point ahead of Reutemann who was himself three points up on Jones. Those three points (and several others) were made by Carlos in what Jones thought was a dishonest way, by disobeying team orders to let Alan finish in the lead. He was extremely bitter about both Carlos and Williams and the whole sorry story was a pale rehearsal for the Piquet–Mansell conflict of 1987. The fact was then and remains true today that Williams only honours the Number One position in certain circumstances, and those circumstances, as Frank sees them, are racing circumstances, not contractual. It has led to trouble at Williams many times and I find it totally misguided, because 1981, like 1986, was a year in which a Williams driver could have been champion. Neither of them was because Frank could not make his mind up and give clear directions; and also because Patrick Head, his partner, has never had any interest in which driver wins so long as his car does. Well, Williams as a constructor won that championship, but they lost the respect and loyalty of Alan. Not wholly, obviously, because he retained his respect for the team and for Frank personally; he just wasn't going to race for them or for anyone any more.

So back home to Australia and to Bev and his son Christian Alan went. With no one expecting he would stay long staring at sheep and barbecuing steaks. In fact, he managed to stay away two years, being lured back only for the occasional one-off race, and then, overweight but as combative as ever, he was offered a contract by Karl Haas, by Ford and by Beatrice, Haas's sponsor, that he could not refuse. It was money in the bank and back to fun and glory.

Alan could not have known that the man who made the Beatrice deal would be sacked and Beatrice drop out; nor could he know that the Cosworth-designed Ford turbo in his car would be consistently down on power and that Ford and Duckworth would give Haas endless excuses but no real immediate support or remedy. What he thought he knew before the season started was that a mate of his, Pete Collins, the current team-boss at Benetton, would be boss at Haas. Instead, Haas had fallen back on what he knew and what he knew was two Americans – Teddy Mayer and Tyler Alexander – for whom Alan had, not to put too fine a point on it, no respect of any sort. As he said all season, 'Those two dummies managed to push McLaren down the drain, what the hell do you think they're going to do to this team?'

Haas remained loyal too long to them, they remained too long loyal to old ideas, the whole scheme went off half-cocked and at the end of the year a disgusted Haas sold up and went back to American racing while Alan, utterly relieved to see the end of a miserable season, finally quit: this time, he said, for good.

Nelson Piquet

It would strike anyone who has known and observed Nelson Piquet over the years that he is something of a paradox: a creature of considerable warmth and passion, sometimes playful, often delightful, and equally one who is malicious, clever, callous and devious. It really depends on whether you are on the right or the wrong side of Nelson. Those close to him – and none are closer than his mechanics and the people he works with every day – tend to worship the ground he walks on. Those at one remove, like those he has worked for, find him exasperating and wonderful by turn. Those with whom he is competing often find him simply intolerable.

Part of the reason is that Nelson has by now been around a very long time indeed. 1988 will be his eleventh season in F1, a record shared by a number of drivers but by relatively few champion drivers. Lauda put in thirteen years, Fittipaldi the same number and Stewart nine. Since Nelson seems to have no other ambition than to go on driving, as his skills are still great and his combativeness – as 1987 showed – far from gone, he may still be around for years. Or he may quit tomorrow. Neither would surprise me, for above all things Nelson is mercurial and moody.

There are not many clues in his biography to indicate how these traits and his double-sidedness developed. On the whole, he had a plump, rich, satisfying childhood. His family was well placed; they lived well; he lived well. I can't think of anything he has ever said about his youth that would leave one to believe that it was particularly fraught, or even that it was particularly interesting to him. Nelson is not really introspective, nor is he truly very interested in other people. He thinks he knows certain things about his own nature and he submits to other people, often with surprising passivity, but on the whole life just seems to go sliding by, and with it, an absolutely extraordinary racing career. He rates right at the top of the profession in number of victories, in pole positions, in consistent performance.

He, Stewart and Lauda are the only champions in the modern period of F1 to win the title three times. That speaks for a lot of class, especially if one considers that Piquet has, of all modern drivers, been the least mobile: he spent eight years driving for Brabham, however indifferent or good its cars were, and it wasn't until 1986 that he finally decided to shift teams for the first time to join Williams, and in 1988, driving for Lotus, he will be in only his third team. That speaks for a lot of loyalty. Or a lot of laziness.

Nelson will tell you about his beginnings in racing and he makes it all sound indolent, natural and easy. It was what he always wanted to do, he started early, his father put it together for him, something like a miniature track, a go-kart, and he just went on from there. He doesn't so readily mention that he was a natural athlete to start with, that he had a sunny, happy-go-lucky disposition and that his mother was a very determined lady who did much to advance his early career, putting the deals together that eventually enabled him to go racing seriously.

In fact, all in all, it is very easy to underestimate Nelson. And Nelson's determination. The lazy cat has his claws. As we shall see.

But first, the driver.

Perhaps the most curious fact about Nelson is that he has won his three championships over a period of seven years: his first in 1981, a second in 1983 and a third four years later in 1987. In between, he has often been in the doldrums. People who have worked with him a long time ascribe this to an essential lack of motivation, and I remember Gordon Murray, who has been as close to Nelson as anyone, telling me that Piquet often had to be treated as one would treat a lazy child, he had to be 'goosed'. Some of the bad years are of course ascribable to inferior cars, but the truth is that apart from one race for Ensign in 1978, Nelson has always worked at the top levels of the sport. He has not been with the no-hopers.

Another oddity about Piquet's career is that his twenty grand prix victories, though they come at regular intervals – and sometimes almost by surprise – are very evenly spaced. Only in 1986 did Piquet succeed in winning four grands prix in a season: otherwise, even his championship years show a maximum of three. This is revealing on several counts. The first is that Nelson has never been a *dominant* driver, but rather a steady one. If you consider the record of comparable champions – Prost and Clark with seven victories in a season, Stewart, Hunt and Andretti with seven, Lauda three times with five – it becomes obvious that, regardless of the equipment supplied, Nelson has never taken a single season by the throat and truly run it his way. A corollary of this, since it is impossible to win a title without scoring more points than your opponents, is that Nelson would seem to have been a steadier driver than many. But that in turn is belied by the fact that Piquet's three championships have all been won by tiny numbers of points. In 1981, he eked out victory over Reutemann by a single point; in 1983 over Prost by two; and in 1987, over Mansell – who wasn't driving in the last two races – by 12. Everything suggests that if Mansell had been driving, Piquet's victory would at best have been yet another narrow one.

I once discussed him with Gordon Murray, then Piquet's engineer at Brabham, for the two of them were, at the time, virtually inseparable. My first question related to Nelson's mechanical ability, which is known to be phenomenal, in the sense that not only does he have an extraordinary feel for the car, he has a genuine love of all machines, of tinkering, of fixing, improving. On his beloved boat, Nelson would spend hours doing the sort of little improvements and maintenance jobs that most of us postpone to another day: as he said, nothing made him happier; he liked to live in harmony with machines and nothing made him unhappier than to have even the slightest thing wrong with them.

Murray confirmed Nelson's talent. He said, 'Designing is an immense puzzle, made up of simple ideas and complex variables, of surprising successes and inexplicable failures. But the reason my relationship with Nelson is so profitable is that we speak the same language; we talk to each other through the machine. If you want, he is the instrument on which I play.' In other words, the feedback from a machine which an engineer and a team get from their driver is all-important. In Nelson's career, it is this symbiosis between man and machine that has carried him so far. At Brabham, he and Gordon Murray could be said to have been really joint engineers: Murray provided the ideas, Nelson the practice. At Williams, it was ever Piquet who did the greatest amount of testing and developing: sometimes to Mansell's annoyance. Nor is there any doubt that what prompted Honda to shift their engine, and Piquet, from Williams to Lotus, was that very same ability: running the Honda engines at Lotus in 1987, the Lotus chassis was simply not up to its engine; it is that which Nelson will be asked to help out with.

When I asked Murray about Piquet's ability as a pure driver, he described Nelson as 'both refined and natural'. He went on to say that few drivers in his experience were 'willing to put as much time into the more boring parts of the F1 driver's job as Nelson. He will test for you endlessly; he will repeat simple exercises, concentrating on one aspect of a car. I think at heart he is deeply competitive, but

I would say that even more than the competition, Nelson simply loves to drive. Nothing else gives him as much pleasure.'

Nelson himself once told me that it was the 'joy of getting something right' that made the onerous business of racing such a pleasure for him: 'You get a problem, it is your job to solve it. You try this, you try that and in the end you find out what the problem is.' If you grasp that this is essentially a solitary task, then you grasp one part of the essence of the man, for most of his pleasures are solitary. I remember him once rhapsodizing about racing at Silverstone – which I suppose one could well think of, outside of a race, as being a high, bare heath – and saying how wonderful it was 'to be alone out there, sometimes spotting a hare'; how he 'liked to see the single trees go by and how alone I feel when I'm in the car going fast and that's all there is in the world'.

The sea, the high air (since Nelson has taken up flying), these are huge, empty spaces. The problems they pose are those of survival in a hostile void. They are not those nasty, niggling problems which have to do with human emotions, with conflict, with jealousy, with opinion or even thought. Another time, sitting at pierside along the old yachting basin on the Ile Nôtre Dame in Montreal, Nelson said that 'racing is as much about getting away from the world as anything else'. And I think that is very true of Nelson as a driver. In a cockpit, he is at last in his own world; no one can interfere with him, no one can tell him what to do. For him, the F1 car is the ultimate form of 'no problem', his and Reutemann's favourite expression.

On the track, as anyone could observe during the 1987 season, Nelson operates best on his own: the presence of another car near him can make him positively skittish and I remember Rosberg once telling me that Piquet was so good a natural driver that the only way you could beat him was to drive right up his back or alongside him: 'he is very difficult to get by, but once you do, he seems to enjoy it and he'll just wait until *you* have a problem.' At least twice in 1987, for instance, Piquet and Mansell, at the peak of their rivalry, sought to share the same stretch of road; in both cases, Nelson was seen to take a corner quite wide. It certainly wasn't to let his rival through; it was to create space for himself.

That brings up the question of direct combativity. Now, I happen to think that 99 per cent of the time, Nelson is a pussycat. You couldn't, in the right circumstances, meet a nicer man. Not perhaps the most articulate man in the world, in part because he seems to think in some no-man's land between Portuguese and English, but certainly one of the more engaging. He greatly likes to make fun of others; he pulls faces like a kid; he imitates and mocks the solemn; he is completely at ease and sometimes uproarious when with his own kind; at describing his own race he is without a peer, complete with noises, gestures and stream-of-consciousness talk. But prick him and he bleeds, loudly and copiously. His ego is nice; his superego is arrogant.

Much of this is protectiveness. When Nelson left Brazil to come and race in Europe, he had his hard times. He liked the companionship of the lesser formulae, but he was also a young man in a hurry. Not particularly big and certainly not especially strong, Nelson also lacked – and lacks to this day – the kind of public persona that is supposed to accompany the glamour of high-level racing. Between weakness and shyness, he often fails to appear at his best.

His frailty was a real problem in his early days. I can recall his passing out on the podium in Brazil once, completely dehydrated; and who will forget the day in 1981 at Las Vegas when he won his first world championship and had to be carried out of his car, vomiting and quite unable to stand up, to receive his accolade? By the time he came around to his second championship in 1983, Nelson had started taking his body seriously, doing training and building up his strength: he knew the question mark hanging over his fitness was simply an invitation to other drivers to push him as hard as they could during a race. To do such a thing, to concede that his abilities needed improving on, was something of a difficulty for Nelson. Like all the naturally gifted, he had so far thought that he could win on his own, by sheer skill, and I remember – in 1980 when in fact Nelson already came close, despite being only in his second serious year in F1, to being champion and was kept at bay only towards the end of the season by Alan Jones – contrasting the two men; Jones the bull and Piquet the cat. There was more to it than just the physical contrast between the two men, the splendid rudeness of the Australian and the almost constrained politeness of the Brazilian, the power of the one and the subtlety of the other, there was also a question of background: Jones's long, slogging years bashing his way to the top, Nelson's slow, almost imperceptible progression, so silky-smooth that one hardly noticed how he was scoring.

In the 1981 championship, which could easily have been a second title for Alan Jones, but wasn't because Carlos Alberto Reutemann refused to be up-staged and cost Jones some vital points, it was intriguing to see how Nelson, a cunning tactician, was able to exploit the rivalry between the two men. Jones and Reutemann swopped wins in the first two races of the year; then, in Argentina, Nelson snaffled victory from the pair of them, repeating the feat at Imola when the European season started. Reutemann won at Zolder, but Monaco brought solace only to Jones and Piquet went off in a shunt. Spain brought little joy to any of the three leaders, nor did France. At Silverstone, Reutemann scored a second place but in the next race at Hockenheim, Piquet, after a notable duel with Prost, was the winner. From then on, it was a battle for placings. Others won; the three clung to their finishing power and it was ultimately Piquet who slipped through at Las Vegas when Reutemann's car faded on him, and though Jones won, it was Piquet's fifth place that won him the title. One had to feel a little sorry for Reutemann: he came within a point of a title he never did manage to win.

In 1983, Piquet's great rival was Alain Prost. In Brazil, Prost led for a lap, then it was Piquet's race all the way. It was his home, and Nelson – unlike his fellow driver at Lotus this year, Ayrton Senna – is really at home in the clamour and confusion of Brazil. After a fruitless Long Beach, the F1 family returned to Europe and Prost outdrove Piquet handsomely at Le Castellet, Nelson nonetheless taking second. At Imola, Prost drew even. The two men raced on fairly even terms right up through Silverstone, where Prost stretched his narrow lead to six points.

I saw Piquet after that race, and he was neither disconsolate nor sanguine; the championship just didn't seem to matter that much to him at that point. He is a man who takes one race at a time. That may be what Piquet said, but one can be easily tempted to believe that Piquet was beginning to play one of his characteristic games: that of letting his opponents underestimate him. In that respect, he is part cool and part wily. After Germany, Prost was nine points ahead and after Austria, 14. Prost admitted in private that the title did seem to be a realistic possibility: his lead seemed comfortable, his car was the better of the two and with his remarkable finishing ability, he had begun to feel he was in with a good chance.

At Zandvoort, with so much at stake, the two collided, a crash which Prost admitted was his fault and about which Piquet, after his initial anger, was complaisant. 'We'll see in Italy,' he said. And in Monza Piquet pulled a splendid victory out of the hat, after a long drought. With Prost having to retire, his lead was now a mere five points and at Brands, the two men fought a furious duel, but Piquet led from start to finish, Prost finishing just behind him. That put it all down to the last race of the season, in South Africa. Prost's Renault let him down and Piquet's third place, driven with great caution, was just enough to give him his second title.

Compared to the duel that took place in 1987, 1983 was a calm season, a year in which the majority of the smart money was on Prost, but Piquet was the man who came up with the money.

I'll return to 1987 shortly, but meanwhile, some explanation has to be given for what happened in the intervening years, when Nelson seemed to go into somnolence and decline. The obvious explanation for 1984 and 1985 and their relative failures – Piquet could do no better than fifth and eighth in the title stakes – is that his Brabham was an ageing car, that some of Gordon Murray's more radical solutions did not work out, that team-boss Bernard Ecclestone paid less attention to his team than to the intrigues of the sport as a whole and that as a result Brabham fell from the front line to the rear guard: in 1984 it garnered a pathetic 38 points compared to McLaren's 143.5 and in 1985, a disastrous year, it could manage no more than 26 while McLaren again dominated.

Some of Brabham's decline, however, must be laid at Piquet's door. Either he wasn't preparing the Brabham cars with his old efficiency or other factors were beginning to interfere with his thoroughgoing professionalism. In fact, those were a pair of years in which Nelson seemed increasingly morose, and I am inclined to believe he is one of those drivers who either reacts strongly to defeat or submits to it with some apathy.

Additionally, however, it must be said that Nelson's personal life in those years was something of a shambles. He seemed to me to have fallen into a sort of thrall: he was sleepy, pooped-out, withdrawn. He had troubles at home with his girlfriend Sylvia; he was restless; she was demanding. Piquet simply became distracted. Murray could blame the BMW engine, which proved a frail instrument subject to violent explosion; others could point to neglect and say the team relied too heavily on Piquet, continuing its tradition of having only one front-line driver and leaving the second car pretty much to God's will. Certainly neither of the Fabi brothers in 1984 or Hesnault and Surer in 1985 were of great help and by 1986 Brabham had declined to the bottom of the table, with only Arrows scoring fewer points.

By that time, however, Piquet had taken the great leap. With Ecclestone's consent and best wishes, he had moved over to Williams. Certainly, the move was a wrench. Nelson had lived inside Brabham for eight years; he knew everyone associated with the team intimately;

it was home. On the other hand, as he said to me at the time, it was plain that he was no longer learning anything at Brabham, that he had lost some faith in Murray, though still greatly admiring his innovative genius, and that he had a career to rebuild. When I asked him why he had taken so long to make up his mind, he said ingenuously, 'I am a little lazy about making decisions.'

After two years of deep frustration, Keke Rosberg, despairing that the Williams would ever be competitive, had finally hung up his gloves; an opening became available; Piquet had faith in the Honda engine (and his own contacts with the Japanese manufacturer); he thought that with Nigel Mansell as the Number Two driver he would get all the attention which had been lacking at Brabham; he admired designer Patrick Head's skill and economy in design; he liked Frank Williams's utter, obsessive devotion to racing pure and simple, in such contrast to Ecclestone's more hands-off approach; it just seemed, he said, 'the right sort of place to be, the place to make a new start'.

Indeed, Nelson appeared in the right place at the right time, for both 1986 and 1987 were – though marred by a tragic accident to Frank Williams himself – triumphant years for the Williams team and the Honda turbo engine. That they were not easy years for Nelson is another matter, and the responsibility for that must lie squarely with the Williams team, which had a number of in-built defects. The first was its reliance on the extraordinary attention to detail paid by Frank, and when that went and Frank was unable to take charge as he had in the past, that flaw began to show. Head was busy designing. Never the most tactful man, he did not get on well with Nelson, nor was he as intimate with or as reliant on him as Gordon Murray had been. The second defect was a racing policy which allowed both drivers to win if they could, although contractually there was a Number One and a Number Two driver and Piquet was their Number One. As it had with Reutemann and Jones, this led inevitably to friction between Piquet and Mansell, a mutual dislike which, as time went by, neither driver took much care to disguise.

This led to the formation of cabals within the team, with much effort wasted by the two drivers and their supporters within the team being at cross-purposes with each other. Nelson has admitted to me since that he greatly underestimated Mansell as a driver when he arrived in the team and, indeed, until the very tail end of 1985, when Nigel pulled off his first two F1 victories and proved himself, there was no reason for Nelson to think Nigel would be a dangerous rival. His record up to that point had been honourable but mediocre. At Lotus he had been in the shadow of Elio de Angelis, whose father paid a lot of the bills, thus making sure that Elio got the lion's share of the attention. But even had it not been for that factor, the Nigel who had raced prior to Brands Hatch 1985 was widely seen as little more than an honest, journeyman driver. He was rash, aggressive, uncontrolled, uneconomical and prone to accident and error. Thus Nelson's attitude was pardonable misjudgement: nothing indicated that Mansell would mature so quickly into a dangerous, tenacious and painstaking adversary.

Furthermore, Piquet thought that his Number One position guaranteed him privilege, and the 1986 season was not very old before he was already complaining that Mansell was getting equal if not better treatment than himself. Further, as the championship battle became a quadrangular dogfight, one of the most closely contested seasons I had ever seen, Piquet was fighting not just on one front but on three: inside Williams, he had to fight off Nigel's challenge; on the track he had to fight a redoubtable Prost, who he knew was every bit his equal in skill and intelligence; and in his own psyche he had to fight off a third challenge from the fast-rising and equally brilliant Ayrton Senna, with whom he did not get along at all and who was, back in Brazil, already beginning to assume the mantle of being Piquet's successor. 'I am not dead yet,' Piquet said to me firmly one day.

Nelson withstood Senna's challenge in Rio, but in Jerez, Senna drove an absolutely superb race in the rain to win, while Nelson was forced to retire. At Imola, it was Prost's turn to enter the title challenge in a big way; Piquet finished second behind him. In Monaco, it was Piquet's turn to fail to finish; Prost won, Senna came third and Mansell fourth. In Belgium Nelson again failed to finish and his three rivals all scored points, Mansell winning one of the better races in his life. Piquet found himself fourth in the title race with 15 points, while Senna had 19, Mansell 18 and Prost 23. The battle heated up in Montreal when all four finished up in the points, but Mansell again doggedly led most of the race. With Detroit coming up and Nigel known to be a street-race specialist, the kind of man who could endure its bumps and indignities without flinching, Piquet knew he had a problem.

He wasn't voluble about it, but one could sense the tension in the man. He began mumbling that the Williams team was favouring Mansell because he was English, and he complained about his testing schedule. It was always hard to talk to Nelson and know how serious his gripes were: they were delivered off the cuff, apparently without intent; they were a form of winding-up, of sowing distrust among his opponents while giving himself added motivation. But when he again failed to finish in Detroit, a race which Senna won in style, his complaints began to be more open. He had his own coterie of Brazilian journos to whom he would throw tidbits of gossip, knowing they would be picked up eventually within the team. By then he was lagging seriously behind Prost in the championship, Senna was second and even Mansell, his Number Two, was 10 points up on him. All in all, if you were used to things going your way, it was understandable that a little wormwood seemed to have entered Nelson's life.

Mansell was now on a quite genuine high; the Honda engine was devastating the opposition; in his own rather cheerful and optimistic mind, it must have seemed after France that Prost, leading him by a point after a sequence of beautifully contrived finishes, despite a weakening engine, was his principal rival. True, Senna was not far behind, but the Lotus was beginning to reveal its own frailties; as for Nelson, he was a good 16 points off the pace. At this point Nigel began to answer Piquet's criticisms with some of his own; the British press, eager to see him win, picked them up and matters grew daily more contentious. When Nigel subsequently completely outdrove Piquet at the British Grand Prix at Brands, the battle between them was well and truly joined: something Prost was to profit from heavily in the months to come.

In Germany, Piquet drove away from the opposition and put himself right back in the thick of the race; then, in the inaugural race at the Hungaroring, a few kilometres outside Budapest, won again; whatever his complaints, they had been suddenly hushed, and Piquet, receiving the press after his victory, was all bonhomie. In a long, gruelling race in great heat, Prost had spun off; Senna, despite leading for thirty-two laps, had been relegated to second place; and the arch-rival, Mansell, had finished third a lap down. With two victories on the trot, Nelson was able to say, 'That ought to show them who is the Number One driver in this team.' 'Them' clearly meant Williams and did not endear Nelson to Nigel's many partisans.

The championship, however, remained balanced on a knife edge, and after Austria, where Prost restored his fortunes, Mansell had 55 points, Prost 53, Piquet 47 and Senna 42. Slightly more worrying for the Williams team was that neither car managed to finish at the Österreichring: was the Honda engine fallible after all? In Italy, Prost was disqualified on a technicality, and Piquet beat out Mansell after

Nigel had held the lead for more than half the race. Senna's chances were now getting remote, Piquet was a mere five points behind Mansell and Prost three behind Nelson. It was a three-cornered race and there were only three races to go. In Estoril, the four heroes of the season occupied the first four places. Prost's second place kept him in contention, as did Nelson's third, but heading for Mexico, it was Mansell who had a stranglehold on the championship with a 10-point lead: not unassailable, but likely to be difficult to dislodge.

In the horrid smog of Mexico City, however, Berger suddenly chose to win his first race, relegating the big four to the next four places. Once again, Prost was the big winner of the internecine rivalry between Piquet and Mansell: his six points narrowed the gap between himself and Mansell to six points, with Piquet nine points down. As both Prost and Mansell would have to shuck off some points, since only the best eleven results counted towards the title, Nelson was in with more than a random chance, but he had to win at Adelaide to overcome Mansell, and finish well ahead of Prost. As it happened, frustrated for so long during the season, Alain chose Adelaide to score his fourth victory of the season, but only after Nigel Mansell had lost a wheel – and, with it, his chances of the championship. Nelson had to content himself with third place, a point behind his team-mate in the final standings.

I think the result greatly frustrated Nelson. He had done his best and yet been bettered. Further, he knew that within the unwritten rules of the team, if Nigel continued to finish ahead of him, Mansell would be the *de facto* if not *de jure* Number One. During the inter-season, his appreciation of the sticky waters in which he found himself grew, particularly when Nigel, for the first time, was paid a sum commensurate with his new status of potential champion, a sum that came close to equalling what Nelson, in the second year of his contract, was being paid. If money could talk, it would say that money is how driver status is measured, and Nelson was seriously disturbed. He made representations to Honda and was again assured that his Number One status remained unchanged.

The 1987 season, with Frank slowly recovering from his accident but still confined to his wheelchair, began in an atmosphere of high tension and turned out to be, in the end, another race for the title among the same four competitors as in 1986. Prost, the reigning champion, had his difficulties with a TAG/Porsche engine that had seen better days; Senna, though he had (ostensibly) a Honda engine identical to that mounted in the Williams car, found his

Ducarouge-prepared chassis was not up to the power of the engine and was never a real threat for the title. It thus narrowed down, in fact – and certainly in the popular imagination – to a straight *mano a mano* between Piquet and Mansell. That was also, from the start, how the two men saw it, and what made the season particularly interesting, at least to any unbiased observer, was the ebb and flow of sympathy for the two men. Much of that feeling, which ran pretty high at times, was carefully nurtured by the press. The British press, as one might expect, was – with few exceptions – solidly behind Mansell: he had deserved the title in 1986, he outfought Piquet on the circuit, he was the worthy winner. In the rest of Europe, however, and in the paddock, there was a surprising undercurrent supporting Piquet. A great part of the French and Italian media, for instance, had a simply irrational dislike of Mansell. To them, Nigel was bullish, stupid, surly and just the kind of unglamorous champion they hoped would never reign. They found his devotion to his family disingenuous and even offensive; the Williams press officer kept Nigel well protected and when they did get unpaid interviews, they found them full of banal statements and tributes (which they did not believe) to what a wonderful team Williams was. The team itself had long earned their collective opprobrium by being such superpatriots that they had hung a card on their motor-home saying, 'British Press Only'. That didn't endear them. Then, though Frank Williams himself is a good linguist, no one else at Williams was much of one; Nelson can get along in French and Italian, but Nigel neither knew a word or cared to learn one. Small beer, but important in PR.

But racing is racing, and no sooner had the season started, in Brazil, than the battle was under way. It was another hot race on another hot day, cars kept coming in to change their tyres and Nelson was an early victim of rubbish thrown on the track and sucked up into his side-pods; the race order changed bewilderingly as first Piquet and then Senna led. The canny Prost then took the lead, having moved up from fifth place. Senna was using the new Lotus 'active', computer-controlled suspension and finding it hard to control: he held second until there were only eleven laps to go. Prost took the lead after his first tyre-change and never lost it, despite having to stop a second time. Mansell and Piquet, who had been first and second on the grid, both had disappointing races; though Piquet's car was overheating, he finished second and Mansell, with a badly deflating rear tyre, just limped into sixth. Round one to Nelson.

At Imola during practice, Nelson had a very serious crash indeed, spinning off at Tosa and slamming right through the guard rail. I remember rushing off after Syd Watkins, the official F1 medic, and being told, 'Nelson's OK. At least, he knows who he is!' Certainly, however, he was going to be in no position to attack Imola's demanding circuit. Saturday, after many of the Goodyear tyres had revealed excessive blistering, they sent to England for replacements and Senna won pole position. On Sunday, the first start aborted and on the restart, though Senna led for a lap, Mansell went round him magisterially and took over a lead which he never abandoned.

By Belgium, Nelson had recovered from his injuries, though still aching; he and Mansell shared the front row, Mansell's time being a new record for the circuit. Mansell made a terrific start, but the race was stopped by a spin by Streiff in which Palmer got unavoidably involved. Some forty minutes later, the race re-started and this time Senna slipped through both Mansell and Piquet to take the lead, but as Senna went on and Mansell followed him, Senna seemed to brake too soon and Nigel was right alongside him around the long bend. Senna did not give way, they touched and both spun off. Later, in the pits, Nigel actually assaulted Senna: he was alarmingly high, the adrenalin flowing, and there had been some provocation, but Mansell's behaviour did nothing to improve his image. Nelson took over the lead, but it was not to be for long. Prost soon caught up to him, overtook him and Nelson had to retire with a busted exhaust pipe. No points for Mansell or Piquet, but those were still early days.

In the charnel house of Monaco, Nigel and Senna were on the front row next to each other: as they were known not to be the closest of friends (and not merely because of the incident in Belgium) and had already managed to wipe each other out three times before, apprehension ran high. Mansell ran away from Senna at the start and had the race in his grasp until a failure in his turbo put him out of contention, with some critics saying that if he had run a more conservative race, he might have finished. Nelson, meanwhile, though not entirely fit and not liking the circuit ('I tell you the truth, I hate this place'), still managed to finish second behind Senna.

At Detroit, Senna and Piquet were among the only four cars to finish the full race distance. Senna won, Nelson notched up another second place and Mansell had all sorts of problems, including heat-exhaustion and cramp, barely managing to be classified fifth. The next race was in France, where it wasn't expected that the championship leader, Ayrton Senna, would be able to repeat his street-circuit triumphs. The Ricard circuit, even without the curve that had taken the life of Elio de Angelis, is a real man's circuit, a place for the swift and the brave: no chicanery and gewgawdom about it. Mansell was again on pole – he was to make a habit of it all year – and Prost was alongside him. I rate this as one of the best races Nigel ever drove. The race was planned by Williams for one tyre-stop only and Mansell, Piquet and Prost were tightly bunched until a twitch and a half-spin by Piquet let Prost by him. Nelson changed tyres on lap thirty and then lay third behind Mansell and Prost, but when they both went in for fresh rubber on lap thirty-six, Nelson was able to take over the lead.

Mansell re-entered the race like a man with his backside on fire. He got rid of Prost in no time at all and within ten laps he was right up to Nelson. Nelson took the Beausset corner a bit wide and Mansell nipped past him. Enraged, Piquet made his charge: from some twenty seconds back, he picked up nigh on two seconds a lap until on lap sixty-five he had caught right up with Mansell. Then he made a decision to stop for another tyre-change and though the change worked to the extent that he again clawed back seconds on Mansell, a stall in the pits had lost him extra time, and all his efforts proved unavailing. Nelson was pretty surly after that race, surly and defensive: his engine hadn't stalled in the pit-lane, he said, it simply stopped; his decision had been taken because his tyres were wearing rapidly and unequally. Yet another second place and, more galling yet, second to his chief rival. To those who said, and I was among them, that it looked as if he had made his first mistake in letting by at le Beausset, Piquet replied that Mansell had forced his way in and he had simply moved out to prevent an 'accident'.

It was at about this time that the long-suppressed bitterness between the two men began to surface. Piquet renewed his accusations that Williams were favouring Mansell and giving him superior equipment and he began to express his 'disappointment' with the way he was being treated by Williams. On this subject, which was to remain contentious throughout the season, it must be said that Nelson had some small justification. One had but to observe the Williams and Honda motor-homes, where the two drivers hung out, to sense that Nigel rather than Nelson was the fair-haired boy. This was, of course, vigorously denied by the team, or rather by its various spokesmen, each of whom had his own contribution to make. None, it might be added, on behalf of Nelson. To Williams, it looked as though Mansell was out-driving Piquet and as if Piquet was defending himself by off-the-track retaliation.

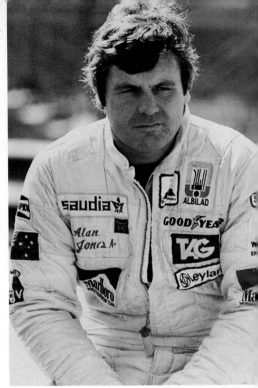

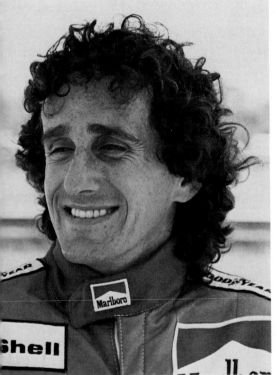

Tot up the money all those sponsors are worth: Hunt, Jones and Prost

Previous page: *Colin Chapman and Fittipaldi at Brands in* 1971

Above: *Jody Scheckter in his triumphant Ferrari*

Below: *Master James: Hunt in the No.1 McLaren*

The reigning world champion: Nelson Piquet

In fact, Nelson was fairly boiling. At Silverstone, I cornered him in the Williams motor-home for a good half-hour and had the whole story out with him: he gave me a long string of examples, of testings he was supposed to do, of remarks Patrick Head had made to him, of internal team politics, of his contract being dishonoured, winding up by saying, 'Williams is shit, I really don't want to drive for them any more. They make promises and don't keep them.' He said a lot more, regrettably unprintable, with scarcely veiled attacks on some of the lesser figures around Williams, including its press officer and its sponsor-relations man, Sheridan Thynne. It was hard stuff, but the interview somehow revived Piquet, even at Silverstone, where the 100,000 crowd's hostility towards him, and favouring of Mansell, was part of the air he had to breathe.

For a long time, Nelson led the race as Mansell was in extremis with severely unbalanced wheels, but two laps from the end, Nigel caught up with Nelson and with an almost exact re-run of his passing manoeuvre at Ricard charged home to win. The end result, another second place for Nelson, another win for Nigel, put the two drivers equal on points, both on 30 and one point behind Senna.

At Hockenheim, luck finally turned a revived Nelson's way. Mansell's car was the unlucky one on the day – its engine seized at about the one-third mark – and Nelson was locked into what looked like a hopeless battle with the world champion, Prost. Nelson had no instrumentation and was getting his fuel consumption by radio from the pits: he turned up his boost, hoped his fuel would last and charged after Alain. In his own mind, it was too little, too late, but then fate intervened and Prost pulled over to the side with a broken alternator and Nelson won, giving him a clear lead in the championship.

Things continued to go well for him in Hungary. Mansell led the early part of the race, with the Ferraris of Berger and Alboreto in pursuit, but Nelson first saw Berger and then Alboreto drop out ahead of him, putting him second but with Mansell well and truly out of sight and irrecuperable. But with six laps to go, a wheel nut fell off Mansell's car and he came to a halt, to sit dejectedly on the guard rail as his rival drove past to his second consecutive victory. It seemed the tide had truly turned for Nelson and he was jubilant. There was a fair amount of recrimination within Williams and considerable talk in the Italian press, particularly, that the two men were now deliberately nobbling each other's cars; in one such report, Nelson was said to have offered his own mechanics a double bonus if he won the title. In fact, each driver had his own engineer, his own mechanics and his own information: things had reached such a pass that whatever Nelson learned in practice would not be passed on to Nigel, and vice versa. At this point, someone within Williams should have taken the matter in hand, but as usual, the same bland denials were made and nothing was done to stop a rapidly deteriorating situation. From Nelson's point of view, the situation was entirely satisfactory: he had made his point and he had an 18-point lead over Mansell in the title race.

Between Hungary and Austria, Nigel took off to the mountains for a week's rest and psyching-up with his personal physician and guru. During that week, an ugly abscess developed in a tooth and Nigel had to have a wisdom tooth extracted. Nigel didn't look too well when he arrived at the Österreichring, but characteristically, he put his troubles behind him and set a provisional pole position that shattered the previous year's record. Not to be outdone, or out-psyched, Nelson proceeded to batter the record down still further. As it rained on Saturday, Friday times remained the official times, so that Piquet and Mansell started side by side.

On start one, Piquet led from Boutsen, Mansell and Berger, but behind them there was a chaotic and massive pile-up; forty minutes later, on start two, Mansell's clutch gave out, he was stuck on the start line and another massive pile-up occurred, this time with twelve cars involved. On start three, Nigel took it easy and Nelson moved into an early lead with Mansell behind him some fifteen laps later. On lap twenty-one, Mansell glided calmly by Nelson and that was that: Piquet's championship lead was reduced, but another second place kept him reasonably safely 15 points up on Nigel.

It was there in Austria that the fur really began to fly inside Williams. I had dined with Mr Nakamura, Honda's sporting director, and I had some inkling that things were not exactly going well between Honda and Williams. The reasons were several, but from the Honda point of view, they came down to two. The first was that Williams had 'dishonoured' them and their contract by refusing to take a Japanese driver into the team. Nakamura was insistent that this had been a part of the deal all along. The second was that Williams had not honoured its contract in relation to Nelson by not giving him the perquisites and privileges due to a Number One driver. Both statements were true, though both were strongly contended by Williams, where Frank himself said, 'No one tells me who drives for my team.' Others added, for him, that no one at Williams picked which driver would win, either: both had absolutely equal equipment and it was up to the better man to prove his worth on the circuit.

Another long talk with Nelson confirmed the rumours already circulating, that Nelson would no longer be driving for Williams: in an elaborate move, Honda transferred its engines for 1988 away from Williams to McLaren, Senna moved to McLaren in the place of the luckless Stefan Johansson, Piquet took his place as 'undisputed' Number One at Lotus, and Williams was out in the cold. This was when the claws really showed in Nelson. By making his move first, he had put the cat among the pigeons and it was quite clear from our conversation that his major motive in the move was to '****' Williams. Not only did he intend to win his third championship and thus prove his point vis-à-vis Nigel and Williams, but because of his ties to Honda, he was going to take that all-conquering engine away with him. It was his moment of triumph and revenge and he savoured it in a way that showed me that the idle, easy-going Nelson of yesteryear was no more.

The questions in the championship now became two: how would Williams react to a driver who was no more than a lame duck, and how would Honda try to ensure that Nelson went to Lotus as world champion? It was common knowledge that Honda thought Williams and Piquet had lost the 1986 championship through intra-team rivalry and caused the Grand Old Man of Honda a needless loss of face in Adelaide the year before. The Japanese can be pretty unforgiving. But what could Honda do? The answer lay in the microchips which control and monitor engine functions throughout the race. These are controlled by the Honda engineers in the pits and Williams admitted to me that they had 'no control whatsoever' over what the Honda engineers did. Ergo, if they wanted Nelson to be world champion, they had a wide variety of ways to do so.

With that in mind, much discussed in the paddock, and with Nigel acknowledging to me that this was no less than a sad truth, we all moved to Monza, and there Piquet won; in Portugal Prost won and Nelson was third. The totals read: Piquet on 67 points, Mansell on 43. It was theoretically possible, with three races to go, for Nelson to lose his lead, and when Mansell won in Spain, only eighteen points separated them, with Nelson being the more likely to have to shed points. Some controversy accompanied the Mexican Grand Prix, where Nelson had obviously been pushed when his car stopped on the first lap; then a major shunt involving Derek Warwick caused the race to be divided into two parts. Mansell eventually won the 'aggregated' race and the gap between the two men was now reduced to 12 points.

History records that Mansell, perhaps tense, perhaps overeager to prove a point, had an almighty accident during practice at the Suzuka Circuit in Japan, and to all intents and purposes Nelson, as the Japanese might have wished, became champion, even though he failed to finish the race, his engine clogged with debris. He failed to finish in Australia, too, but by then it was all over. Mansell had wisely decided to stay home in the Isle of Man and recoup his strength and Piquet wasn't trying all that hard. He was trying to enjoy his third victory while realizing that it hadn't *really* been won on the track, but by default, and that that would always be held against him.

As I said to start, Nelson has always been a paradox and will always remain one. It is no good going by externals and there is as much grit in the man as there is smarm. Altogether, the fracas of the two years at Williams proves something that I have always held: that the last people in the world likely to understand the strained, stressed and tortuous minds of grand prix racing drivers are those who employ and abuse them. It is never pleasant to watch the complacency with which they decide the fates of others and the egotism with which they pursue their own goals. They are short-sighted. Apart from Enzo Ferrari, there is not a constructor – be he Ron Dennis or Frank Williams or Bernard Ecclestone – for whom the public has any particular esteem or in whom they have any special interest. The sport belongs to those who wage it on the track, at the risk of their lives. That the two – drivers and constructors – grow annually to resemble each other more and more in their cunning and conniving, their manoeuvring and politicking, is no argument to the contrary. Until he joined Williams, Nelson had never really had to behave like the big-shot drivers about him; he'd always been modest, agreeable and easy. Maybe that ease will now return to him, but in the overheated atmosphere of Lotus, and without Colin Chapman's whip, and whipping, hand, I have my doubts and I greatly dislike seeing the nice turn sour.

Keke Rosberg

When the word 'professional' was invented, it was clearly designed for a character like Keke, a man who defies Archimedes' law and whose purse fills constantly, is rarely dipped into (try extracting so much as a cup of coffee out of him!) and yet is never full enough to please. 'I'm a paid driver,' Keke announces, 'that's what I do in life . . . Being a professional is looking after your own bloody future. No one else is going to look after it for you.' There's the man all right: forthright, no-nonsense Keke. According to his parents he's always been that way, except for his one weakness, an inability to get up in the morning. If he had been able to wake up, Keke might now be a dentist, because that was his original idea. Sure, he loved racing, he raced since he was a kid, but as a profession? That was another matter. But anyway, he failed his exams twice: once from sloth, the second time because he didn't wake up in time.

Both his parents – his father a veterinary surgeon, his mother a chemist – raced. Keke raced karts, motorbikes, anything he could lay his hands on. Once father and son raced together in Lahti: the father's last race and Keke's first. That was in the spring of 1965.

Keke of course is a Finn. About whom most of us know very little. What Keke knows is that 'there aren't that many ways to get a Finn into F1. The biggest single-seater race we ever had in Finland was an F3 race. Finns have no opportunity to be seen.'

In reality, he is very proud of being Finnish – even if he was actually born in Sweden! They are, he once told me, a practical, hard-working people with just enough of the devil in them to make them interesting. Keke has more than a bit of the devil in him. As funny as Alan Jones he isn't, nor as laid back as Nelson Piquet. But mischief he dearly loves. His kind of charm is all his own and his wit is that of the man who likes to score points: against other people or against himself. What others might consider to be telling remarks against himself, he thinks of as the truth and therefore worth saying. How many drivers would admit that what interests them most in the sport is its marketing? Mind you, the marketing Keke is most interested in is the marketing of himself.

But there's something endearing about this statement of aims on his part: 'I was racing go-karts and I couldn't understand why I should be riding go-karts and paying for it. I was paying too much and I still couldn't afford to do it the way I wanted . . . I couldn't really compete. So I decided to quit go-karts and go into motor racing and, having looked at the sport, I was convinced I could get other people to pay for my pleasure. It sounds awful, but that's the way it started.'

In its own way, Keke's story is that of the talented journeyman who makes his way to the top by sheer determination, a lot of application, the minimum few lucky breaks and the ability to exploit at all times every opportunity he has, no matter how infinitesimal. As he rightly says, it takes *years* to make an F1 driver, even when the opportunity comes along, which it does to very few. To make a driver at all also takes years, which is why most champions have spent apprentice years in so many different formulae. When a driver is young, he is quick; when he is quick he often overestimates himself and is foolhardy.

> Very few young drivers . . . have the maturity of mind to put in a whole competitive season. They can do a one-off and make an impression, but they can't fight against the odds and keep up the pace through a whole year. What still hits me about F1 is that it matures you so quickly. It is the best form of character building in the world, mainly because in F1 you learn to take the bad with the good. Up to that point you've been moving up the ranks . . . then you're in F1 and you've supposedly made it; only to realize that you haven't made anything at all. You have to start all over again, from the very beginning.

Keke's beginnings were hard. First, his parents were both against his taking racing seriously. 'When I bought my first racing car,' Keke says, 'my father thought I was being bloody stupid because I only had a tiny income as a computer trainee and there I was getting into a sport he *knew* could get to be like a drug.' The car was a Mustang with a big V-8 engine and Keke's father knew he was being naive. 'I simply believed in myself,' Keke says, 'as though that was all you needed to go racing.' Keke soon realized he knew nothing. At his first race, someone else prepared his car for him: his own mechanic was a vet and barely knew one end of a screwdriver from another. And as Keke adds, 'even at that first race I had a sponsor'.

The apprenticeship was not only long, it was immensely wearying and difficult. The man who really gave him his chance to prove himself was Fred Opert. 'Opert gave me the opportunity to race all over the world. If it had wheels, I drove it. In a single year, he and I did five continents in F2 and F Atlantic.' Finnish karting champion for five seasons out of eight, Scandinavian and European champion in 1973, Keke by 1974 had seven wins in F Vee-1300 and other formulae in 1974: twenty-one races, fourteen placings. The next year, twenty-one more races, ten wins and five further placings. The shift to F2 in 1976 was less immediately successful: fourteen races and tenth in the F2 championship. And so it went. By 1978, Keke was doing thirty-eight races. He was fifth in the European F2 championship, second in F Atlantic, champion in F Pacific – more significantly, he'd been given his first chance to race in F1.

The chance came through Teddy Yip, one of the world's most colourful characters – on his seventieth birthday he invited all the girls he'd known in his life to a gigantic party, presenting each of them with jewels – and long a figure on the edge of F1. Teddy had made his money buying up timber in Burma at the end of the war and investing it in property, mainly in Macao. He adored motor sport but, apart from drivers – Depailler, Piquet, Jones all drove for him – he had no talent for spotting people who could run his team for him. Teddy's team was no winner, but Keke had at least made it to the top. Yip paid Keke $1000 a race, but Keke had also developed expensive tastes: here a big Mercedes, there a penthouse. 'I wasn't doing all that on $1000 a race,' Keke recalls. 'I was racing every weekend or doing something else (profitable!). It's my bread-and-butter theory: the bread from racing, the butter from elsewhere.'

Yip's was a one-off chance: Yip couldn't keep his promises to test, to develop the car, so Keke was left with a brief record in F1 while running all over the world racing in everything else he could lay his hands on. Keke's first race in an F1 car was in South Africa and he retired; his second was a non-championship race at Silverstone which he won. The rest of his races for Yip's Theodore team resulted in failures. Gunther Schmid of the ATS season offered Keke another one-off behind Jochen Mass in Sweden and Keke jumped at it: he may have finished fifteenth, but it was the first time a Finn had ever crossed the finish line in an F1 championship race. As he wrote his father, he felt he had somehow 'arrived'. People knew who he was, he had a few nibbles, he was around to be seen. He also felt he had outgrown F2 and that he no longer wanted to race so much in

America: 'The money is better, but Europe is the heart of racing.' 1978 he considered his year of apprenticeship in F1: his poor results were not his fault, his relatively good ones were achieved by his own skills.

Nonetheless, 1979 was another year of scrambling around for jobs, of driving here, there and everywhere. In the Can-Am series he was often on pole: rarely did he finish. In F1 he had nine races for Walter Wolf; no points resulted. By 1980, Walter Wolf's team merged with Fittipaldi: the ex-champion wanted to make a comeback and chose Keke to be his Number Two. It was to be a particularly bitter year for Keke. As he says of Emerson, 'a man who's really grown up would know a return isn't on'. F1 was a different world from when Emerson had been a winner. 'Emerson hadn't really grown up. He kept fiddling about with the team and interfering with the professionals who were trying to run it in a professional way.'

One of those 'professionals' was Peter Warr, the current Lotus team-manager, and a man for whom Keke has a great deal of respect; another was Harvey Postlethwaite, now at Ferrari. 'It was really thanks to Peter that I managed to survive those years with Fittipaldi with my head still screwed on. Peter was supposed to be running a racing team, but he wasn't; he was running a creditor's office from dawn to dusk.' As for Keke's relations with Emerson, they went well enough 'until I started beating him, which was pretty early on in the season'. But the team was so underfinanced that it couldn't work properly: 'We had less good everything than the rest of the field: less good gear-box parts, less good engines. A team with those financial resources can't run properly; it has to skimp.'

Without much choice in the matter, Keke signed on for another two years at Fittipaldi, though he didn't expect the contract to last to term: 'There was no future for me in that team personally. I am an egotist; I am interested in my own future . . . I wasn't liked. They didn't believe I could do the job. To be more specific, Emerson didn't like me . . . For the last six months of 1981 I was working out how to get out of the team . . . I hadn't been paid for ten months.' Keke's problem was 'how could I create a situation in which I could leave but make sure I was paid before I left?'

The balance sheet for 1980 was not that awful. As Keke said, 'My tenth place in the championship, *ex aequo* with Daly, Watson, Jarier and Villeneuve, is highly satisfying for a first complete championship season in F1. Many drivers have made worse beginnings and gone on to better things.' 1981 was a desert, but better things were just around the corner. Alan Jones had retired; Williams needed a replacement. Presumably, Keke was to be thought of us a back-up for Carlos Reutemann, who was staying with the team.

Keke's longish history with Williams — four seasons in steady decline from his championship — parallels that of the other champions who have driven for Frank and Patrick Head, a Jones or a Piquet. There is the initial flush of fervid love and then a long period of exacerbation and disappointment. Keke's view of Williams and the team and how constructors behave in F1 is germane to every champion and worth listening to:

Just before I was signed up by Williams, Frank ran about telling everyone he's signed the greatest driver . . . A week later he told one of my sponsors, 'Well, you know, you kind of need a driver but the driver's not very important, he's just there to drive the car round in circles.' That's the way the game goes. It's a very commercial world and you say what you have to say at the time you have to say it.

I like to think Frank thinks better of me than that . . . I am as close to Frank as I can, being only a driver . . . He's a very close man and a deeply competitive man whose life is utterly based on competing twenty-six hours of every working day. He is utterly unrelenting . . . Like Frank, I don't enjoy looking into myself. I enjoy looking into others. Why not myself? Maybe I'm afraid of finding something I don't like. Maybe that's the way with Frank, too.

I'd have thought that having lived through the really fraught situation between Carlos Reutemann and Alan Jones, where those relations deteriorated seriously and damaged the team, Williams would have appreciated better than most teams how important communication and human relations are. But that's just not the way it is. It's not that way at Williams and it's not that way in most teams. What I have learned is that in F1 the main question seems too often to be who stuffs whom first. That isn't the attitude I brought into the sport. It's an attitude I've had to learn the hard way, right through my heels.

History records that Keke won his championship in a year in which the different teams were so well balanced — Williams, Renault, McLaren and Ferrari — that the smallest margins made the greatest difference: eight drivers finished within two grands prix of each other;

19 points separated Keke as champion from Michele Alboreto, joint seventh. History also records that Keke is the only champion to have won only one grand prix during his championship year, a fact which made many sneer at his championship as though the title was only valid if its holder was a regular visitor to the podium. My memory of the championship is very different: it was a vital, vibrant and exciting year from start to finish.

It began, however, in the mire of politics. The drivers' strike at Kyalami during the first race of the season is described in the chapter on Niki Lauda. It was a strike to which Keke was the most absolute outsider. 'I thought it was ridiculous,' he says.

If it had depended on me alone, I would have gone right through the so-called picket line, got into my car and raced. After years and years of work I had finally made it to the top: to a first-class team in F1. Now I was being asked to take part in a strike that I knew had not the slightest chance of succeeding. I was really conned into the strike without knowing what had been planned . . . Strikes are no way for intelligent people to achieve their aims . . . Much of the strike garbage was his [Didier Pironi's] doing; it was like a high point of his life . . . I was not interested in doing anything that could jeopardize my career.

Such an attitude naturally did not sit well with the drivers who supported the strike, but then Keke is not a joiner by nature. I remember the weekend as being burningly hot: in every sense. Tempers were hot, the track was hot. Keke finished fifth in a race which Arnoux led for most of the race but Prost won despite a puncture. Fifth was better than Keke had done in the whole of 1981 and he was delighted with the result: at the altitude of Kyalami, the Ford/Cosworth engine was hardly a match for the Renault turbo.

The F1 family was supposed to go on to Argentina next, but politics interfered with that and the race was cancelled, so after a long, enforced break, the teams all went to Rio. There, Keke qualified third, three places up on Lole Reutemann, his team-mate. The heat was again tremendous and after Villeneuve went off trying to pass Piquet where there was no room to pass, the race became a beautiful, classic duel between Nelson and Keke. Nelson won and duly passed out on the podium. Keke was second. But Renault and Ferrari protested the race, saying that the two leading cars had altered the weight of their cars with water tanks. Keke was furious at the time and went about muttering between races that the sporting authorities were trying to make a French champion. Frank Williams told him to shut up so as not to prejudice the Williams case. In fact, the water tanks had been used in Kyalami and they were used again after Brazil; not only that, but other cars and drivers in Brazil itself used similar tanks. But Nelson and Keke both had their points taken away by the bureaucrats in Paris because their cars were under the 580-kilo limit. As Keke was to say, 'Why just Piquet and Rosberg? Why not the others?'

Just before the next race, in Long Beach, Reutemann unexpectedly retired – thus probably avoiding a major problem for Keke, for Carlos was ever a problem to his team-mates. A fine driver and a gent, Carlos was also stubborn to a degree, proud as only an Argentine can be and extremely arrogant about his standing within a team. Keke was now the undisputed Number One driver. I remember that as doing wonders for his morale and Keke had begun to take on the mantle of the cock-sure star which was to be his persona for the rest of his racing career: up to then, he hadn't dared!

That year's Long Beach provided plenty of thrills. Keke had a memorable duel with Gilles Villeneuve, who finally went off attempting, once again, the impossible. On the day, Lauda was unbeatable and Keke finished an excellent second. Keke would have been leading the championship then if it hadn't been for FISA upholding the protest from Rio. 'I was extremely bitter about it. That was part of the bad blood that led to the Imola boycott. The sport was at war again and I was disgusted.'

The Imola boycott, ah, memories. Keke didn't race. Only Tyrrell of the teams represented by FOCA participated in the race; the others all refused to race. Keke watched it on television and I remember it chiefly for a superb duel between Pironi and Villeneuve in which Pironi clearly outclassed the fiery Villeneuve and overtook him superbly in the closing stages of the race, then refused to shake his team-mate's hand on the podium. Regrettably, it was Villeneuve's outrage at Pironi's 'disloyalty' that was to lead Gilles into one final, and fatal, error in the next race, at Zolder. Keke was furious to be missing the race: 'If a race is going on, we should be there. I thought I'd have a real chance at the championship and we weren't even racing!'

Zolder was where the new Williams 08 first appeared, and what a triumphant car it was! Keke knew right away the car was going to be outstandingly good. Keke qualified third, but shortly before the end of practice 'we heard Gilles had had a terrible crash. I was numb.

I didn't want to talk to anyone. It didn't really hit me then; I suppose I was kept intact by the fact that I had a job to do.' On race-day, Keke's engine blew up during warm-up; it affected his confidence, as probably did thoughts of Villeneuve's death. After four laps, Keke got by Arnoux: it was the first time he had led a F1 race. On the second-to-last lap, pursued by John Watson, Keke made a mistake: he tried too hard to get by Surer, locked his rear tyres and spun off. He finished second, but both Keke himself and the team were disappointed. It was a race he should have won. It was really a psychological failing, and a valuable lesson:

> I was still upset by those anonymous people in Paris taking away my six points in Brazil, in effect saying Rosberg didn't deserve those points. The politicians had deprived me of a chance to race at Imola and now I'd blown another possible three points. All right, the points were gone, but it still rankled . . . I felt that Frank was under a lot of pressure . . . It was one of several low points that year and if a driver reaches that sort of low, then there's trouble.

Coming into Monaco, Prost led the championship, followed by Watson. Keke was third. And Monaco was a race that Keke, unlike many drivers, really liked. 'It's not a race in the strict sense of the word. No street race is. But to my mind it's head and shoulders above any other grand prix in Europe: because of its unique setting, because it's the best street circuit in the world.' The problem at Monaco is to get pole position: 'That's the only place to be, given that opportunities to pass are few.'

Pole position he did not make. He was third on the grid and in the race was too often blocked. He was eighth into the first corner, but was soon sixth when Arnoux spun and Giacomelli retired. Alboreto was next: 'He is a gentleman and let me past.' Andrea de Cesaris was not made of the same stuff: 'His attitude is that if someone's on his tail trying to get by, he should prevent it by any means.' The two men fought it out for forty long laps and Keke's car was so hard to handle that he took the skin off his hands just holding onto the wheel. Keke knew he was faster than de Cesaris, but in Monaco, that helped not at all. He made another mistake: he misjudged a passing attempt by an inch and a half, hit the kerb and broke his suspension. It was his first retirement and it hurt.

Detroit, another street circuit, was next. The place wasn't ready and took two days to prepare. Rain fell steadily. When the race finally got going, it was stopped when Patrese ran into a wall and a tow-truck came out on the circuit. On the re-start, Keke was in second place alongside Prost. Keke got by him without about an inch to spare between his car and the wall. Then Watson drove one of his miraculous races, moving from seventeenth past Keke in a matter of relatively few laps. Keke took after him, but his gearbox gave way: on a street circuit he now had neither third nor fourth gears! Miraculously, he finished fourth even so and held onto third place in the championship. But Watson was now a definite threat and Keke left Detroit deeply worried about his chances. As he admits, 'Weariness was setting in. I was doing all the testing. I had asked to do it and Frank gave it to me. That was part of the concentration on the main thing, winning the championship.'

Montreal was not promising for Williams; the turbo-powered cars generally held the edge. 'My attitude going there was: what chance have I got on that circuit? There were some circuits where I knew I would be handicapped, and Montreal was one of those.' Friday he was good, leading both practice sessions; Saturday it started to rain: his engine blew; the spare car was undrivable. Again, an accident marred the race. Riccardo Paletti didn't see Pironi's car stalled on the grid and hit him in the rear: he died instantly in the ensuing fire. Two hours later, the race re-started and after a reasonable start, Keke kept dropping back. A gearbox problem, again, and Keke was now only fifth in the championship: for three races he had only three points to show. 'That was the low point of the season: a mistake at Monaco, a poorly performing car at Detroit, failing to finish in Montreal and problems piling up. It's not the sort of situation calculated to make you cheerful . . . but when you're on the inside you know what you have to do is simply pick up the pieces and work all the harder. You have to tell yourself the game isn't over.'

It was at that point that Frank Williams tried to trade Keke away to another team. Luckily, Keke did not learn about it until eighteen months later. Still the move, however covert, and typical of Williams's attitude towards drivers, made some sort of sense. They had been all-triumphant with Jones in 1981; here they were languishing with Keke and his new team-mate Derek Daly. At the time, Keke was still a relative unknown; his results were spotty; though extremely hard-working, he was undoubtedly an egotist and a man who made waves. Temperamental differences between Keke, Frank and Patrick Head undoubtedly led to the Williams decision. In the end, the move did not work out and the team started to put the pieces together again. Keke put in a frantic schedule of testing.

At Zandvoort, Keke was seventh on the grid, failed to make a good start, got into a pack and took some time settling in. Pironi and Piquet were up front and as Keke says, 'The last ten laps I drove on the absolute limit . . . On the last lap I had Piquet in sight, then I was right up on him; on the final straight I was right on his tail. The car, the tyres, the engine had nothing more to give.' Third place was at least a positive result, but Pironi's win put him at the top of the table and even Keke admitted after the race that he looked to be the best bet for the title. Still, Zandvoort had pulled the team out of a slump. 'Watson hadn't scored and it was now a three-way battle for the title . . . The championship was too tight for anyone to build any solid hopes on.'

Brands Hatch was next and Keke knew 'in his bones' that it was going to be his race. The circuit favoured the Williams and disadvantaged the turbos. Keke won pole on Friday, beating his own record by a full second. Saturday afternoon, however, the car was not performing well, though Keke kept his pole position; on Sunday morning the car was even worse. Then at the start, his engine would not fire up: it was a warm day and it vapour-locked. 'A disappointment but no disaster. I said to myself, "You're going to win from the back and that will look even better."' Keke did catch up to the rest of the grid by Clearways, but by then he had a serious understeering problem. Some fifteen laps into the race, he had worked himself up to sixth, but his front tyres were going to be a problem. When he came into the pits to change them, Keke could see the team was in despair. 'There's nothing worse for a driver. He's sitting there in the car, fuming and waiting for something to be done. He thinks he can still save the race . . . Not only was their world falling about their ears; mine was too, and it was my race.'

When he did get going again, his engine misfired and stopped. The tyre problem was a serious one (the compound was new and relatively untested); the team hadn't solved it. It was there that Keke got out of his car and I will never forget his shouting at the team: 'Now we're equal,' he yelled. 'I blew Monaco and you've blown this race for me.' He was furious; he felt betrayed. Worse yet, he and his championship chances were heading for a series of ultra-fast circuits which definitely favoured the turbo engines.

The first of these was Ricard. The grid was headed by the two Renaults of Arnoux and Prost and the race was one in which Arnoux was under orders to let Prost win, which he failed to obey. Keke was in trouble throughout the race: no wing, no handling, worn tyres. He only just managed to finish fifth and fell back to fifth in the title fight, with Hockenheim coming up. There were still 45 points to be won in the race, but Keke never liked Hockenheim and his attitude was negative. On the Friday, he was only tenth; on Saturday it rained. Only a few drivers went out testing. Pironi set an excellent time; he didn't need to go out again, but he did, running behind Prost and Daly in a cloud of spray. He saw Daly's brake lights but not Prost's. The result was an accident which ended Pironi's career and his chances of the championship. Fate had intervened.

Keke raced in his spare car. 'It wasn't a pleasant race . . . Tambay led the race with Arnoux behind him. I more or less inherited third place after Prost and Watson dropped out. That at least kept my chances alive . . . but once again my car had been unsatisfactory, I'd had to wrestle it . . . and to cap it all, when I got back to England my house had been emptied of everything I really cared for.'

Keke and Niki had had words at several races and when the drivers turned up in Austria the papers were full of Niki's judgement that it would be a disaster if Keke won the championship. Niki's reasons were his own competitiveness, his love of 'needling' the opposition and Keke's refusal to take part in Niki's safety-minded politicking. When I asked Niki what he had against Keke, his answer was quite simple: Keke was brash, selfish, self-concerned, a relative parvenu in F1; he lacked the manners and the poise of a champion.

Despite all that, the race was sheer perfection. I have seen no better. Elio de Angelis won it, but by a margin so infinitesimal I can still hardly credit it. Keke was in considerable pain from a foot and he was held up for a good part of the race by Jacques Laffite whom he was lapping. But once past him Keke was right on Elio's tail. The race, everyone could see, was going to be decided on the final corner, a long right-hand downhill curve. 'The truth is,' Keke relates,

I wasn't brave enough to get past Elio on the last corner. I could have done it. That is, if it hadn't been for the championship being at stake and for the fact that it is such a quick corner, I could have gone straight over the kerb on the inside . . . But at the top of the hill I hesitated too long, trying to figure out which side I should go on the way down . . . The only chance left for me was to out-accelerate him coming out of that corner. It didn't work, but I wasn't far off. A hundred more yards and I would have made it.

In fact, Keke lost out to Elio by 5/100ths of a second.
Still, his second place had put Keke back in the lead of the championship and he was beginning to take his chances seriously:

Once you're ahead, after all, it is up to others to take it away from you . . . The only oddity was that here was Rosberg leading the championship and he hadn't yet won a grand prix. There were sections of the press that wouldn't forgive me that, but I didn't give a damn. The championship is the championship whether you win it with four grand prix victories or by consistency and a lot of lesser places.

Dijon was next and Keke thought he had a good chance. Practice was a bit disappointing, with the turbos notably faster than the Williams car, but Keke made a good start in the race, just avoiding a collision with Lauda. Prost led with Arnoux second and Keke closing in on René. But then he came up to lap his nemesis, Andrea de Cesaris.

To the best of my memory, there is only one occasion when I've come close to losing control over myself during a race. Dijon was that time. There I was running third and catching up on the leader at about 1.5 seconds a lap. Then I came up against Andrea. He was very quick on the straights, very slow in the corners. I lost eleven seconds behind him. He just would not let me past.

Keke did everything he could. As he said,

If it had been possible I would have got out of the car in the middle of the straight and hit him as hard as I could straight in the face, climbed back in the car and gone on . . . Would I have shoved him off deliberately? I don't know. I was very close to doing so. We were both going down the straight at 170 m.p.h. and I banged him with my front wheel on his sideboards. I couldn't get any closer.

Eventually Andrea lost it: faced with a choice of going off or losing a corner entirely, he went off. Keke took Arnoux and then caught Prost three laps from the end. It was his first grand prix victory.
Fatigued, deprived of his privacy, frantically trying to capitalize in

business on the possibility of the title, Keke was not at his best at Monza. Watson lay just behind him in the championship and Prost was still in the hunt. The weather was memorably hot. Keke thought it best not to try too hard. He needed only one point. Driving carefully in eighth place, he heard a bang, thought it was a tyre and slowed down. In fact it was his rear wing that had broken. The pit-stop took two minutes and he rejoined the race fifteenth. Prost span off: that ended his title chances. Watson finished fourth, keeping himself in contention. The race was a disappointment for Keke, but the race was now down to two men – and one race, Las Vegas.

There, on the track, the temperature was 130 degrees. The best he could do on the grid was sixth. The pressure was getting to him. 'I knew the situation perfectly well. The task ahead of me was to finish the race in a certain position without even thinking about what Watson might be doing. It seemed entirely possible to me, but you never know; you never stop thinking about what can go wrong.' The Renaults led at the start and Keke lay sixth, battling with Mario. Mario's suspension broke and he got by. That put Keke fifth. If Watson won and Keke retired, he was pipped at the post. The pressure was all on Watson, who in fact drove a brilliant race. Alboreto led. What if Alboreto retired? Then Watson would win. If Watson won and Keke retired, it was all gone. 'It was my fifty-second grand prix and everything I'd been working for since the start of my career was at stake.'

Alboreto won ahead of Watson, Keke kept fifth and was champion. All he felt was pure relief and off he went to San Francisco for the celebrations.

I was too tired to enjoy the party properly. I think that is probably characteristic of winning the championship. There is a sudden deflation as you let go on your control and realize how exhausted you are. I'd been through despair and hope and mental stress. When it was over, it was like a balloon. You let the air out and all there is left is a pile of rubber. That's how I felt.

It takes a braver and less greedy man than Keke to stop racing with a championship, particularly since a lot of people tried to make him feel as if he hadn't *really* won it. So Keke raced on. But, as he says, 'it's very difficult for a team that's been on top for four years to find itself suddenly – or maybe not so suddenly – in the shit . . . It's sometimes not merely that you're bad, but that other people have suddenly got very good.'

The 1983 season was bad, the part of a long decline at Williams. The low point was at Zandvoort, when the best the world champion could do was qualify twenty-third on the grid; then, having run a pretty good race and worked his way up to twelfth, he found after ten laps everything falling apart – as it had been doing all year. The final insult was to reach the end of the race, limping home, and find Frank and Patrick with their bags packed just trying to forget their frustrations by leaving the track. 'The entire second half of 1983 was like that. The cars were very bad. They were underpowered: they were pigs to drive.' And Keke had another year to serve at Williams. And at Williams there were egos just as big as his. And from there on, it was just downhill. The Honda turbo was to save them in 1984, but it took time to break in and Patrick Head made a major design mistake from which the team never recovered.

Also, by then, Keke had found out how Frank had tried to trade him away during his championship season with the team. After Keke found out about 'that piece of disloyalty', things could not be the same within the team.

> I knew all along that Frank was a hard man to get close to, I knew he was obsessive, neurotic in some ways, but it's my nature to like people . . . When I found out about that, I said to myself: I can't figure out people who behave like that, I won't ever know what makes them tick, they're too unlike me. And I stopped trying to read Frank's mind.

Fortunately, his marriage to Sina and the birth of a son did a lot to keep Keke's basically sunny and settled nature on top. I visited him in Ibiza at the worst of his troubles with Williams, and though he was understandably bitter, he was never personal about the failures at Williams. His patience was simply and understandably running out. He was helpless. He couldn't put any pressure on the team. They were not in a listening mood. As soon as he tried insisting, they 'slipped out of my hands; if I persisted, there was an explosion'. The team as a whole was bottoming out and 1984 was the bitterest year of them all: so many hopes dashed, so much promise gone.

The 1985 season was much, much better, but relations within the team were never properly rebuilt and by 1986, Keke had moved to McLaren: they were successful, Prost was champion, but Keke wasn't.

His heart had gone out of the business; he was tired; he wanted to be with his family; he had matured, and though the professionalism remained just as much a feature of his life, he thought he could do better by retiring and devoting himself to his other concerns. Including money, which always rated high with Keke.

In a way, his career is an oddity among championship careers. He won his title in the most minimal way in a season of great difficulty and frustration. He won it by sheer application. Then, when he should have been at the top, Williams collapsed under him, a collapse that was as much moral as professional. I think it is fair, in judgement, to say that Williams cheated Keke of the success he could have had, that he gave of his best and they gave considerably less than that, and that had Keke been less loyal to Williams and gone earlier to McLaren, where he would always have been welcome, he would have won many more races and quite possibly at least one other championship. As a driver under adverse conditions, Keke was a nonpareil. Who can forget his race in the broiling heat and potholes of Dallas? Or the first time the 200-m.p.h. limit was beaten at Silverstone? Too testy in his early days, too egocentric in his good years? I think Keke was all the things that have been said about him, but he was also a far better driver than he has ever been given credit for. I know that when I talk to his colleagues about the great champions of the Seventies and Eighties, there is not one who has raced against him who does not have the greatest admiration for his verve, his professionalism and his manners both on and off the track.

Alain Prost

It is 1980 and a remarkable young French driver has just scored a sixth place in Argentina a week earlier. The front three in that race have been Alan Jones, Nelson Piquet and Keke Rosberg. Prost's first F1 point has come in the company of three world champions. We are in Guaruja, which is on the Brazilian coast below São Paulo, staying where most of the drivers in those days stayed between the Argentine and Brazilian grands prix: a handsome, colonial-style hotel with tiles on the walls, a big pool and room to roam around. The South Atlantic beats lazily on the sand across the street. It is an evening when Alain apparently does not want to go out with McLaren. In his first fortnight in F1 he has already found out that life at the top can be pretty cloistered: you see the same people all the time and those people talk about racing all the time. John Watson, who is his co-driver at McLaren, has gone down the road to Emerson Fittipaldi's house for a party; Alain is a new boy. Twenty-four years old, he either hasn't been invited or he doesn't want to go. He is standing around the lobby doing nothing.

We strike up a conversation. Pretty boring, I say, or something like that. Alain looks up. He has to look up, being pretty short. He has a lot less hair then than now; he doesn't have his own trendy style and he's on his best behaviour. Also it's in his nature to be polite. This is the world he wants to be part of; at the same time, he doesn't want to be owned by it. Not boring, he answers, but there must be other things in life than just hanging around the hotel. Ho, I think, what's this? A driver who thinks for himself? He says Jacques Laffite is the only driver he really knows at all, but Jacques always goes off fishing in the Andes between the races, so he's kind of stuck down here. What he's really itching to do is to go over to Santos and watch what used to be Pele's team play football. He likes football and his idol is the great Michel Platini. But football is on Sunday and Sunday is race time; besides, today isn't Sunday.

So I say, why don't we go out to dinner? Someone's told me there's a fabulous little fish place a few kilometres up the road. He says, great. Then we have to find this place. Everywhere except on the beach there are dead-water inlets; you practically can't see the reeds for the mosquitos swarming. The natives, trouserlegs rolled up, are trawling for crabs with their toes. Alain stares out of the window of my car, excited as a little boy. He's never been anywhere, really. And this is something else he always wanted: to travel, to move around, to see new sights. But, you know, not just luxury hotels.

Night is falling, that dusk-filled, moist Brazilian summer night. We take several wrong turnings, Alain trying to read the concierge's map out on the flats where there are no road signs and barely a road. Finally we find this thatched cottage of a place, open on all four sides, and we sit down. What there is to eat is written on a blackboard, but Alain can't read Portuguese. I say he ought to try the *siri*, which are local crabs *au gratin*. Dish after dish arrives and something comes over quite plainly: this young man has no idea how you're supposed to talk to people, certainly not journalists, to whom you're supposed to talk about your car, your ambitions, who's who and what's what. Instead, Alain talks about whatever comes into his head. His family, what it was like when he was young, how he feels somehow different from everyone else because . . . Well, it's hard to explain, but they seem sort of sophisticated and he feels like a new boy in school and the rest of the drivers, except for Jacques, aren't all that friendly. Arnoux, who drives for Renault, strikes him as a bit crazy: you're never even sure he's looking at you, says Alain. Jabouille is nice and helpful, but he's got his own problems. Villeneuve's at Ferrari, but he's another crazy in his own way, though he's one hell of a driver – mind you, first he's got to survive, the way he drives.

Then, too, Alain's got problems with his English, which isn't all that hot yet. Anyway, he's got time to learn. The first race? Not that many drivers score points first time out. Well, he was a lap back, wasn't he? A lot of people didn't finish, there were only nine who did. So he just drove as sensibly as he could. What he wanted most was not to make a mistake or wreck his car. Otherwise he thought they might be angry with him at McLaren.

He made an impression on me that first night, and in F1, if you make friends at all with a driver, it's usually through luck. Because he's standing around in a lobby, with nowhere to go. He didn't just make an impression on me, I liked him. And I've liked him ever since.

The next weekend I watched him in operation at a party the team's sponsors, Marlboro, were throwing at some fancy house. The place was swarming with gaudy Brazilian society women, voices like mynah birds, more jewellery than they could carry, sagging under furs despite the heat, with their husbands in full fig, swarthy men with as much gold on them as their wives had diamonds, with Marlboro PR people going around introducing Watson (who managed always to look vaguely embarrassed – and surprised there were other people in the world) and Prost to São Paulo high society. The young man I'd seen in Guaruja in a Marlboro T-shirt and jeans was being charming and polite to all these people as if he'd never done anything else in his life, and that weekend he moved one rung up the ladder to fifth place.

It was already clear that Prost was a natural and that he'd make it. You can always tell. There is something about a future champion that you can spot in their earliest days. Not necessarily in the car, because they may be in what the F1 family calls a 'shit-box' – and that year's McLaren was hardly a world-beater, nor did Prost score many more points – but by their demeanour. Future champions are drivers without bullshit, without pretensions; they are people who get on the job and learn whatever they can from anyone. They don't want just to learn about their trade – they have to know something about that or they'd never have made it into F1 in the first place – but about all aspects of life: about money, about how to get smarter, about women, about life, about places, politics. Everything is grist to their mill. And what was striking about Alain, and what made him absolutely distinct from the start in my mind, is that he wanted to be tops, but not just in racing. He was voracious in everything he did, and whatever he learned, he applied. By the time of that party, he could read a menu in Portuguese and make pleasant remarks about how delicious Santos crabs were. He was also open, generous, honest and straight from the start; even more extraordinary, he hasn't really changed that much. Real champions are serious about their jobs: they work at them, they concentrate. And even in those first races, when Alain was learning the absolute basics of racing in F1, Alain could concentrate in a way that I've rarely seen equalled, perhaps only by Niki Lauda on his better days. That concentration was absolute and when Alain got out of a car at the end of a race, it was always as if he were emerging from a decompression chamber; it took him some time to come back to the ordinary world.

Prost's overall record is matched by only a very few. He has won nearly a quarter of his races (twenty-eight victories out of 121 races) and only Fangio, Stewart and Clark beat him on that count; in 1988, he finally beat, in only his eighth year, Jackie Stewart's all-time record of twenty-seven victories, which had stood for a decade and a half;

his productivity in results and the regularity of his finishes are of the very best; after a fifteenth place in the championship standings in his very first year (he was already tied with the former world champion Emerson Fittipaldi and ahead of champions Jody Scheckter and Mario Andretti), he finished fifth, then fourth, twice second, twice first, and fourth in 1987, a year in which his McLaren was far from being as competitive as it had been in previous years.

If this suggests that Prost is an accomplished driver, that is only half the story. The French call him *le Professeur*, or the Prof, for he combines, perhaps to a greater degree than any other driver in the modern period, all the qualities required of a championship driver. He is, for instance, Lauda's superior as a qualifier and, though combative to a high degree when necessary, he also has all Lauda's ability to judge a race tactically and make the best of his opportunities. As a preparer of cars he has few equals – he was integral to the development of both the Renault and the McLaren, the only two teams he's ever raced with. His 'natural' skill may not equal Piquet's or Ronnie Peterson's, but it remains outstanding and his style is far more economical than the latter's and more free of mistakes than the former's. He is the sort of driver you can never count out of a race: even in the most adverse circumstances, he seems to know what to do, how to handle any given problem. He is absolutely outstanding in his preservation of his resources, tyres, fuel and engine. Tactically and strategically, he is quite masterful, and when I once asked him what was the difference between race strategy and race tactics, he said that the former was what one might consider before, but the latter was what was forced on a driver during a race; the former was an ideal scenario, the latter a reaction to circumstances which changed lap by lap.

Temperamentally, he is almost ideal for the task. He is cool, rational and very seldom angered and, when angered or disappointed, seldom sulks. It is true that in his years at Renault, he was hard tested in this department and failed, on occasion, to retain his absolute self-control; on the other hand, the provocation there was extreme. Physically, he has enormous stamina, works out with great care – though not without enjoying life – and now, compared to the young man I first met in Brazil, has become an all-round athlete: perhaps not perfectly smooth on the tennis court or the golf course but, by dint of hard work, extremely efficient. Efficient in the sense that he uses the other sports he practises, especially skiing, at which he excels, on behalf of his driving. They are both relaxation and training, and one of the most curious sights I recall was playing golf just behind him last year and watching him *run* the entire course while still being able to stop and relax between his runs to strike the ball smoothly. He told me afterwards he had done the eighteen holes in a little under ninety minutes, something that would greatly please any club secretary!

As Alain is the first French world champion in F1, credit should here be given to the schooling and support which he has enjoyed throughout his career. He was spotted early, brought up through F. Renault and F3 with good, farseeing sponsorship from the French petroleum giant Elf, and arrived in F1 with relative ease. Corresponding to this advantage is an equal disadvantage: as the 'official' French candidate, Alain was from the start the subject of the sort of scrutiny by his national press that is more generally reserved by Italians for their drivers.

Here, the difference between Alain and his French colleagues who more or less overlapped his early years is instructive. By the time Prost reached F1, his friend Jacques Laffite — together they own a golf course, together they played tennis and golf — had already been about for six years. The essential difference between them was no more than a matter of the teams for whom they raced: Laffite spent seven years in the relative wilderness with the Ligier team, a ramshackle, often disorganized but high-spirited 'private' team run by the former Rugby star Guy Ligier. Laffite's team, ever hampered by financial privation and by a basically old-fashioned, untechnological approach to the sport, was always condemned to be a middle-of-the-road team, not one of the majors. It served splendid meals, it was fun to be around, it was relaxed, but the bibulous Ligier proved something less than the kind of strict disciplinary leader that an F1 team needed in a decade of increasing professionalism. Its mechanics often looked, when working on a car, like a dozen men trying to force spaghetti back through a sieve. The atmosphere was one of fun rather than effort.

When Jean-Pierre Jabouille joined Renault in 1977, he had been driving for them in various other formulae for years. He was experienced, intelligent and steady, but his job was to bring the first turbo engine in the sport to the point of reliability and consistency; by the time he had accomplished his task, he had had a severe accident and probably would have been shunted aside even if it hadn't happened. Jean-Pierre Jarier, loose and easy-going, was another of that early generation. Perhaps because of his happy-go-lucky attitude towards the sport, he languished for years in Don Nichols's Shadow team and never managed to finish better than third.

René Arnoux, a real whacko from Grenoble, was a sort of throw-back to the earlier days of the sport: undoubtedly quick, utterly brave, personally dissolute, he lacked the one essential quality of the modern racing driver, intelligence. On his day he was more than able to win races; seldom did he have a clear idea why.

That background may well have been why Prost was hailed from the start as the true standard-bearer of France, and why there was such a shock when Alain decided one day that he had had enough of socialism and French taxes and was moving his domicile to Switzer-land. But even if having so much expected of one was, after all, nothing more than what any front-line F1 driver has to put up with, the fact is that if a national press is constantly focused on one, one loses as much as one gains: gone is one's private life, a padlock is placed on one's opinions, one is at the service of a sponsor and a nation.

Alain's only true predecessor in the French stakes, then, was Didier Pironi, who had the undeniable advantage of a wealthy background, an easy personality, a dreamy nature – his two great hobbies were astronomy and the sea, the latter causing his untimely death – and the considerable mental powers which, for instance, led him to becoming the drivers' representative. His quintessential niceness, along with his skills in politics and public relations, made him an ideal choice for Ferrari, and because he was driving for Ferrari when the Renault challenge was still hugely important to France, he counted for something less than Alain. Had he not had a disastrous accident in Germany in 1982, he might well have been ranked alongside Prost in the French pantheon.

But the truth is that Prost inherited all those natural, national assumptions and he had the best packing from the start. Elf and Renault made sure that he got the kind of coverage he needed to become celebrated. Journalists and TV commentators followed him everywhere, their bills generously picked up by Alain's sponsors, and Alain often told me that he only felt he could breathe easily when he divorced himself from his French context and settled down with a British team like McLaren. He found in McLaren exactly the opposite of the atmosphere he had lived through at Renault. The giant French manufacturer was, after all, an arm of the government, a nationalized company, a national standard-bearer. As such, Alain felt constrained in his behaviour. Government politics affected his driving future.

Decisions about research, development, testing, finance, management, were all taken at remote levels. Not so with McLaren, where everything was on the spot, the surroundings were smaller and less pretentious, the relationship with his sponsors more agreeable, the team more familial and the pressures were taken off his back. In fact, he was a changed man.

Renault was all along a difficult team for him. He arrived with much being expected of him and had, first, to learn how to drive a turbo-charged car (something that in those days required quite a bit of skill on the part of a driver accustomed to the normally aspirated Cosworth engines), and started the season involved in a pile-up at Long Beach. In the next race, in Brazil, both Prost and his team-mate Arnoux crashed. It was not a distinguished start to a new career. But beyond misfortune, the second problem Prost faced was that the Renault engine, in its third year of development, was still more than a little unreliable: it showed flashes of great promise; it disappointed as often.

Alain scored his first points for Renault in Argentina, finishing ahead of Arnoux, but at Imola, which came next, neither Renault finished, a sad story which continued at Zolder, Monaco and Spain, with the result that Renault reached Dijon in July with nearly nothing on the scoreboard. There matters took a turn for the better, for Alain scored his first grand prix victory in a race interrupted by rain, which left him well-placed, at the re-start, to finish in the lead. In Germany, Prost finished second and Arnoux didn't: it was perhaps the beginning of a rivalry between the two drivers which was to poison relations between them in the future. Nonetheless, in most eyes, Prost was already clearly the cleaner driver and the more consistent finisher; his Number One position in the team, though tacit, was an acknowledged fact. Prost won again at Zandvoort and at Monza, finishing a second place at Las Vegas. The least one could say of his first year at Renault was that he had been in contention throughout the latter part of the year: as soon as the turbo engine's problems seemed to have been resolved.

In fact, 1981 was a year of transition in which many drivers had a crack of the championship. Piquet won the championship from Reutemann by a single point; Alan Jones was third, only four points off the pace, and Laffite fourth, two points behind Jones and one ahead of Prost: the first five drivers were all within one grand prix of each other in the final standings.

The general opinion around the paddock was that Alain had been somewhat unlucky not to win the championship, even if he had been favoured by the stewards at Dijon. He had led races and had stupid failures; some of his retirements were due to incidents beyond his control. That adjective, 'unlucky', was to stick with him for some years, as Alain was to become the 'almost-champion'. Keke Rosberg's year, 1982, was to provide another close finish to the championship, with Prost finishing fourth, just 10 points away from Rosberg.

It was a season that might have gone better for Prost if details on the Renault had been worked out with proper care. Beginning with a pair of fine wins in South Africa and Rio, the latter rendered somewhat controversial because Piquet and Rosberg, both of whom finished ahead of him, were disqualified, Prost looked well on his way. But at Long Beach his brakes gave out; at Imola his engine blew up; in Monaco a myriad problems put him back in seventh place, three laps down; in Detroit and Montreal the car again betrayed him; at Zandvoort the engine did him in; in England he could finish no better than sixth.

His 1982 season might also have ended otherwise if Prost had not been traduced, or felt he had been traduced, by René Arnoux on a number of occasions, and it was the first time that I have ever observed a crack appear in Prost's otherwise easy disposition. In Prost's mind, he was the team's Number One driver. I don't think anyone differed. Except Arnoux. But Arnoux was something of an anarch, and team policy was – as it often is when two drivers are both doing well and are capable of winning – that the driver in the lead should be given the greater chance of winning the championship. On more than one occasion, once flagrantly, Arnoux had disobeyed the golden rule. As a result, relations between the two drivers, never good, had deteriorated seriously: in France, despite clear team instructions, Arnoux had severely jeopardized Prost's chances of winning and Alain, forced back into second place when no other driver could challenge either of them, was enraged at the end of the race. Enraged and in tears.

There was a gigantic scene outside the Renault motor-home and neither driver heaped glory on himself, with Arnoux accusing Prost of whingeing and Prost acting rather like a spoiled child whose toy has been snatched from his hand, and calling Arnoux 'stupid' and 'unworthy to race'. By the end of the season, Arnoux had been moved along to Ferrari, where he continued to be irregular and only moderately successful, and the ultimate travelling driver, Eddie Cheever, took his place. At least with Cheever there was no question of who was Number One. Unfortunately, however, given Cheever's more modest level of achievement, the burden on Prost was even greater.

By 1983, Prost had already racked up seven pole positions; he had five victories under his belt, had led many races and finished as many times as his car would allow him. His skills were obvious and he was already being wooed by a number of major teams. This was not merely because of his driving skills, but because of his application, off circuit, to the myriad other duties which befall a grand prix driver. It was Prost who tested endlessly for Renault and had the lion's share of developing the car. It was Prost who was the front-line rep for Renault and his sponsors; Arnoux, with his hophead's eyes and scruffy appearance, his unreliability and bouts of sexual incontinence, was a far less appetizing prospect. Prost had, in fact, become the 'ideal' driver, the one who can offer a team as much support off the circuit as on.

In all this, there is a share of calculation, and Prost was never short of that quality. From the start he seems to have known both what was expected of him and what he wanted for himself. Less obviously ruthless in this respect than a Jones, a Rosberg or a Fittipaldi, less obvious in his manoeuvres, less flamboyantly playing the role of 'star', he nonetheless knew how to turn any situation, any opening, however small, to his advantage. Rather like Stewart, Prost was canny and shrewd rather than loud and demanding. He placed his investments carefully; he lived with some modesty; he was discreet about his private affairs; when he could, he fled the limelight: it was as though, unlike many, he had no need of a specific image with which to project himself onto the world stage.

But within Renault, things were beginning to deteriorate. The company was putting pressure on its sporting division to obtain more spectacular results. Its advertising heavily reflected its – and Elf's – participation in F1, but so far its overall results, while always promising, had been disappointing. The year 1983 was to be its high-water mark, but still fall short of the goal which it had set itself – the championship – and short of what the company's leadership demanded in return for the continuing drain on its resources. In a major nationalized company that had its ups and downs on the open marketplace, but a long tradition of union disruption and politicization, it was becoming ever harder to justify to a militant work force the budget expended on an apparently fruitless quest for the world championship and the enormously high (by the standards of the day) wages paid, to Prost in particular.

The man who felt most of the pressure was the sporting director Gerard Larrousse, the man directly under the gun. An amiable well-organized administrator, Gerard felt that the shortcomings of his engines and chassis were not necessarily his fault. There were inevitable delays as, back in Paris, Renault engineers, acting in committee, thrashed out solutions. Jean Sage, the team-manager and a former driver himself, did his best to put a good front on matters, but it was clear that 1983 was the make-or-break year. The Renault turbo engine, meanwhile, had been passed on to Lotus as well, in an attempt to increase development and cut costs; other turbo engines were beginning to make headway – the BMW, the Ferrari, the Hart – and later that year, the Honda was to enter the field. Renault had been the pioneer; it was time it capitalized on its greater experience. It had, in Prost, a driver of the greatest quality. What was wrong with the team?

It was an unhappy and resentful year for Alain, a season of discontents. As usual, it began badly, with Prost on the first row in qualifying in Brazil, but failing to finish. Long Beach, which came next, was known not to be a Renault circuit, and once again Alain had to retire. The French Grand Prix at the Ricard Circuit was unusually early that year, in April, and Prost won it handsomely: the track's long straight particularly favoured the power of the Renault turbo. At Imola, with a car that suffered all sorts of problems, Alain managed to finish second, well behind Tambay's Ferrari. In Monaco, Prost was on pole, but as always on street circuits, his car suffered from throttle lag and handling problems and he could do no better than finish third behind Rosberg and Piquet.

When racing returned to Spa for the first time in many years, Prost showed his mastery of the difficult conditions and the trying circuit, overcoming a hugely determined early charge by the surprising Andrea de Cesaris to win in style. Another street circuit, Detroit, followed, and again the Renault was nowhere. The car was simply not up to sinuous circuits and tight corners and Prost was furious: it was as though Renault had one half of the car right but couldn't get the other half right. What was the point, he asked rhetorically, in having a car that was so superior on quick circuits and so inferior on the slower ones?

For a good part of the year, the championship race was delicately balanced between Alain, Nelson Piquet driving a BMW-powered Brabham and René Arnoux over at Ferrari – Arnoux having a particular point to make with regard to Prost. In Canada, the next race, Arnoux and Prost were side by side on the front row, but minor problems dropped Prost back to fifth place; but at Silverstone, Alain won again once he had conquered Tambay's Ferrari and Piquet – as delicate and masterful a piece of hauling-in as one could hope for. Hockenheim, which should have offered the Renault a major opportunity, was a great disappointment: Arnoux won it going away and Prost could do no better than fourth. At the Österreichring, Alain took his revenge, beating out Arnoux in a thrilling finish, by a mere six seconds.

At this point Nelson Piquet began to make his presence in the championship felt in a big way. He was on pole at Zandvoort but was put off by Prost in one of Alain's very rare mistakes. The next two races, Monza and the Grand Prix d'Europe at Brands Hatch, Piquet won on the trot. The best the Renault would allow Prost to do was a single second place at Brands. They came to the last race of the season, at Kyalami, with Prost holding on to the slenderest of leads, 57 points to Piquet's 55. It was just not to be Alain's year: a third place gave Piquet four points to overtake Alain.

What I found fascinating about it was to watch the way Alain handled the pressures of an 'almost' championship. At the beginning of 1983, he had used his brain to tell him that early success does not mean much, that the season is long, that much may go wrong during the year and others may just as likely have a lucky streak. It wasn't until Austria that Alain began to realize that he really just might be champion. With his usual diffidence, he continued to deny it publicly; privately he would admit that the idea was working from the fringes of his mind to the middle. When he suffered a mechanical failure in Monza (and Piquet won), it should have knocked the stuffing out of the man. Instead, I remember him well – with the personal bodyguards Renault had laid on for him, his own personal motor-home – coming back after the race, shrugging and saying 'such things happen'. He went on to a victory celebration (for the race in Austria) and handled it with aplomb.

The schedule for that week is revealing. Prost was at a critical moment in the championship, but . . . After Monza he had a Monday lunch, then a session testing wet tyres at Clermont Ferrand for Michelin. Wednesday he went to Paris to sign on with Renault for another year: somewhat unwillingly, because he was even then moving to Switzerland. Thursday he was in Lyon for a TV show, Friday he rested with his parents, only to be back in Paris on Sunday for another TV appearance (Renault and Elf both have gargantuan appetites), lugging two heavy suitcases and the laundry his mother had done for him. The same night he dined with Larrousse and Monday early he left for Geneva for three days with his wife and young son, whom he took for a long walk in the woods: 'We didn't discuss philosophy,' said Alain. Then he came to Brands, I saw him early Friday morning, and he finally admitted, 'Yes, I'd be awfully disappointed if I didn't win the championship.'

Well, he didn't. Not in 1983 and not in 1984.

The interseason was probably the most difficult part of the year for Alain. Persistent rumours linked him with the pretty and charming wife of one of his superiors in Renault; the gossip columnists of France (with no more mercy than the tabloid press in England) pursued him to beyond and back. Alain denied the rumours, but to no effect: to me, he admitted he had been indiscreet. At the same time, John Watson, who had had a satisfactory but not earth-shaking season with Lauda at McLaren, was pushed by his agent to ask for a gigantic sum – something like three times what he was realistically worth – and got the sack. That left a vacant seat at McLaren, a scandal at Renault (Alain said he walked out of his own accord, Renault said he had been 'dropped', and the truth is that Renault did a deal with McLaren) and Prost signed with Ron Dennis.

With his private life torn to shreds, his wife understandably upset, a move to Switzerland which infuriated the xenophobic French press and all socialists – whom he directly accused of causing his move – and a new drive in a new car in the same team as Niki Lauda, Prost was a chastened man the next time I saw him: very quiet, very reasonable and very much happier. He'd taken as much rest as he could, he'd worked on his physical fitness, he'd patched up his marriage and he'd put France and the French firmly behind him.

The 1984 season, which Lauda wrested from Prost during the very last race at Estoril, has been covered in the chapter on Niki: suffice it to repeat that Prost raced throughout that year, a year which he told me he had expected to spend 'learning' and from which he did not expect to emerge champion, with great intelligence and efficiency. The record speaks for itself: he won seven races, two more than Lauda, finished second once, third once and fourth once: ten finishes is the points out of sixteen.

With Lauda gone in 1986, Prost swept the board, winning his first, and long-postponed, championship by a massive margin over Michele Alboreto. True, McLaren favoured him over Lauda; the margin of his superiority over his team-mate, however, leaves little doubt that

Prost earned his title. At the end of the year, he was delighted and relieved but not in the slightest changed from the man we had known for all those years. True, he admitted, coming so close so often had made him 'superstitious' – which in a man who sleepwalks by night and has found himself on the roof of a house he was once staying in, is no surprise – but in the long run he said he had 'a streak of fatalism' in his nature: what would happen would happen and he wouldn't worry too much about what didn't happen. As always, he was utterly devoted to his work, and his first thoughts on clinching the championship were about getting right down to work to prepare for a second championship the year following.

The year 1986, of course, will always be engraved in the British mind as the year in which Nigel Mansell 'lost' the championship when a tyre blew during the very last race in Australia. The fact is, championships are not lost; they are won, and Prost won his second championship by sheer consistency. His McLaren was in no way the equal of Mansell's Honda-powered Williams, yet he stayed in the championship race throughout the year: four victories, four seconds, three thirds and two sixths, thirteen finishes out of sixteen races. It is that sort of driving, making the most of what you have, that makes champions.

By then Prost was, like Mansell, a very experienced driver. His philosophy of driving has really never changed from his beginnings. He has never been one for the outright, balls-out win; he does not specialize in the sort of show which wins pole positions; he does not necessarily believe that to win he must lead a race. He knows that finishing is more important than winning, conservation more vital than show. Like his mentor, Lauda, he has come to learn that more races are won from the back than from the front, that it is harder to work out one's possibilities if one is leading and being pursued than if one is behind and doing the pursuing.

By his own exacting standards, 1987 was a definite let-down for him, and he acknowledged as much during the season. In the first place, the Williams-Honda so dominated the season with Piquet and Mansell that no other driver was really in with a chance, Williams scoring nearly twice as many points during the season as any other team. In the second place, with Niki retired and Stefan Johansson taking his place, Prost was denied two invaluable aids: the exchange of information with Lauda which had been so fruitful in the preceding seasons and the pride of racing within the team against another of the sport's great champions. Thirdly, there is little doubt in my mind that the departure of McLaren's chief designer, John Barnard, to Ferrari adversely affected the team. True, Barnard produced no instant miracle at Ferrari, but what he did produce was something like a vacuum at McLaren. Gordon Murray, who had left Brabham, took up some of the slack, but it was hard to ask him to achieve, with what was basically a Barnard-designed car, what he might have achieved with his own design. Fourthly, the mighty TAG/Porsche engine began to reveal first its age and then the German firm's lack of interest in continuing to develop it, with the result that on all levels – electronics, reliability, fuel-consumption, on-track intelligence and in a dozen smaller ways – Porsche managed to make the 1987 season a villainous one for Prost. Finally, besides the natural let-down after two successive championships, I felt throughout the year that Prost's relationship with the team was less successful than in previous years. Perhaps it was that Ron Dennis had catapulted himself into the stratosphere, perhaps that Ron needed to spend so much time gathering in the money necessary to success that he began to neglect detail, perhaps it was the absence of Barnard's fire, perhaps the retreat towards the boardroom of Marlboro's John Hogan, always a tempering influence. The most Prost would say of his last year was that it had been 'deeply disappointing' both professionally and personally. He admitted that there might have been some 'slack' in the team and that, given the constant failures of his engines, he had 'allowed himself to become discouraged'.

Perhaps in the end it was that old 'fatalism' that got to Alain. But I rather think the real reason was that Alain was already, at the start of 1987, beginning, like many another champion before him and like all the truly intelligent ones, to look ahead to the day when he could do something else, when he could broaden his mind and his experience, when he could truly live and not be a slave of his skills, when he need no longer fear – he who has never had a really serious shunt – the accident that could end his career. It happens to all the best ones: some day they realize that F1 racing is not all there is to the world. I would not be in the least surprised, should he fail to win his third championship in 1988, to see Alain retire. By the end of the season he will be thirty-three and have spent more than a decade racing, nine years of which will have been in F1. If he does, it is well known that he wishes to move up into racing management, preferably of an all-French team, though it is just as probable that he could continue at a management level at McLaren.

I don't think they could pick a better man. In my day, he has been the most complete driver I have seen – complete as a person and complete as a professional, a true champion in every sense of the word. If there is one thing that distinguishes him from Niki Lauda in the definition of a true champion, it is that, to date, Prost has not been struck down by adversity and survived; and if Niki has one weakness that is not in Prost, it is that his temperament has often overruled his mind.

Index

Firestone Tyre Company, 86–7
FISA, 9, 46, 68, 89, 145
Fittipaldi, Emerson, 16, 17, 22–31, 36,
    56, 60, 62, 63, 71, 101–9, 121,
    142, 154, 157
Fittipaldi, Maria Helena, 30
Fittipaldi, Wilson Jr, 22, 29, 101
Fittipaldi, Wilson Sr, 22
FOCA (the Formula One Constructors'
    Association), 9, 117, 145
Ford, 120
Forghieri, Mauro, 35
Formula Ford, 100
Foyt, A. J., 84
French Grand Prix, 48, 104–5
Fuji, 75–7, 90

Gardner, Derek, 16, 68, 107–8
Giacomelli, 117, 146
Ginther, Richie, 5
Granatelli, Andy, 85
Grand Prix d'Europe, 51–2
Gurney, Dan, 14, 85

Haas, Karl, 83, 88, 96, 120
Hailwood, Mike, 17, 61, 101, 104
Hawthorn, Mike, 1, 3–4
Head, Patrick, 115, 120, 128, 135, 143,
    147, 152
Herd, Robin, 15, 34, 56
Hesketh, Lord Alexander, 57, 60–2,
    109, 113
Hesnault, 127
Hill, Graham, 1, 4–5, 6, 13–14, 15, 61,
    85, 86, 101, 103, 113
Hockenheim, 135, 149–50
Hogan, John, 42, 44, 52, 63–4, 167
Honda, 123, 128, 131, 136–7, 166
Horsley, 'Bubbles', 60–1, 62
Hulme, Denny, 1, 24, 61, 101, 102, 103,
    104, 107
Hungaroring, 130
Hunt, James, 9, 12, 28, 41, 42, 56–80,
    84, 90, 91, 97, 109, 111, 122
Hunt, Susy, 58–9, 65–6

Ickx, Jackie, 6, 24, 25, 86, 97, 106, 107
Imola, 132–3, 145
Indianapolis 500, 84–5
Interlagos, 90

Jabouille, Jean-Pierre, 118, 155, 158
Jarama, 68, 108
Jarier, Jean-Pierre, 142, 158
Johansson, Stefan, 53, 137, 166
Jones, Alan, 23, 42, 76, 77, 79, 99,
    112–20, 125–6, 128, 139, 141,
    143, 147, 154, 160
Jones, Parnelli, 87–8

Kerr, Phil, 102, 105
Kyalami, 44–5, 67, 81, 144

Laffite, Jacques, 44, 48, 118, 149, 154,
    155, 158, 160
Langhorne, 84
Larrousse, Gerard, 50, 163, 165
Las Vegas, 151
Lauda, Marlene, 37, 41, 52
Lauda, Niki, 1, 2, 12, 17, 27, 28,
    32–55, 56–7, 60, 62, 65, 66–9,
    74–8, 79, 90, 92, 97, 103, 107,
    108, 109–10, 121, 122, 145, 149,
    150, 156, 157, 165, 166, 168
Le Mans, 3–4
Levegh, Pierre, 3–4
Ligier, Guy, 158
Long Beach, 67–8, 87, 145
Longines, 74
Lotus, 5, 6–7, 17, 24–6, 63, 65, 85,
    88–95, 102, 107, 122, 123, 129,
    137, 138
Lunger, Brett, 40–1, 113
Lyons, Pete, 76

McCormack, Mark, 45
McDonald, John, 44, 45–6
McEnroe, John, 12
McLaren, Bruce, 13, 14, 18, 22, 85, 86
McLaren team, 26–7, 28, 42, 44,
    46–51, 54–5, 57, 64–5, 68,
    69–70, 74, 101–7, 137, 143,
    152–3 154–7, 159–60, 165–7

Statistics

GIUSEPPE FARINA
Total Grand Prix contested 33
Total number of victories 5
Total World
Championship points 116⅓ (128⅓)

Team & World Championship position

1950	Alfa Romeo	1st
1951	Alfa Romeo	4th
1952	Ferrari	2nd
1953	Ferrari	3rd
1954	Ferrari	8th
1955	Ferrari	5th

JUAN-MANUEL FANGIO
Total Grand Prix contested 51
Total number of victories 24
Total World
Championship points 245 (277½)

Team & World Championship position

1950	Alfa Romeo	2nd
1951	Alfa Romeo	1st
1953	Maserati	2nd
1954	(Maserati	1st
	(Mercedes	
1955	Mer.edes	1st
1956	Ferrari	1st
1957	Maserati	1st
1958	Maserati	14th

ALBERTO ASCARI
Total Grand Prix contested 32
Total number of victories 13
Total World
Championship points 107½ (139)

Team & World Championship position

1950	Ferrari	5th
1951	Ferrari	2nd
1952	Ferrari	1st
1953	Ferrari	1st
1954	(Maserati	24th
	(Ferrari	
	(Lancia	
1955	Lancia	–

MIKE HAWTHORN
Total Grand Prix contested 45
Total number of victories 3
Total World
Championship points 112½ (127½)

Team & World Championship position

1952	Cooper	4th
1953	Ferrari	4th
1954	Ferrari	3rd
1955	(Vauxhall	–
	(Ferrari	
1956	(Maserati	11th
	(BRM	
	(Vanwall	
1957	Ferrari	4th
1958	Ferrari	1st

JACK BRABHAM
Total Grand Prix contested 126
Total number of victories 14
Total World
Championship points 253 (261)

Team & World Championship position

1955	Cooper	–
1956	Maserati	–
1957	(Cooper Climax	
	(Cooper F2	–
1958	(Cooper Climax	17th
	(Cooper F2	
1959	Cooper Climax	1st
1960	Cooper Climax	1st
1961	Cooper Climax	11th
1962	(Lotus Climax	9th
	(Brabham Climax	
1963	(Lotus Climax	7th
	(Brabham Climax	
1964	Brabham Climax	8th
1965	Brabham Climax	10th
1966	Brabham Repco	1st
1967	Brabham Repco	2nd
1968	Brabham Repco	23rd
1969	Brabham Ford	10th
1970	Brabham Ford	5th

PHIL HILL
Total Grand Prix contested	48	
Total number of victories	3	
Total World Championship points	94	(98)

Team & World Championship position
1958	(Maserati	10th
	(Ferrari F2	
	(Ferrari	
1959	Ferrari	4th
1960	Ferrari/Cooper	5th
1961	Ferrari	1st
1962	Ferrari	6th
1963	(ATS	–
	(Lotus BRM	
1964	Cooper Climax	19th

GRAHAM HILL
Total Grand Prix contested	176	
Total number of victories	14	
Total World Championship points	270	(289)

Team & World Championship position
1958	(Lotus Climax	–
	(Lotus F2	
1959	Lotus Climax	–
1960	BRM	15th
1961	BRM	13th
1962	BRM	1st
1963	BRM	2nd
1964	BRM	2nd
1965	BRM	2nd
1966	BRM	5th
1967	(Lotus BRM	6th
	(Lotus Ford	
1968	Lotus Ford	1st
1969	Lotus Ford	7th
1970	Lotus Ford	13th
1971	Brabham Ford	21st
1972	Brabham Ford	12th
1973	Shadow Ford	–
1974	Lola Ford	18th
1975	Lola Ford	–

JIM CLARK
Total Grand Prix contested	72	
Total number of victories	25	
Total World Championship points	255	(274)

Team & World Championship position
1960	Lotus Climax	8th
1961	Lotus Climax	7th
1962	Lotus Climax	2nd
1963	Lotus Climax	1st
1964	Lotus Climax	3rd
1965	Lotus Climax	1st
1966	(Lotus Climax	6th
	(Lotus BRM	
1967	(Lotus Climax	3rd
	(Lotus BRM	
	(Lotus Ford	
1968	Lotus Ford	11th

JOHN SURTEES
Total Grand Prix contested	111	
Total number of victories	6	
Total World Championship points	180	

Team & World Championship position
1960	Lotus Climax	12th
1961	Cooper Climax	11th
1962	Lola Climax	4th
1963	Ferrari	4th
1964	Ferrari	1st
1965	Ferrari	5th
1966	(Ferrari	2nd
	(Cooper Maserati	
1967	Honda	4th
1968	Honda	7th
1969	BRM	11th
1970	(McLaren Ford	17th
	(Surtees Ford	
1971	Surtees Ford	18th
1972	Surtees Ford	–

DENNY HULME
Total Grand Prix contested 112
Total number of victories 8
Total World
Championship points 248

Team & World Championship position
1965	Brabham Climax	11th
1966	(Brabham Climax	4th
	(Brabham Repco	
1967	Brabham Repco	1st
1968	(McLaren BRM	3rd
	(McLaren Ford	
1969	McLaren Ford	6th
1970	McLaren Ford	4th
1971	McLaren Ford	9th
1972	McLaren Ford	3rd
1973	McLaren Ford	6th
1974	McLaren Ford	7th

JACKIE STEWART
Total Grand Prix contested 99
Total number of victories 27
Total World
Championship points 359 (360)

Team & World Championship position
1965	BRM	3rd
1966	BRM	7th
1967	BRM	9th
1968	Matra Ford	2nd
1969	Matra Ford	1st
1970	(March Ford	5th
	(Tyrrell Ford	
1971	Tyrrell Ford	1st
1972	Tyrrell Ford	2nd
1973	Tyrrell Ford	1st

JOCHEN RINDT
Total Grand Prix contested 60
Total number of victories 6
Total World
Championship points 107 (109)

Team & World Championship position
1964	Brabham BRM	–
1965	Cooper Climax	13th
1966	Cooper Maserati	3rd
1967	Cooper Maserati	11th
1968	Brabham Repco	12th
1969	Lotus Ford	4th
1970	Lotus Ford	1st

EMERSON FITTIPALDI
Total Grand Prix contested 144
Total number of victories 14
Total World
Championship points 281

Team & World Championship position
1970	Lotus Ford	10th
1971	(Lotus Ford	6th
	(Lotus Turbina	
1972	Lotus Ford	1st
1973	Lotus Ford	2nd
1974	McLaren Ford	1st
1975	McLaren Ford	2nd
1976	Copersucar Ford	16th
1977	Copersucar Ford	12th
1978	Coperucar Ford	9th
1979	Copersucar Ford	21st
1980	Fittipaldi Ford	15th

NIKI LAUDA
Total Grand Prix contested 171
Total number of victories 25
Total World
Championship points 420½

Team & World Championship position
1971	March Ford	–
1972	March Ford	–
1973	BRM	17th
1974	Ferrari	4th
1975	Ferrari	1st
1976	Ferrari	2nd
1977	Ferrari	1st
1978	Brabham Alfa	4th
1979	Brabham Alfa	14th
1982	McLaren Ford	5th
1983	(McLaren Ford	10th
	(McLaren TAG Porsche Turbo	
1984	McLaren TAG Porsche Turbo	1st
1985	McLaren TAG Porsche Turbo	10th

JAMES HUNT
Total Grand Prix contested 92
Total number of victories 10
Total World
Championship points 179

Team & World Championship position

1973	March Ford	8th
1974	(March Ford	8th
	(Hesketh Ford	
1975	Hesketh Ford	4th
1976	McLaren Ford	1st
1977	McLaren Ford	5th
1978	McLaren Ford	13th
1979	Wolf Ford	–

MARIO ANDRETTI

Total Grand Prix contested	128
Total number of victories	12
Total World Championship points	180

Team & World Championship position

1968	Lotus Ford	–
1969	Lotus Ford	–
1970	March Ford	15th
1971	Ferrari	8th
1972	Ferrari	12th
1974	Parnelli Ford	–
1975	Parnelli Ford	14th
1976	(Parnelli Ford	6th
	(Lotus Ford	
1977	Lotus Ford	3rd
1978	Lotus Ford	1st
1979	Lotus Ford	10th
1980	Lotus Ford	20th
1981	Alfa Romeo	17th
1982	(Williams Ford	19th
	(Ferrari Turbo	

JODY SCHECKTER

Total Grand Prix contested	112
Total number of victories	10
Total World Championship points	246

Team & World Championship position

1974	Tyrrell Ford	3rd
1975	Tyrrell Ford	7th
1976	Tyrrell Ford	3rd
1977	Wolf Ford	2nd
1978	Wolf Ford	7th
1979	Ferrari	1st
1980	Ferrari	19th

ALAN JONES

Total Grand Prix contested	116	
Total number of victories	12	
Total World Championship points	199	(206)

Team & World Championship position

1975	(Hesketh Ford	17th
	(Lola Ford	
1976	Surtees Ford	14th
1977	Shadow Ford	7th
1978	Williams Ford	11th
1979	Williams Ford	3rd
1980	Williams Ford	1st
1981	Williams Ford	3rd
1983	Arrows-Ford	–
1985	Lola-Haas-Hart-Turbo	–
1986	(Lola-Haas-Hart Turbo	12th
	(Lola-Haas Ford Turbo	

NELSON PIQUET

Total Grand Prix contested	138
Total number of victories	20
Total World Championship points	378

Team & World Championship position

1978	(Ensign Ford	–
	(McLaren Ford	
	(Brabham Ford	
1979	(Brabham Alfa	15th
	(Brabham Ford	
1980	Brabham Ford	2nd
1981	Brabham Ford	1st
1982	(Brabham Ford	11th
	(Brabham BMW Turbo	
1983	Brabham BMW Turbo	1st
1984	Brabham BMW Turbo	5th
1985	Brabham BMW Turbo	8th
1986	Williams Honda Turbo	3rd
1987	Williams Honda Turbo	1st

KEKE ROSBERG
Total Grand Prix contested 114
Total number of victories 5
Total World
Championship points 159½

Team & World Championship position
1978	(Theodore Ford	–
	(ATS Ford	
	(Wolf Ford	
1979	Wolf Ford	–
1980	Fittipaldi Ford	10th
1981	Fittipaldi Ford	–
1982	Williams Ford	1st
1983	(Williams Ford	5th
	(Williams Honda	
	Turbo	
1984	Williams Honda	
	Turbo	8th
1985	Williams Honda	
	Turbo	3rd
1986	McLaren TAG	
	Porsche Turbo	6th

ALAIN PROST
Total Grand Prix contested 116
Total number of victories 28
Total World
Championship points 401½ (406½)

Team & World Championship position
1980	McLaren Ford	15th
1981	Renault Turbo	5th
1982	Renault Turbo	4th
1983	Renault Turbo	2nd
1984	McLaren TAG	
	Porsche Turbo	2nd
1985	McLaren TAG	
	Porsche Turbo	1st
1986	McLaren TAG	
	Porsche Turbo	1st
1987	McLaren TAG	
	Porsche Turbo	4th